Frontline Intelligence *1*

New Plays for the Nineties

D1101911

Hush by April De Angelis, **Digging for Fire** by Declan Hughes, **Somewhere** by Judith Johnson, **East from the Gantry** by Edward Thomas

Frontline Intelligence *1* is the first volume in an anthology series of the most original and exciting new plays for the nineties.

Hush premièred on the main stage of the Royal Court, London in 1992: 'Weird, surreal . . . but also wry, witty and genuinely imaginative . . . De Angelis's darkly haunting play.' *Guardian*

Time Out award winner *Digging for Fire* was staged by Rough Magic in Dublin and the Bush Theatre, London in 1992: 'This is a sad, funny, revealing and *important* work.' *Irish Independent*

Somewhere was first performed at the Liverpool Playhouse Studio and subsequently on the Royal National Theatre's Cottesloe stage in 1993: 'Eloquent, highly charged drama. . . . Johnson catches the jumpy aggression of adolescence in her edgy, witty script.' *Independent*

East from the Gantry, the third in the 'New Wales Trilogy' was produced by Y Cwymni and premièred at the Tramway, Glasgow in 1992: 'A free-wheeling three-handed comedy . . . there are moments of uproarious humour and bizarre storytelling in Thomas's unique portfolio of ideas exploring that world of living on the edge that is what Celticism has always been about.' *Guardian*

Each play has an afterword by its author and the volume opens with an introduction by Pamela Edwardes, Editorial Director at Methuen Drama.

in series with

Plays by Women: Volume Two (ed. Micheline Wandor)
Claire Luckham, *Trafford Tanzi*; Rose Leiman Goldemberg from Sylvia Plath, *Letters Home*; Maureen Duffy, *Rites*; Olwen Wymark, *Find Me*

Plays by Women: Volume Six (ed. Mary Remnant)
Cordelia Ditton and Maggie Ford, *About Face*; Maro Green and Caroline Griffin, *More*; Byrony Lavery, *Origins of the Species*; Deborah Levy, *Pax*; Eve Lewis, *Ficky Stingers*

Plays by Women: Volume Seven (ed. Mary Remnant)
Kay Adshead, *Thatcher's Women*; Claire Dowie, *Adult Child/Dead Child*; Lisa Evans, *Stamping, Shouting and Singing Home*; Marie Laberge, *Night*; Valerie Windsor, *Effie's Burning*

Plays by Women: Volume Eight (ed. Mary Remnant)
April de Angelis, *Ironmistress*; Mary Cooper, *Heartgame*; Janet Cresswell and Niki Johnson, *The One-Sided Wall*; Ayshe Raif, *Caving In*; Ena Lamont Stewart, *Towards Evening* and *Walkies Time*; Joan Wolton, *Motherlove*.

Plays by Women: Volume Nine (ed. Annie Castledine)
Marieluise Fleisser, *Purgatory in Ingolstadt, Pioneers in Ingolstadt, Avant-garde, Early Encounter, I Wasn't Aware of the Explosive*; Maureen Lawrence, *Tokens of Affection*; Sheila Yeger, *Variations on a Theme by Clara Schumann*

Black Plays: Volume One (ed. Yvonne Brewster)
Earl Lovelace, *The Dragon Can't Dance*; Winsome Pinnock, *A Rock in Water*; Maria Oshodi, *Blood, Sweat and Fears*; Benjamin Zephaniah, *Job Rocking*

Gay Plays: Volume Three (ed. Michael Wilcox)
Crowe and Zajdlic, *Cock and Bull Story*; Paul Selig, *Terminal Bar*; Timothy Mason, *Levitation*; J R Ackerley, *Prisoners of War*

Gay Plays: Volume Four (ed. Michael Wilcox)
Eric Bentley, *Round 2*; Gerald Killingworth, *Days of Cavafy*; Neil Bartlett, *A Vision of Love Revealed in Sleep*; Joe Pintauro, *Wild Blue*

Lesbian Plays: Volume One (ed. Jill Davis)
Jill Posener, *Any Woman Can*; Women's Theatre Group, *Double Vision*; Jackie Kay, *Chiaroscuro*; J W Fleming, *The Rug of Identity*

Lesbian Plays: Volume Two (ed. Jill Davis)
Debby Klein, *Coming Soon*; Catherine Kilcoyne, *Julie*; Sandra Freeman, *Supporting Roles*; Sue Frumin, *The Housetrample*; Cheryl Moch, *Cinderella: The Real True Story*

Frontline Intelligence *1*

New Plays for the Nineties

Hush
April De Angelis

Digging for Fire
Declan Hughes

Somewhere
Judith Johnson

East from the Gantry
Edward Thomas

Edited and introduced by Pamela Edwardes

Methuen Drama

Methuen New Theatrescripts

First published in Great Britain 1993
by Methuen Drama
an imprint of Reed Consumer Books Ltd
Michelin House, 81 Fulham Road, London SW3 6RB
and Auckland, Melbourne, Singapore and Toronto
and distributed in the United States of America
by Heinemann
a division of Reed Publishing (USA) Inc,
361 Hanover Street, Portsmouth, New Hampshire NH 03801 3959

ISBN 0–413–67680–3

A CIP catalogue record for this book is available at the British Library

The front cover photograph is of Andy Serkis as Dogboy in the Royal Court production in 1992. Photo: John Haynes.

Typeset by Hewer Text Composition Services, Edinburgh
Printed in Great Britain by Clays Ltd, St Ives plc

Contents

Introduction

Why 'Frontline Intelligence'? I first came across the term used in this context in speaking to Rob Ritchie, a former literary manager of the Royal Court Theatre in London. Now designated Britain's National Theatre of New Writing, that theatre, more than most, has trusted writers to give us frontline intelligence of what is happening in the world not just by performing the plays of established writers but also by setting out to provide a platform for new, young voices. It is no accident that all these 'new plays for the nineties' have been produced at venues with a commitment to new work. *Hush* by April De Angelis was premièred at the Royal Court Theatre; Judith Johnson's *Somewhere* was a joint commission by the Liverpool Playhouse Studio and the Royal National Theatre in London; the two remaining plays were both produced by companies founded and led by writers: *Digging for Fire* was written for Rough Magic in Dublin by its producer/director Declan Hughes, and subsequently transferred to another 'new writing' venue, the Bush Theatre in London; and Edward Thomas wrote *East from the Gantry* for his own Welsh company Y Cwymni, the play premièred at the Tramway in Glasgow, a theatre space first created by Peter Brook to house *The Mahabharata* and which has since retained a reputation for the highly original theatre which the venue's character demands.

There is, however, another sense in which this volume justifies its title. A successful new play at any one of the venues I have mentioned is an event celebrated and debated in the national press and seen by anything between 2,000 and 20,000 plus people. These figures are impressive compared to the 750 odd readers of a first novel; a novel though is a transportable object and may be acquired by any would-be reader at little cost beyond the cover price, while mere geography will prevent most people from seeing the first production of a new play. The publication of these playtexts offers those people frontline intelligence of what has excited theatre audiences in London, Liverpool, Dublin and Glasgow over the last year.

Every decision I have taken in selecting plays for the volume has been a decision about the quality of a piece of writing. I find it intriguing to discover how, speaking in many dialects and styles, these plays all comment on the rapid social change of the last thirteen years and ask 'Is this the world we wanted to create?' Not one of the plays seeks to lay out a Marshall Plan for economic and social recovery but all point to defeats and victories of the spirit which suggest where some kind of positive movement could have been made or might yet be made. If an imaginative piece of writing can articulate and crystallize the hopes and fears of a generation then there is much to learn from these new voices. And to anybody who doubts the power of the playwright to speak for our time and longer, I would quote Arthur Miller's riposte 'Give me the name of a Greek shoemaker'.

Pamela Edwardes, 1993

Hush

April De Angelis

Hush was premièred at the Royal Court Theatre, London on 6 August 1992, with the following cast:

Louise	Marion Bailey
Denise	Debra Gillett
Rosa	Dervla Kirwan
Tony	Stephen Dillane
Colin	Will Knightly
Dogboy	Andy Serkis

Directed by Max Stafford-Clark
Designed by Sally Jacobs
Lighting by Johanna Town
Sound by Bryan Bowen

Part One

The stage area is roughly divided into two parts. The beach and the house. The house is one room with a sofa, some cardboard boxes and a small, old, round sidetable which sits near the sofa. Both pieces of furniture are covered in a dust sheet. The room looks dusty, unlived in. The beach may encroach upon the house surrealistically.

Scene One

The house. **Louise** *enters. She stands for a moment in the room. She pulls off the dust sheet. She bundles it up. She exits.*

Scene Two

The beach. **Rosa** *and* **Denise** *sit on the beach. They look out to sea.*

Denise   I like beaches in winter.

Rosa   More than in summer?

Denise   Not more. But I like them.

Rosa   I hate beaches.

Pause.

Denise *leans back.*

Denise   That's better.

Pause.

Much better.

Rosa   Better than what?

Denise   Better than cleaning.

Rosa   But you're a cleaner.

Denise   I'm not a cleaner.

Rosa   You clean things. That's what you do.

Denise   That may be what I do at present. I may do that at present but that's not what I am.

Rosa   What are you then?

Pause.

You're having a crisis.

Denise   I am not.

Rosa   You're stuck. Horribly stuck. Festering. Your youth is dwindling away.

Denise   It is not.

Rosa   Drip by drip.

Denise   That's all you know.

Pause.

That's all you know because I'm leaving.

Pause.

Rosa   Leaving?

Denise   I've just got this weekend then I'm finished. I only decided on Tuesday. I've been meaning to tell you.

Pause.

I've got to do something. With my life. Start a new life.

Rosa   Doing what?

Denise   I'll think of something.

Rosa   What?

Pause.

Denise   I went to this woman last week. She's got this booth in Camden Market. She tells you things. She held my hand and she said 'do you mind if I swear?' She said she swore when she got going. She said I should watch my back. I thought to myself 'is that symbolic?' But then I thought 'no, not for two pounds fifty'.

Pause.

She meant my lower back. She said me or my husband would have problems in that area.

Rosa   You haven't got a husband.

Denise   I know.

Rosa   She sounds like a bucket of shit.

Denise   I could have a husband. I could have. In the future.

Pause.

Rosa   Did she talk to any dead people?

Denise Not that I noticed.

Rosa They usually do. That sort.

Pause.

Bury me.

Denise What?

Rosa In the sand.

Denise What for?

Rosa Fun.

Denise That sand's grubby.

Rosa Go on.

Denise Unsalubrious.

Rosa If you don't do it I'm going to swallow a stone.

Denise You wouldn't?

Rosa I would. Then your new life would be unnecessarily complicated.

Denise That's blackmail.

Rosa Start with the feet.

Pause.

Denise *begins to bury* **Rosa**.

Denise I don't know.

Rosa What?

Denise You. You're disturbed.

Rosa Did she swear then? That woman?

Denise No.

Rosa Didn't she even let a fuck slip?

Denise I don't think I inspired her.

Rosa What a disappointment, after all the build up.

Denise She said there was a stranger on my horizon. A ginger man.

Rosa How repulsive.

Denise What's wrong with that?

Rosa Pubes. Ginger pubes.

Denise Rosa!

Rosa   Will you do my head?

Denise   Your head?

Rosa   Bury my head.

Denise   What for?

Rosa   The experience.

Denise   It's a bit extreme.

Rosa   Go on.

Denise   You won't be able to breathe.

Rosa   We can use that straw.

She points to a straw in the sand.

Denise   We don't know where it's been.

Rosa   Don't be finicky.

Denise   It's probably swarming with germs.

Rosa   Give it here.

Denise   I don't know how you can.

*She beings to bury **Rosa**'s head.*

Don't let on to Louise.

Rosa   Thus they committed her to the sand. And the deserts of time blew over her wiping out forever from the eyes of men all last trace of her ethereal beauty.

Denise   Put the straw in.

*She covers **Rosa** up. She sighs. Lies down next to the mound.*

Pause.

Louise *enters. She carries a young tree. She places it down.*

Louise   I bought a tree.

Denise *sits up.*

Denise   Louise.

Louise   Well?

Denise   It's nice.

Louise   It was bloody expensive. For a tree. I said to the man at the garden centre, 'Is this really the price?' and he said, 'yes', like he thought I was mad. I said I could go and dig up a tree for free.

Denise   What did he say?

Louise   He said that would be against the law.

Denise   He was probably right. It probably is against the law.

Louise   I know he was right. It's just the principle of the thing. A tree should be free or very cheap.

Pause.

Denise?

Denise   Yes?

Louise   I just wanted a word.

Pause.

You know you're always welcome to come down here at weekends. With us. Now we're getting the place sorted.

Denise   Thanks.

Louise   Also, also . . . you've been smashing.

Denise   Oh . . . no. I haven't.

Louise   I'm not just talking about dusting. I mean with Rosa. Us. It's been smashing. So any time you want a weekend by the sea . . .

Denise   Thanks.

Louise   Just let me know.

Denise   Thanks.

Pause.

Louise *notices the mound.*

Louise   What's that?

Pause.

Denise   It's a mound.

Louise   What's that sticking out of it?

Denise   It's a straw.

Louise   Am I missing something?

Denise   It's Rosa.

Pause.

She wanted me to bury her.

Pause.

Louise   Don't you think that's rather sick. In the circumstances?

Denise   I didn't think.

Louise   Obviously. Can she breathe?

Denise   The straw.

Louise   I see. It's incredibly unhygienic. She could get hepatitis.

Denise   Sorry.

Louise *approaches the mound.*

Louise   Rosa?

Pause.

I think you should come out now.

Nothing happens. **Louise** *removes the straw and throws it away.*

(*to* **Denise.**) You better dig her up.

Louise *picks up the tree*

I'm going to plant this somewhere it can be seen. From the sea.

She exits.

Denise   Shit.

Rosa *breaks out of the sand.*

Rosa   I could have hepatitis.

Denise   It's not funny.

Rosa   If I did you'd feel guilty. You'd feel terrible. Your new life would be blighted.

Denise   God knows what she thinks of me.

Rosa   She thinks you're an idiot.

Denise   It's like I've delivered a blow to my own karma.

Rosa   You should have told her it was yoga. An advanced form of yoga.

Rosa *gets up. She begins to dust herself down.* **Denise** *helps her.*

Rosa   I had sex.

Denise *takes little notice of this. Continues to brush off sand.*

Last time I was down here. Don't you want to know what it was like? His dick?

Denise   Not particularly.

Rosa That's a lie. Everyone wants to know that sort of thing. I'll draw it for you in the sand if you like.

Denise Would he be likely to walk by and see it?

Rosa He wouldn't know it was his if he did. It's like not recognising your own voice on tape.

Denise *has finished brushing* **Rosa** *down. She sits down dispirited.* **Rosa** *draws in the sand.*

Denise That's not to scale is it?

Rosa It's enlarged to the power of seventeen.

Denise I'm glad to hear it.

Rosa *stands back to look at what she's drawn.*

Rosa You don't believe me. You can't take anything in.

Denise You're not leaving that there.

She rubs it out with her foot.

Rosa You'll miss me when you go. You'll miss my little ways.

Scene Three

The house. **Louise** *and* **Tony**. **Louise** *is holding a spade. In the other hand she holds some sheets of A4 from which she is reading.* **Tony** *listens intently.*

Louise. . . . bulging red, pulsing red, engorged and red. Red red red. The eye of the traffic light blinked at him with meretricious self assurance. It seemed to signal to him some preposterous urban omen, some secret sense of his own deficiency; a ghastly plot to deprive him of his 'droight de seigneur'. He felt the raw sewage of panic bubbling irresistibly and the next bit's scribbled out.

Tony Yes.

Louise Is that it?

Tony That's as far as I got.

Pause.

Louise Well . . . I think it's gripping.

Tony Gripping?

Louise Yes. Quite . . . gripping.

Tony Do you get the nightmare quality? Does the nightmare quality come through?

Louise   It certainly does come through.

Pause.

He's at the traffic lights is he?

Tony   It's just this chapter. I know at bone level if I can crack it I'm home and dry. He's at his worst point you see.

Louise   I see.

Tony   He's struggling. Struggling. I'm making it bloody difficult for him.

Louise *twizzles the spade.*

Louise   Good.

Tony   But he survives. He survives. And on the way he learns something about human goodness.

Louise *looks closely at the spade.*

Louise   Jolly good.

Tony   The last page is almost filmic. He watches the sun come up over the city.

Pause.

It's rather wonderful isn't it? To think of all those people down the ages who have watched a sunrise with hope, with a sense of new possibilities.

Louise *holds up the spade.*

Louise   Do you think this is sufficient.

Tony   Sufficient?

Louise   For digging?

Tony   I should think so.

Louise   I bought a birch.

Tony   A birch.

Louise   I can remember Jo saying she liked them once. I don't know. She changed with the wind.

Pause.

Tony   A birch is great.

Pause.

To me books are terribly important. They're like little mouths on the world. People need those, Louise.

Louise   Yes.

Tony   They need those like they need lungs.

Louise   Yes.

Tony   You're not just saying yes, are you? You do see what I mean?

Louise   I have to go and dig a large hole shortly, Tony. I expect that's distracting me.

Tony   Sorry.

Louise   I can't tell you how much I've been longing for today. Longing to put it all behind me. A year. I've never known a year like it.

Tony   Poor Louise.

Louise   I want this whole business finished. Over.

Tony   It is over. It's practically over.

Louise   There's thirteen hours to go yet. I counted.

Tony   That'll fly by. Fly.

Pause.

Louise?

Pause.

Do you still have faith in me? Faith that I can do it?

Louise   I don't know how many times I can say it, Tony.

Tony   Of course. Of course.

Pause.

I shouldn't ask. Not today.

Louise   That's OK.

Tony   Do you need any help? With the hole?

Louise   I'd rather do it by myself. Catharsis.

Tony   It's like with this character I'm writing. There's a struggle but he wins through. And in the end, things turn out his way. In the end things are OK. Things are, in the end.

Pause.

Louise   Is anniversary the right word?

Tony   There isn't another one.

Louise   Doesn't seem right.

Tony   That's the English language for you. Never a synonym when you need one.

Louise   I'll be outside.

She exits.

Tony *picks up sheets of A4, scans them. Scribbles something in one of the margins. Thinks.*

Denise *enters. She is carrying a bucket of water and a sponge. She sees* **Tony**. *Stops.*

Denise   Sorry. Are you working? I didn't realise.

Tony   Don't mind me.

Denise   I wouldn't like to think I was putting you off or anything. You know, interrupting the creative flow.

Tony   You go ahead.

Denise *takes the cloth off the small table.*

Denise   Dusty. (*Whispers.*) Sorry.

She begins to wash the table with the cloth.

She hums.

Denise   I hummed. It was automatic. Shall I do this later?

Tony   No. No. I'm just thinking really.

Denise   I don't know how you think of things. I mean, how do you think of things?

Tony   The million dollar question.

Denise   I suppose it is.

Pause.

I wish I was good at something.

She continues to wash over the table.

Tennis or nursing. Something.

Tony   You are. You are good at something.

Denise   What?

Tony   Everyone's good at something.

Pause.

For example, I know you as a cleaner. You're a very good cleaner.

Denise   Oh God.

Tony   Don't put yourself down, Denise. Where would we be without cleaners?

Denise I meant something like a vet or a solicitor. Something I could have enthusiasm for. I keep waiting. Waiting for something to come along. Only nothing comes along.

Tony It will. It will.

Denise It will?

Tony Things happen to people. They happen. People have a destiny. One morning you'll wake up and something will happen. You'll stumble on something inside you.

Denise Do you think?

Tony Absolutely. Absolutely. People have amazing resources inside of them. Amazing. I used to work with this old Polish guy. He told me that he'd bricked a woman up inside a chimney. Bricked her up for years inside a chimney.

Denise Why did he do that?

Tony She was a Jew and he saved her life. He hid her from the Nazis. He kept one brick loose and he used to pass food back and forth by means of removing the brick.

Denise He removed the brick?

Tony Yes. And amazingly, she survived.

Denise God.

Tony Yes.

Pause.

Denise What happened to her family?

Tony Well, they died. They died. But the point is she survived. That's because people have a lot of good in them. A lot of good which they find at the right moment.

Denise Yes, yes I see.

Tony The African elephant.

Denise Pardon.

Tony The African elephant will be saved in the nick of time by international co-ordination and agreement.

Denise Oh good.

Tony It's the same thing. Pulling that extra bit out of the bag and surprising even yourself.

Pause.

Denise I'm thinking of going to Tibet.

Tony Really?

Denise Yes.

Tony Fantastic.

Denise Yes.

Pause.

It's very spiritual. There's a lot of monks in Tibet.

Tony Ah.

Denise You can't turn round for the monks.

Tony So that's what you'll do?

Denise Do?

Tony When you leave us.

Denise Oh well. Yes. Maybe. I've got the brochures.

Tony Well. Good luck.

Denise Thanks.

Tony I think you're very brave. Setting out. It will be a whole new life.

Denise *begins to cry.*

Tony Denise?

Denise Sorry. This is stupid. It's just now it's come to it. Going. It doesn't feel like I imagined it would.

Tony God. Look. I haven't got a handkerchief.

Denise That afternoon. That time . . . when we . . .

Tony Look . . .

Denise I shouldn't have brought it up.

Tony You're a lovely girl, Denise.

Pause.

Denise Sometimes I think 'Christ, what is going to happen to me?' I mean I haven't got anyone.

Tony You'll meet someone. You'll meet someone.

Pause.

Denise I'm sorry. I shouldn't have brought it up. About before.

Tony   Don't worry. Don't worry. That's fine.

Denise *begins cleaning the table once more.*

Denise   Apparently it's like a bowl.

Tony   What is?

Denise   Tibet.

Pause.

Apparently over the centuries all this good karma has collected in that bowl. Like rain.

Pause.

I'd like to sit right in the middle of that bowl like sitting at the bottom of a pool and feel all that good stuff wash over me. Till I was as clean as a stone in the sea.

Pause.

This table's coming up nice.

Scene Four

At the edge of the beach Louise is digging. **Rosa** *watches. The tree is beside them, ready to be planted.*

Louise   What do you think?

Pause.

The place. It's a nice spot.

Rosa   It's alright.

Pause.

She didn't like trees.

Louise   I thought everybody liked trees.

Rosa   I never heard her say she did. I never heard her say 'I love trees'

Louise   It's not the sort of thing people do say. Not out loud. Anyway, I said like, like trees. You love people or dogs. You admire vegetation.

Rosa   She never liked people.

Louise   That's not true. You know that's not true.

Rosa   She never liked you.

Louise   We were sisters. Sisters fall out all the time.

Rosa   Normal people like their sisters.

Louise   Well, often people aren't normal. That's the tragedy of it.

Rosa   You think she wasn't normal.

Louise   I never said that.

Pause.

Rosa?

Pause.

We rub along alright together, don't we?

Pause.

Rosa   Yes.

Louise   Good. I'm glad.

Pause.

Rosa   I hope that tree dies.

Louise   You shouldn't say that. That's an awful thing to say.

Pause.

She didn't do it on purpose.

Pause.

The worst bit's over now. We can put the worst behind us.

Pause.

Do you want to help me plant it?

Rosa   She fucked left right and centre. That house was a shit-hole when we lived there.

Louise   It's rather heavy. I'll need someone to hold it. While I put the earth back.

Rosa   You ought to get Tony or someone to give you a hand.

Rosa *moves away. Sits facing away from* **Louise** *and the tree.*

Louise *struggles with the tree alone.*

Louise   (*to herself*) Bastard tree.

Louise *manages to right the tree and stamps earth round it. She stands back.*

Rosa   Tony's here. Right in the nick of time.

Tony *and* **Denise** *enter.*

Tony   It's a smashing tree.

Pause.

You got it up on your own then?

Pause.

Louise   We should have thought of something. Something to say.

Tony   We could have a few quotes. Poetry.

Pause.

I can't remember any.

Pause.

Denise   We could sing something.

Tony   The Internationale.

Louise   This isn't the time for flip remarks, Tony.

Tony   Sorry.

Rosa   I'm not singing anything.

Denise   I meant like a hymn.

Louise   Jo wasn't that way inclined.

Tony   Man is descended from a sea-squirt. She sent Louise the article.

Denise   Oh.

Tony   Didn't she? Louise was in the Christian Union at college. Jo had a campaign.

Denise   What's a sea-squirt?

Louise   A sort of stomach on a stick that sucks up excreta from the sea bed.

Tony   Jo knew how to mass her ideological troops. She could be very persuasive.

Louise   I wan an easy target.

Tony   It put poor old Lu off.

Denise   We're not really descended from sea squirts?

Rosa   Tony might be.

Louise   I think we should get on with this.

Pause.

I think we should say anything we want.

Pause.

Hello. Anything. We'll do that.

Silence descends. They gather round the tree.

Tony. You go first.

Tony   Do you think it should be me?

Louise   Yes. Go on.

Tony *takes a step or two forward towards the tree. Slight hesitation. Everyone watches.*

Tony   Hello Jo. It's me. Tony speaking.

Pause.

I'm still here. Still with Louise as you can probably guess. Louise has planted a pretty smashing tree here. For you actually, naturally. The house is getting a good clean up. I must say it's great being by the sea. I've always liked the sea.

Pause.

This is a bit like an international call, isn't it?

He laughs.

I'm still slogging away at the old typewriter, every spare moment. Still teaching in between the real work, writing. Don't laugh but my last book *Salamander Days*   got a mention in the *Sunday Times*. I don't think that was 'the book'. You know, not 'the book'. But who knows, maybe this next one?

Pause.

So . . . so . . . I can't think of much else. The world's still going round. 30km a second. (*Short laugh.*) Yes. We're all still trying. I realise . . . I shouldn't have said that earlier. About the sea . . . Sorry. Anyway, nice to chat. Over and out, Tony.

He steps back.

Was I alright?

Louise *steps forward.*

Louise   Hello Jo. It's a year on. A year on. We all miss you. Rosa's here. She's with me now.

Pause.

Louise *steps back.*

Rose?

Rosa *does not move.*

Pause.

Denise *steps forward.*

Denise Jo. You don't know me. I've seen your photo. I help Louise out. Well, I'm just finishing. I did a bit of housecraft, you know, hoovering. I know Rosa.

Pause.

You've got a lovely daughter.

Pause.

I don't believe in God, but I do, you know, believe in something. Something more than just us. Just us here. I mean a force. A benevolent force. A force field even. Something big. Creative. Something that's in nature. I think whales are closer to it than we are. Closer to living it. I mean they don't do any damage, do they? They just do a lot of swimming and that's not because they're stupid. That's just the way they've evolved. They keep the same partner forever. There's got to be something. I heard about this woman who kept seeing a cat out of the corner of her eye and there was nothing there. Nothing. Not a real cat. But something. You know. Something.

She loses her thread. Steps back.

Louise Rosa?

Rosa I'm not talking to a tree.

Louise Why not?

Rosa It was in a shop a few hours ago.

Louise It might be a good thing. It might make you feel better.

Rosa When you die you rot. That's what she said. Slowly at first but then surprisingly quickly.

Louise Maybe we could leave you here alone. For a bit.

Rosa Do what you like.

Louise *touches* **Rosa**'s *arm.* **Rosa** *moves away. They leave* **Rosa** *by the tree.* **Rosa** *stares at the tree.*

Rosa There was a little girl and she had a little curl right in the middle of her forehead. And when she was good she was very very good. And when she was bad she was horrid.

Rosa *kicks some sand at the tree. She exits.*

Scene Five

Denise *alone on the beach. She makes a circle of stones in the sand. From her bag she takes a book. She takes off her shoes and places them with her bag outside the circle. She sits in the centre of the circle with the book. She thinks for a moment then closes her eyes and runs her hand over the pages of the book until she has chosen a place to open it. She hesitates once or twice then finally opens it. She opens her eyes, looks at the book. Turns it the right way round and reads.*

Denise   A tree is not a suitable place for a wild goose.

She thinks.

A goose?

She closes her eyes. Repeats the process.

Colin *enters.*

Denise *opens her eyes. Reads.*

Denise   The tusk of a gelded boar brings good fortune.

Colin   But is not easy to come by nowadays.

Denise *starts.*

Denise   God!

Pause.

I was just . . . talking to myself.

Colin   Can I see your book?

Denise   My book?

Colin   Yes.

Denise   What for?

Colin   Just to have a look.

Denise   I don't know you.

Colin   Is it new age?

Denise   I don't know you from Adam.

Colin   I'm just interested.

He goes to step into the circle.

Denise   Don't.

Colin   What?

Denise   Come in here. The circle.

Colin   Oh. The circle.

Pause.

What happens if I do? Go in.

Pause.

Will I sprout horns?

Denise   This is typical. A woman. A woman alone on a beach. It's like a red rag to a bull. To a man.

Pause.

Denise *stands up and walks over to him, still keeping inside the circle.*

Remove yourself. Shrivel. Become extinct.

Pause.

Sometimes I look in men's eyes and know something's wrong. They've got eyes like pebbles.

Pause.

Pissing dirty pebbles.

Pause.

Colin   I was a friend of Jo's.

Pause.

Denise   A friend of Jo's?

Colin   Yes.

Denise   Jo's?

Colin   Yes.

Pause.

Denise   Oh.

Colin   Colin.

Pause.

I saw you earlier. With Rosa.

Pause.

Denise   Do you live round here then?

Colin   Not far.

Denise   It's nice round here, isn't it?

Colin   It's alright.

Denise   The colours of the houses . . . are nice.

Colin   I can't say I've given it much thought.

Denise   That's understandable. As a visitor I'd notice that sort of thing you see. As a visitor. Whereas you, being an inhabitant would be more likely to take it for granted. As an inhabitant.

Pause.

The people are nice though. Friendly.

Colin   A lot of rich bastards live round here. They creep down from the cities. To escape the mess they've made. It's like an infection.

Pause.

Denise   That's an interesting way to look at it. An infection.

Pause.

Colin   So you're a friend of Rosa's.

Denise   Yes. In a way.

Colin   That's nice for her.

Denise   Nice?

Colin   For her to have a friend.

Denise   Oh. Oh. Yes.

Pause.

It's a lovely beach.

Colin   It's filthy.

Denise   Is it?

Colin   And the sea. That's full of crap. Pollution.

Denise   How awful. I mean. The sea.

Colin   I don't know. There's a sort of justice in it. An equality in destruction. No one can enjoy it now. Not even the bourgeoisie.

Denise   I suppose so. God, that's true. Yes. I can see that. The bourgeoisie. God.

Pause.

Here.

She hands him her book.

Open it. Any page you like.

He does so.

Read it.

Colin   (*reading*) Published by Mushroom Press Limited, Northampton.

Denise   Not that page.

Pause.

You ought to call round some time. See the house. For old times' sake.

Colin   I'd like to. I may do that.

Denise   I'm leaving tomorrow.

Colin   Mind the circle.

Denise *looks down. She has dislodged some of the stone.*

Denise   Oh that.

Scene Six

Somewhere along the beach.

Dogboy. *He has a dog with him. This is theatrically imagined. He is playing with his dog. The dog leaps to fetch something he holds.* **Dogboy** *pulls his hand away each time.*

Rosa *approaches. Watches.*

Rosa   Is that your dog?

Dogboy *continues playing with dog.*

What's its name?

Pause. **Dogboy** *still splays.*

Dogboy   Yelp.

Rosa   That's the noise a dog makes.

Dogboy   That was the idea.

Rosa   It's an ugly dog.

Dogboy   It doesn't have a very good diet.

Rosa   You should feed it better.

Dogboy *stops his game.*

Dogboy   What's it to you?

Rosa   I could work for the RSPCA.

Dogboy   Fuck the RSPCA. Spying eejits.

Rosa   You're paranoid.

Dogboy   And you're a polaroid.

Rosa   Is that supposed to rhyme?

Dogboy   Please yourself.

Pause.

Rosa   You live on this beach.

Pause.

How d'you get a bath?

Dogboy   A bath. Madam muck.

Rosa   Madam muck yourself.

Pause.

My mother drowned in that sea.

Dogboy   Was she a good swimmer?

Rosa   Quite good.

Dogboy   My dog's a fucking brilliant swimmer.

Rosa   It might do it good to go in salt water.

Dogboy   Maybe.

Pause.

Rosa   I want to do it again.

Dogboy   Alright.

He lies down. **Rosa** *undoes his flies, sits on him. She begins to move on top of him. After a bit she stops.*

Rosa   You're crying.

Dogboy   So. I'm human.

Rosa   That dog's whining.

Dogboy   Sometimes I want to kick it when it does that.

Rosa   You wouldn't though.

Dogboy   No. I'd feel bad afterwards.

Rosa *climbs off him.*

Rosa   I might as well go then.

Dogboy   I'm looking for a cave.

Rosa   What cave?

Dogboy   A dry, sandy cave,

Rosa   There's no caves round here.

Dogboy   There could be.

Rosa   I used to live down here. I lived down here years. I never saw a cave.

Dogboy   You can't see the best caves from the outside.

Pause.

I tell you what. This dog is a bloody good watchdog. Aren't you girl? Eh? When I sleep, she watches. Don't you girl? Eh?

Rosa   There's no caves.

Dogboy *begins to sharpen a stone against another stone.*

Dogboy   This is how people made tools. How they made tools in the old days. Stone on stone. Stone on stone. They made things with blades. That's how they slit throats. Animal throats. They did it at the neck where the skin's soft. Where the blood is. Where there's a lot of blood to come out. Blood and air would bubble out.

He continues to sharpen the stone.

I've been working on this. Look.

He shows **Rosa**.

You can touch it. Touch the edge.

She doesn't touch it.

Go on.

She touches it.

Ow! Sharp, eh? Hurts.

He lays it flat against his cheek.

Warm. It's warm.

He begins to sharpen it again.

Rosa   We should have used something.

Pause.

Precautions. Before. When we did it.

Dogboy   How old are you?

Rosa Fifteen and one month.

Dogboy You're under age.

Rosa Only legally.

Dogboy The law's the law.

Pause.

Rosa What would you do if I was? If I swelled up bigger and bigger?

Dogboy I'd see you alright.

Rosa How would you?

Dogboy You'll see what I'll do.

Rosa I'd have to leave school.

Dogboy You'd go back though. After. There's no prospects without an education.

Pause.

Rosa You couldn't do anything. If I was.

Dogboy You'll see. What I'll do.

Rosa You've only got a stone. A stone and a dog.

Dogboy I've got something else.

Rosa What?

Out of his coat he brings a magazine.

Let's have a look.

She reaches for it. He whisks it away.

Dogboy In a bit.

Rosa Is it filthy?

Dogboy It's mine. There's people in here, their faces shine.

Rosa That's the paper. The quality of the paper.

Dogboy Shine. Like saints.

Rosa It's the paper. Give it to me.

Dogboy Wait.

She grabs it.

Rosa *looks at the magazine.*

Rosa Do you read it?

Dogboy Yes.

Rosa Fucking queer.

Dogboy Get lost.

Rosa You stole it.

Dogboy I found it.

Rosa Put your hands in dirty rubbish.

Dogboy I found it.

She hits him with the magazine.

Rosa Queer bastard.

Dogboy Don't hit me.

She hits him with it again.

Dogboy I'll set the dog on you.

Rosa Shiny faces.

She hits him again.

Dogboy Get off!

Rosa Fucking queer. Fucking queer in the head.

She hits him.

Dogboy Don't hit me.

Rosa You'll be crying soon.

She begins to tear up the magazine.

Dogboy It's mine.

Rosa Boo hoo.

She continues to tear it.

Dogboy Don't tear it!

Rosa Fucking queer bastard.

Dogboy Fuck you.

Rosa *throws the magazine to the ground.*

Rosa Crying bastard. Like saints. Don't you know anything? You couldn't do anything if I was. Could you?

Dogboy *kneels down. Smoothes out a bit of the magazine. Begins to read.*

Dogboy Have the days of sticky-back plastic passed us by? Covering old jars with this new range of designer plastics performs a miracle of recycling and can create a matching set of storage containers for the cheap and cheerful kitchen.

Pause.

Sometimes I see people. In their windows. Sometimes they're black bastards. Sometimes they're women or men in shirts. They close their curtains and they yawn. Sometimes I close my eyes and I see myself going in. Often they're asleep. I've got my stone in my hand or in my pocket. I stick it into their hearts or their necks.

He goes over to **Rosa**. *He touches her stomach.*

Is it in there?

Scene Seven

The house

Louise *is sorting out stuff in the boxes. While she does this* **Tony** *is typing on a small manual typewriter. He sits at the small table* **Denise** *has cleaned earlier. He draws a page out of his typewriter. He looks at it. Laughs.*

Louise   Is that a funny bit?

Tony   This guy. I've got this guy in his bedroom. I've decided to keep the place vague. Eastern European.

Louise   It's not vague if you happen to come from Eastern Europe.

Tony   Queues, greyness, a tendency to weep. You know.

Louise   Sounds like London.

Tony   Anyway, this guy has just been overcome with paint fumes. He's stumbling about and he mistakenly gets into his wardrobe which has a faulty catch . . . and he can't get out.

Tony *laughs.*

Pause.

You have to read it really.

Louise *is unfolding a banner which she has taken out of one of the boxes. She reads.*

Louise   'Women unite to reclaim the night.' This would probably fetch something on the memorabilia market. Jo never threw anything out. She was either a hoarder or extremely disorganised.

Tony   The paint fumes are an analogy. The bewilderment of new ideas. What will happen when the man comes out of the wardrobe?

Louise (*folding banner*) He steps in a paint tin?

Tony This is an amazing time, Louise. An amazing time to be living in. Huge empires are breaking up. It's like the end of the ice age. Watching the ice cracking. All warm-blooded species rejoice!

Louise *holds up a jumper with a huge CND symbol on it.*

Louise Do you think Jo ever wore this?

She examines it.

It's a monstrosity. I expect she did.

Tony Recently people have died for their ideas. Laid down in front of tanks and the tanks have rolled over them and they've been squashed.

Louise I don't expect they imagined that would happen. Not when they lay down.

Tony But they took the risk. That's the human spirit. It gives me a great sense of optimism.

Louise *has tried on the jumper. It is very big. It reaches her knees.*

Louise Subtle, isn't it?

Pause.

All this is going, Tony. Everything. Today. I can't stand this stuff hanging around any more. We've come down here the odd weekend and it's like we've been afraid to touch anything. We've been tip-toeing around, thinking things are sacred. This isn't a shrine. It's my house now, mine and Rosa's. This is day one, Tony. Everything has to be dead and buried from today. That's what I want.

Tony What I want is for this book to be better than the last. That's what I want.

Pause.

Then it will reach more people.

Louise Everything's so dusty. Dust is mostly human skin. Flakes of human skin. Did you know that?

Pause.

She's been with me a year now, Rosa. A year. But it's not right. There's something between us. Distance. Why should there be? Sometimes I look at the back of her head and my throat aches.

Pause.

She knows I'm lying.

Tony   You're not lying.

Louise   I cast a light on things. A comfortable light. That's a deception. You can smell that. Rosa can.

Tony   You took the best option. And in all probability you were right.

Louise   You can't build something on a lie. It's roots keep humping up the earth.

Tony   Jo went swimming. That's all we know.

Louise   That's not all we know.

Pause.

She had problems. We know she had problems. Living down here. She hid down here. Dreaming. Living off ideas. How do you explain seventeen empty cans of baked beans in the washing machine? She went up and down like a yo-yo. There's a name for that.

Tony   She was obviously a very untidy woman. That doesn't prove anything. It's supposition.

Louise   What about the phone call? Days before she phoned me. She said she hadn't bothered to get dressed for three days. Three days. She said that. She said her hair was going grey. She was depressed about the Gulf. God knows. Something. Those aren't suppositions Tony.

Tony   Everyone was depressed about the Gulf. It was a highly inflammable situation.

Louise   Stop sitting on the fence, Tony.

Tony   It's a question of accuracy, Louise. We just don't know what happened. You couldn't say anything now anyway.

Louise   Why not?

Tony   Well. I think that would be a little insensitive. Not to say irresponsible.

Louise   Don't you understand? It's coming between us. Me and Rosa. The lie is ruining everything.

Pause.

Your book.

Tony   Yes?

Louise   When you ask me my opinion, what do you expect?

Tony   I expect the truth.

Louise   And what if I thought it was turgid, you know, distended beyond it's natural size by watery substances?

Pause.

Tony   I don't see the point of all this.

Louise   What would you expect then?

Tony   I'd expect your honest opinion.

Louise   You wouldn't rather I lied? A kind but cowardly act? Because that's the choice.

Tony   I'd still want the truth.

Louise   Naturally. Anyone would.

Pause.

Tony   Are you trying to tell me something?

Louise   Because that's the choice.

Tony   What I've shown you. You hate it don't you?

Louise   Do you really want to know?

Tony   Yes.

Louise   Really?

Pause.

Tony   Yes.

Louise   You see. People need truth, Tony. Otherwise they resent you. That's understandable.

Tony   My book?

Louise   I haven't got the guts. The guts to tell Rosa.

Pause.

Tony   What about the book?

Louise   I'm not talking about that now.

Tony   You don't understand. I lie awake thinking about that book. Turning it over and over. It's my contribution, Louise. To everything. That's why I do it. To contribute. If I didn't do that who would I be?

Louise   You'd be a teacher.

Tony   I think I'll go out for a bit.

Louise   I was making a point. That's all. A point.

He gets up, exits.

Pause.

Louise *continues to sort out Jo's stuff. She pulls out a dressing gown, past its best, a pink, silky 1930's affair. She examines it.*

Louise This was falling apart. It's rotten under the arms. I expect you sat around in this, fundraising for a Nicaraguan women's rug weaving collective.

She smells it.

It smells. Smells of you.

Pause.

The trouble is your stuff's falling apart.

Pause.

The trouble is you're not quite gone. You're still in the dust. Floating about in the dust.

Pause.

This place was a mess, Jo. You make a mess and then you leave me to clear it up.

Pause.

It's not so much you, how you lived, I was thinking of Rosa.

Pause.

That name. Calling her that. It's quite a lot to live up to, Jo. Political martyrdom. I used to watch her when she was small. I used to think I'd be quite happy for my child not to smear banana on the living room carpet. Something ordinary, like that. But that name's a weight, Jo, a weight.

Pause.

Did you ever think that she might be more like me? Not like you. Like me.

She takes off the jumper and stuffs it with the dressing gown back into the box.

The trouble with you Jo is that you're destructive. The things you touched. Maybe it was just as well. Just as well, what happened. There. I've said it now. I've said it. I didn't want to say it.

Pause. **Rosa** *enters.*

Louise Rosa?

Rosa I need something. From the kitchen.

Louise Rosa.

Pause.

I just wanted to say . . . what I wanted to say was that sometimes . . . sometimes I haven't been as honest with you . . . as honest as perhaps I should have been. But I wanted you to know that from today . . . from today you can ask me anything and that from today I will be honest with you. Tell you.

Pause.

About Jo. Anything.

Pause.

Earlier by the tree, we were talking. Remember?

Pause.

Rosa There is something.

Louise Yes?

Rosa Would you ever have a baby?

Pause.

Louise What brought that up?

Rosa Would you?

Pause.

Louise I can't. I can't have one.

Rosa Why?

Pause.

Louise I did something. Something stupid once.

Pause.

I was young. I didn't understand things. Well, I understood them but I couldn't believe they were happening to me. I missed my time, twice, three times.

Rosa What did you do?

Louise This is twenty years ago. I was at college. I went to my room and hit myself. I hit myself here.

She indicates.

I hit myself over and over. After a bit I started to bleed. It was a very stupid thing to do. I did myself quite a bit of damage. I didn't go to my doctor soon enough. Unfortunately.

Pause.

So.

Denise *enters.*

Denise Hi.

Rosa   The kitchen. I better go.

She exits.

Louise *goes back to the boxes. Picks one up.*

Pause.

Denise   I've been on the beach. Ages. Looking at the sea. It's incredible, isn't it? A human thing. That something can happen to you at a certain moment. At the right moment something lifts you. I met a man on the beach. I mean it's not as if I'm down here all the time or anything. I mean it is odd, isn't it? That just this morning I had a feeling . . . not a good feeling but then something can happen, happen just like that. Like fate. And I feel different. Full. It's as if something can come along..

Louise   A man can come along.

Denise   If you like. And then without me doing anything . . . It's weird. It's incredible isn't it?

Louise   I wouldn't know. I don't have a religious faith.

Denise   Not religious. Like fate. Brilliant.

Louise *exits with box.*

Denise   Brilliant.

Scene Eight

Beach.

Rosa *finds* **Dogboy** *hunched on the sand. He is not wearing his coat.*

Pause.

Rosa   Where's your dog?

Dogboy   It's run off.

Rosa   Has it?

Dogboy   Or someone's done its head in with a rock. There's a lot of them about. Rocks.

Pause.

Rosa   Where's your coat?

Dogboy   Dunno. Up the beach.

Pause.

Rosa   I bought you something.

She hands him a sandwich.

Pause.

Say ta.

Dogboy takes a bite. Swallows.

Dogboy   I feel cold.

Rosa   You shouldn't leave your coat lying about.

Dogboy   I feel cold all the time.

Rosa   You shouldn't have left it.

Dogboy *drops his sandwich in the sand.*

Dogboy   I've dropped it.

Rosa   Didn't you want it?

Dogboy   It was an accident. It'll have sand on it now. I don't like it when they get sand on them.

Rosa   You never wanted it.

Dogboy   I did. I'll eat it now. See.

He begins to eat it where it lies. Animal like.

Rosa   Not like that. Not like that. You're fucking mental. Brain dead mental.

Dogboy   Your mother was mental. She drowned in that sea.

Pause.

Rosa *exits.*

Dogboy   Come back. Come back. I don't mean anything.

Pause.

Something's coming. Something's coming. I can smell it. It has wet teeth. Terrible. Think something. Think it. Think anything. Think it now. Think it. Keep it off me. Can't keep it off me. Can't stop it. Can't stop it.

He gives a cry. He suddenly convulses as if something has possessed him.

Scene Nine

The house. Evening.

The boxes are gone. There is a lamp on. **Louise** *enters with a vase of flowers which she puts on the small table. She exits.*

Denise *enters tentatively. She is over-dressed for the occasion. She is wearing a short dress. She is anxious about this. She perches on the edge of the sofa. She carries a handbag.*

Louise *enters with a bowl of peanuts which she will place on the table. She sees* **Denise.**

Louise   Oh! That's a nice dress.

Denise   It's too much, isn't it?

Louise   Too much?

Denise   You know. Just too much. Uncasual. Over the top. Tarty. Throwing it about.

Louise   Well, I wouldn't say so.

Pause.

Are you expecting anyone?

Denise   Oh no, no, no.

Pause.

No.

Pause.

It's just, if this man wants to call round some time, if he wants to, he might just call round tonight. It might be that tonight might be a good time seeing as I'm leaving tomorrow. Mightn't it?

Louise   I see.

Denise   God, I feel nervous. My hands are shaking.

Louise   Is that the prospect of travelling?

Denise   What?

Pause.

Denise *opens her bag and brings out a bottle of wine.*

I got a bottle of wine. It's Bulgarian. Do you want some?

Louise   No thanks.

Denise   Oh go on. Otherwise I'll just drink it all myself and get slaughtered.

Louise   Well. Alright then. Just a glass.

Denise   I'll get them.

Denise *gets glasses. Sits back down. While opening the bottle . . .*

Sometimes you remind me of a train.

Louise   Thanks very much.

Denise   I meant a train on its tracks.

Pause.

A train going, going, going.

Pause.

It's meant as a compliment. I used to see you leaving for work in the mornings when I had early starts. You had a briefcase and a raincoat and I'd think there goes a woman with enthusiasm. Then I'd imagine you coming back at night. You'd sit down and have a gin.

Louise   There's quite a lot to be done, in between the setting off and the gin.

Denise   Oh, I know. I know.

Pause.

She hands **Louise** *a glass. Takes one for herself.*

Cheers.

Pause.

I meant to ask you. Do you think I'd be good. Any good in a job like yours?

Louise   On a magazine?

Denise   Yes.

Louise   Have you got any qualifications?

Denise   How d'you mean?

Louise   Any qualifications?

Pause.

Denise   Not really.

Pause.

Once I started on a jewellery design course. But it was ever so fiddly. After a bit I just went off it. I left one Friday night and never found the enthusiasm to return. I've matured a lot since then though.

Louise   I thought you were set on going to Tibet.

Denise   For when I got back I was thinking.

Pause.

That was the door.

Tony *enters with his typewriter.*

Denise   It's Tony.

Louise   (*to* **Tony**) What's that?

Tony   It's a typewriter.

Louise   I can see that.

Tony   It's got rather cold upstairs. My fingers were going numb.

He puts typewriter on small table.

Louise   Aren't you being a little anti-social?

Tony   I'm not disturbing anyone am I?

Louise   I don't particularly want to sit here listening to you clatter away on that thing.

Tony   I'll sit in the corner.

Louise   I'll still be able to hear it from the corner.

Tony   I'm at rather a significant juncture.

Louise   I remain unmoved.

Pause.

Tony   Alright. Since there appear to be strong objections I'll proceed in pencil. You shouldn't be able to hear that unless you're listening very hard for it.

Louise   You still won't be joining in.

Tony   Joining in what?

Louise   Conversation. The general free flowing exchange of ideas. You know, the thing people do in your books a lot. Sit opposite each other and talk.

Tony   Fine.

Tony *sits down, folds his arms. Waits.*

Silence.

A long pause.

Denise   Once I got really pissed. Really pissed at this party and then I got really hungry, really hungry, you know, like you do after drinking and so I devoured a bowl of peanuts. A whole bowl, to myself.

Pause.

And then I vomited the lot back up. I sort of regurgitated them. The thing is, the thing is, they came out whole. I must just have swallowed them down without any sort of chewing. Later someone remarked that they shot out like bullets. Ping ping. Ping.

Pause.

I was a bit depressed at the time.

Tony I'm afraid I don't have any vomit stories.

Louise You're just not trying.

Pause.

Denise Was that the door?

Tony Are we expecting someone?

Denise/Louise No.

Denise jumps up.

Rosa *enters.*

Denise *sits back down.*

Denise Rosa.

Rosa There's boxes outside. Boxes of Jo's stuff.

Louise I've been clearing things out. Nothing precious. Nothing we would have wanted to keep.

Rosa I don't want to keep anything. I just saw the boxes.

Louise It looks better in here, doesn't it?

Denise It must be nearly half past. Nearly half past by now.

Rosa Is someone coming?

Tony/Louise/Denise No.

Pause.

Rosa We should burn them.

Louise Burn them?

Rosa The boxes. Pile them up and burn them.

Louise I was thinking of sending them to Oxfam.

Rosa It's quicker to burn them.

Louise It would be quick.

Tony You're not going to burn them?

Louise It's not illegal Tony.

Tony Rosa doesn't really want to. Do you Rose?

Rosa Yes, I do. (*To* **Louise**.) Let's do it now.

Louise Now?

Rosa Then we won't have to see them again. Think of them.

Louise   Like a big finish?

Rosa   A big fire.

Louise *picks up a box of matches. She shakes them.*

Louise   Matches!

Tony   It's a bit of a Nazi impulse, isn't it Louise? They burnt books.

Louise   Don't tempt me.

They exit.

Tony   Sometimes I wonder whether she has any respect for my work whatsoever?

Pause.

Denise   The reason I'd been depressed was because I'd been working at this sandwich making job. I was living with this bloke and we were making sandwiches in his flat. At first I really threw myself into it. I experimented with fillings, I bought a butter dish. We used to drive round delivering sandwiches to local businesses only quite often we never got any orders. We ate quite a lot of sandwiches on those occasions. That dealt quite a blow to my enthusiasm I can tell you. Not to mention the fact that I wasn't getting the correct balance of amino acids in my diet. And that can lead to personality disorders. Like shoplifting or slimming. Then one day we found a cockroach lying upside down in a giant size tub of margarine. It wasn't me that left the lid off. That was when the infestation started. You can never be alone with an infestation. Soon after that he left me. He walked out leaving rent arrears and twenty-seven kilos of cheddar. I lay in bed weeping for days. I don't know if what we had was love but it did provide light relief from all the buttering. That was before I became a Buddhist. I used to watch the cockroaches basking on the walls. They do say in the event of a nuclear holocaust cockroaches will survive to inherit the earth. They used to crawl around in a superior manner as if they knew they could survive intense heat and I couldn't. Cocky bastards. The thing is, I'd never go through that now. Be used like that. Because now I'm different. Transformed by experience.

Pause.

What time is it?

Tony   Seven forty-five.

Denise   It's not too late is it? I mean if you were going to drop in unexpectedly on someone it's not too late?

Tony   I don't suppose so.

Denise   Good.

Pause.

Sometimes I wonder what happens. What happens to people who can't find enthusiasm for things. The way things are.

Pause.

Of course there's always acupuncture.

Rosa *and* **Louise** *enter.*

Louise We've got a blaze going.

Rosa A fire.

Louise It's all going up.

Rosa Burning.

Louise It was fast. It went up fast.

Rosa All the sparks. Flying up.

Louise *puts her arm round* **Rosa**.

Louise It's a good end. A good end.

Denise The door. That was it. The door. I heard it. God. How do I look?

She hurries out.

Denise *returns. She is followed by* **Dogboy**. *He stands in the doorway. He is naked. He holds his stone. He is muddy, bloody.*

Dogboy *barks.*

Pause.

He barks again.

Denise He was there. At the door.

Tony Jesus.

Dogboy *barks.*

He's naked.

Louise Go away!

Dogboy *barks.*

Go away!

Dogboy *does not move.*

Part Two

Scene Ten

The house. A little later.

Dogboy *is sitting on the floor. He has a blanket over him. He seems vacant.* **Denise** *is watching him intently. She stands holding her shoe in one hand, as if to use the heel as a weapon. She is poised.* **Rosa** *stands well in the background as if to disassociate herself. She watches too. She gives no help to* **Denise. Dogboy** *makes a soft grunting noise.* **Denise** *jumps. She looks over to the door. No one comes. She resumes her watch.* **Dogboy** *gives a small whine.*

Denise (*calls*) Louise!

Pause.

Nothing happens.

Fuck.

Pause.

Dogboy *looks at her.*

Dogboy Smell.

Pause.

Smell. Got bigger and bigger. Took me over like an itch. Sea stinks fish. Air stinks salt. Sand stinks sun and dirt. Smell drags me. Leads me circles. Paths and paths. Found old belt. Smells dead horse. Smell pulls me like God.

Denise Shut up.

Dogboy *growls.*

Denise Louise! (*To* **Rosa**.) Where is she?

He growls again.

I'm warning you.

Pause.

She looks towards the door.

I've hit people before. I'm not afraid to. I've drawn blood.

Dogboy *growls.*

Quite a lot of blood.

Dogboy *gets up and snatches the shoe from* **Denise** *with a bite. Holds it in his mouth.*

Denise *gives a cry.*

Denise   Louise!

Dogboy *growls and shakes the shoe from side to side in his mouth.*

Louise *and* **Tony** *enter.*

Denise   He's got my shoe. He snatched it. He was growling.

Tony   Did you provoke him in any way?

Louise   Of course she didn't.

Denise   I didn't. (*To* **Rosa.**) Did I?

Tony   He seemed perfectly calm when we left.

Louise   Well he's not calm now. (*To* **Dogboy.**) Give that back.

Dogboy *backs away. Whines a little.*

Give it back.

Tony   Shouting at him won't get you anywhere.

Tony *approaches* **Dogboy**.

Drop it. Drop it.

Dogboy *drops it.*

Tony   There.

Louise   Bravo.

Tony *picks up the shoe and gives it to* **Denise** *who takes it gingerly.*

That was the easy bit.

Pause.

Rosa. I think you should go upstairs.

Rosa   Why?

Louise   Please don't argue. It's just for the best.

Rosa *exits ungraciously.*

Tony   I'm not sure I can do this, Louise.

Louise   Do I have to do it?

Tony   It's not a question of who does it. It's a question of do we do it at all?

Louise   It's either that or turn him out for the night and lock the doors. You choose.

Tony   It's raining out. It's started to rain.

Louise   Well then. I don't see why we just don't phone the police.

Tony   They'll only throw him into a cell.

Louise   Probably the best place for him.

Tony   I couldn't have that on my conscience, Louise.

Louise   Then there's no alternative.

Tony   It just doesn't seem right.

Louise   There's a fifteen-year-old girl in this house and she's in my care. I have a duty towards her. I've asked you to come up with another solution and I may say that you've failed dismally on that score. This is real life Tony, not one of your novels and in real life things actually really happen and one actually really responds.

Tony   The thing about my novels, Louise, is that they tend to convey a spirit of optimism. Trust and optimism. Both of which are sadly lacking here.

Louise   Give me the ropes.

Pause.

Tony   I'll do it. I'd just like it publicly noted that I do it with a great deal of reluctance.

He approaches **Dogboy**.

Hello.

Pause.

Look. I've got some rope.

He pulls the rope out of his pocket and shows it to **Dogboy**.

Dogboy *pats the bit of hanging rope with his hand. It swings.*

Rope. And I think I'd better explain that although this goes against quite a few of my deeply held principles I'm afraid I'm going to have to restrain you just for tonight.

Dogboy *grabs hold of the rope.*

Ah. He's got hold of the rope, Louise.

Louise   Yes, I can see that.

Dogboy *begins to pull on the rope.*

Tony   I think he wants a game.

Louise   For goodness' sake.

Tony (to **Dogboy**)   Actually, this is the rope I was meaning to employ.

Dogboy *pulls the rope harder.*

Tony   He's pulling the rope quite hard now.

Louise   Well, pull it back.

Tony *does so. A small tug of war ensures.*

Dogboy *suddenly lets go.* **Tony** *loses his balance.*

Now you've had the game. Perhaps you can get on with it.

Dogboy *offers* **Tony** *his hands.*

Tony   He's offering his hands. I think he understands.

Louise   Of course he understands.

Tony *begins to tie* **Dogboy**'*s hands in front of his body.*

Louise   Not in front of his body, Tony. If you tie his hands in front of his body he'll be able to undo his feet.

Tony   I don't think he'd do that.

Louise   Unless you do it properly there's absolutely no point in doing it at all.

Dogboy *puts his hands behind his back.* **Tony** *ties them.* **Tony** *begins on his feet.*

Tony   This whole thing's ridiculous.

Louise   He growled at Denise just now. Didn't he, Denise?

Denise   Yes, he did. Grrr, like that. Then he leapt at me.

Louise   See.

Tony   I can't believe that I'm spending my Saturday night tying a man up.

Louise   It's no use making me out to be a monster. I don't like it any more than you do. I'm just not prepared to take any risks.

Tony   Well, it's done now. It's done.

Louise   Put the blanket over him, so he's warm.

Tony *tucks the blanket round him.*

Tony   There you go.

Louise   Someone should sleep down here for tonight. Just in case.

Tony   Just in case what?

Denise   I will. I'll sleep down here. I don't mind. We could still get a visitor, late. I'll sleep on the sofa.

Louise   Thanks.

Pause.

Everything was supposed to be over today. Now there's this. Something dragging on. It's like Jo doesn't want everything to be over. It's as if she's sent something. To vex me.

Louise *exits.*

Denise *takes the bottle of wine and sits on the sofa. She drinks some of the wine straight from the bottle.*

Dogboy *licks* **Tony***'s hand.*

Tony   He's quite a playful chap, isn't he?

Tony *exits.*

Denise *looks at* **Dogboy***, drinks some more.*

Pause.

Denise   You know what I was thinking. I was thinking if you were driving a car, through, say, slowly moving traffic and you saw me, walking. What would you think?

Pause.

Would you think 'that looks like an attractive person, a person who it would be good to spend an evening with' or would you think 'that looks like a boring person with a funny haircut'? What do you think? Because that was what I was thinking.

Pause.

I don't know why I'm asking you. Look at you. You're a bloody state. How did you get like that? You've let yourself go. There's no need for that.

Pause.

She goes over and lifts up the blanket.

It's not much to write home about. Is it? When you come to look at it.

She puts down the blanket.

Still. When you're in love it changes all that doesn't it? The other person becomes sort of godlike and you feel sort of godlike and it lifts you into another world.

Pause.

Still, it's not much is it, close up.

She gets back on the sofa. Lies down.

There's got to be more than that. Something else I could feel passionate about. A great painting or a political movement.

Pause.

People only join political movements so they can get off with someone.

She closes her eyes.

Scene Eleven

The same. Early morning.

Denise *lies on the sofa asleep. An empty bottle on the floor beside her. The lights come up a bit.* **Rosa** *enters quietly, surveys the situation. She walks quietly over to* **Dogboy**. *She kneels next to him. Whispers.*

Rosa   See that light. That's morning coming up over the sea. Morning comes up that way. Orange. And the sea's dark, dark.

Pause.

You keep your mouth shut. I'm keeping my mouth shut.

She pats her stomach.

Just remember that. Bad dog.

She exits softly.

Scene Twelve

The same morning.

Lights fully up. We can see **Denise** *more clearly. She looks wrecked.*

Pause.

Colin *enters.*

Colin   Hello? Hello?

Denise *wakes. Orients herself.*

Colin *comes fully into the room.*

Colin   The door was open.

Pause.

It's not too early is it? To pop in?

Pause.

Denise   I must look crap.

Colin   I came to see the house, for old times' sake.

Denise   For old times' sake?

Colin   Yes.

Denise   I'm leaving today. Starting my new life.

Colin   Well. Good luck.

Denise   Thanks.

Pause.

You spoke to me first.

Colin   Pardon?

Denise   On the beach. You spoke to me first. I didn't ask you to.

Colin   No.

Denise   No.

Pause.

You approached me. I was minding my own business. I was quite happy.

Pause.

Colin   It's a while. Since I've been here.

Pause.

Quite a while.

Denise   Last night.

Pause.

Last night I thought you might, well . . .

Colin   Well?

Denise   Pop in. I thought you might pop in.

Colin   Well, I popped in this morning. Does it make any difference?

Denise   No. Absolutely no fucking difference whatsoever.

Pause.

Anyway, I'm going to Tibet.

Pause.

Would you go to Tibet?

Colin   Not personally.

Denise   Yet you'd be quite happy for me to go!

Colin   No one's forcing you are they?

Pause.

Denise What's in Tibet? Lots of long dry roads and a load of daft monks.

Colin Not to mention a military occupation.

Pause.

Denise A ginger man.

Colin What?

Denise Nothing.

Pause.

Colin Perhaps I'd better call in another time.

Denise Go on then. Go.

Colin Well. Good luck with everything.

Denise I thought.

Pause.

I thought the only thing, the only thing was two people, two people together.
I thought the only thing was looking at someone and them looking at you. In
your eyes. Close up. That thing. What else is there? Just to be held. Held. I
haven't got enthusiasm for anything else. All my life people have been
avoiding me or taking bits and leaving the rest. I've had to force people. Force
them to be with me. That's not right. Why's that? I thought you looked at me.
That's what I thought. I thought you watched me in that way.

Pause.

Dogboy *whines faintly.*

Colin What's that noise?

He notices **Dogboy** *in the blanket.*

I didn't see him. Is he sleeping?

Rosa *and* **Louise** *enter from outside.*

Denise Oh fuck!

Pause.

Louise It's too late. I've planted it.

Colin What?

Louise The tree. I planted it yesterday.

Pause.

Is there something wrong with it? Is that why you're here? To deliver tidings
of a leaf virus?

Colin I . . .

Louise Because it's not coming up again. It comes up again over my dead body. You shouldn't sell dud trees.

Colin It's not a dud.

Rosa That's Colin.

Colin I knew Jo.

Louise Oh. So this is a social call. I was confused. Yesterday you sold me a tree.

Colin I had a hunch you might be Louise.

Louise (*to* **Denise**) We've been out. Looking at what's left of the fire.

Colin I've been wanting to talk.

Louise We're thinking of using the ashes for the garden. They're supposed to be good for gardens.

Colin It won't take long.

Louise It's a bit hectic this morning.

Denise (*to* **Colin**) You must think I'm stupid.

Colin (*to* **Louise**) I been wanting to talk to Rosa.

Louise I'm sorry. We're busy.

Denise (*to* **Colin**) You must think 'God, she's stupid'. Mustn't you?

Colin (*to* **Denise**) No.

Denise God.

Louise (*to* **Colin**) Perhaps you should write a letter. Put it in the post.

Colin It needs to be said face to face.

Denise (*to* **Colin**) You never wanted me, did you? You wanted to talk to them.

Colin (*to* **Louise**) We met earlier.

Louise I gathered.

Denise You were lovers. You and Jo. Lovers.

Pause.

Pebbles. Bloody pebbles. I was right.

She exits.

Pause.

Colin Hello Rosa.

Rosa He's a communist, Colin. He always wears those trousers.

Colin We spent a lot of time together. Me, Jo and you. Didn't we? Remember once we tried to build a boat?

Rosa We used to switch the lights out when he called round. Then we'd lie on the floor, me and Jo. We were laughing. We used to bite our arms so he wouldn't hear us.

Colin We fell out. We fell out near the end. Before that we were close. We saw eye to eye on things.

Pause.

Rosa. I want to talk to you. About Jo.

Louise She doesn't want to talk about that.

Colin Can't she answer for herself?

Pause.

Look. I didn't come here to fight. It's just that I've been thinking. About what Jo would have wanted.

Louise We've no idea what she would have wanted.

Colin What Jo would have wanted for Rosa.

Louise Rosa is happy where she is.

Colin I'm not saying she's not happy. I'm saying that Jo lived in a certain way.

Louise I know how she lived. This house was a health hazard.

Colin I'm not talking about housework. I'm talking about principles. You have coffee in this house.

Louise Is that some sort of mistake?

Colin I don't suppose you've spared a thought to the plantation workers. The conditions they have to endure?

Louise I'm sure they're awful.

Colin That's right. There's a case of a woman who organised a union meeting and was dead one week later. She was found by her daughter tied to a tree. Both her breasts had been cut off.

Pause.

Louise What exactly are you trying to say?

Colin Jo wouldn't have coffee in the house. She was boycotting it.

Louise   I'm sure that had a devastating effect on imports.

Colin   Rosa knows what I'm talking about.

Louise   Well, now you've said your bit, lectured us on the evils of the coffee bean, perhaps you could go.

Colin   You see, Jo and I talked. We talked of this eventuality. If something happened to her.

Louise   Something happened to her a year ago. It's too late to change anything now.

Colin   I wanted to wait. Until Rosa could make a decision for herself.

Louise   What decision?

Colin   A decision about how she wanted to live. I want you to know you've got a choice, Rosa. That you've still got friends down here. People who thought like Jo did. Me. You can stay with me any time. All the time if you want. There's room. Jo might have wanted it.

Louise (*to* **Colin**)   This year has been a bastard. How you think you can swan in after a bastard of a year and just expect to waltz off with Rosa I can't conceive. I've been the one that's had to deal with everything. Practically deal with it all. It's meant cooking food for someone who won't eat. It's been me persuading them to eat. It's been them refusing. It's been me persuading and persuading. It's been me looking at bodies and saying 'no'. Looking at dead people from the sea who aren't Jo. It's been me lying awake at night just in case I can hear someone crying. Try persuading someone of the value of regular school attendance when their life's just fallen apart. That's real. That's coping. Coping isn't some noble but ineffectual boycott it's real bloody hard life and sometimes I've drunk coffee to keep me going. Rosa may not have been in a position to choose if it wasn't for that.

Colin   It's Rosa's choice.

Pause.

Dogboy *whines.*

Colin   He's whining.

Louise   He's fine.

He whines again.

Colin   Why is he making that noise?

Louise   That is no concern of yours.

Dogboy *barks.*

Colin   He just barked.

Pause.

Don't you think that's a little unusual?

Louise Spare me the analysis.

Colin *approaches* **Dogboy. Louise** *attempts to divert him.*

Louise He's my cousin.

Colin *stops.*

Colin Is he?

Louise Yes. He is. He's my cousin and I'm dealing with this. So please just go and leave him alone.

Colin *draws back the blanket.*

Colin Where are his clothes?

Louise I've no idea. He appears to have mislaid them.

Colin Mislaid his clothes? His hands are tied. Why's that?

Louise That is absolutely none of your business.

Colin Do you treat all your relatives like this?

Louise Don't be ridiculous.

Colin Did you tie him up?

Louise Is that an accusation?

Colin Probably.

Louise We took the decision. He walked in here last night unexpectedly. He was deranged. We gave him a floor for the night. I wasn't prepared to take any risks. He was carrying a weapon. A sharp stone. It might not have been an ideal solution but it's not worked out too badly.

Colin Ideal?

Louise I'm afraid there were no rule books to consult on this one. No boycott sprung to mind. No doubt you would have proposed revolutionary socialism but unfortunately you were unable to be with us yesterday.

Colin I don't think binding a man hand and foot can be considered a solution.

Louise This happens to be the real world not a fairy tale. I don't know why you're complaining. Communism's done much worse things.

Colin I don't think communism proposes the ritual humiliation of the proletariat.

Louise The proletariat! I wondered how long it would be before you dragged them into it.

Colin   Have you got something against the proletariat?

Louise   I might have if they existed.

Colin   This was Jo's house, Rosa. There's a neofascist spouting on about the working classes. There's a man tied up on the floor. It's like poison. You can't stay here.

Louise   Poison. You're poison. Your words are poison. Jo was the sort who swallowed poison. She festered away down here, dreaming. Avoiding life. Waiting for the world to start turning her way. Only it never did. She suckled off stupid words like proletariat and the people and the vanguard and the struggle and it just drained the life out of her. The real life.

Colin   What do you know about real life? You don't even smell real? You're smothered in perfume. Your life's a farce. There's a whole great suffering world out there hungry for solutions and what do you do? Double lock your front door and hope it goes away. Collaborate. Write daft articles for some pathetic publication that celebrates the female orgasm and recommends underwater mascara. Still, you don't have to worry about what's real, do you? You can just make it up as you go along. That's a luxury you can afford. You don't have to pick coffe for 60p a week. And if real life got too close for comfort, you could always crack open a decent bottle of wine and forget it. As long as I'm alright. That's the way it goes, isn't it? What's so pathetic about all this is your attempt to claim some sort of moral high ground. That's what stinks. Jo wouldn't have wanted this for you, Rosa.

Rosa   Jo? Jo shouldn't have drowned.

Colin   You don't want to stay here.

Louise   Yes she does. Rosa wants to stay with me. Don't you?

Pause.

If Jo wanted the best for Rosa she wouldn't have taken her own life.

Rosa   You think she took it.

Colin   It was an accident.

Louise   She took it because of words. Words she lived on. But what happens when the words disappear? I know what it's like to have something taken away. Something taken away and nothing put in its place. That's what people like you do. That's what Jo did to me. I know what it's like to want to pray and know there's nothing there because Jo made sure I knew. I was in pain and there was blood and I knew there was nothing. But then her words slipped away too and I was glad because then she knew what it was like. The proletariat never rounded the corner waving their flags did they? They opted for washing machines and regular supplies of eggs. And who can blame them?

Because those things are real. All those people in dull, ideologically correct Eastern European places who couldn't buy toilet paper didn't stay conveniently behind the words you liked. And the words fell to the side like dead weights and your nightmare started. Well, I could live with mine, but Jo couldn't live with hers. So she died.

Colin It was an accident. Not deliberate.

Rosa She took the blue towel. She said she'd be fifteen minutes. She shouldn't have said she'd be fifteen minutes.

Louise *puts her arm around* **Rosa.**

Louise I know.

Roas Water went in her mouth. In her eyes. She did that.

Colin It wasn't like that.

Rosa I'm glad it went in her mouth.

Colin People swimming, it happens. Cramps, currents. It happens with surprising regularity.

Louise Oh come on. Jo knew what she was doing.

Rosa She shouldn't have said it.

Colin Jo was stubborn. She never gave up on anything. She didn't see the point in giving up, stopping. You see it was me, me that always gave up on things. Not Jo. Jo used to say I let things get to my bones. That I'd let them sink too far. That I was sick with it. She'd never let things sink.

Louise I think you'd better go. Rosa's made a decision to stay with me.

Pause.

Colin (*to* **Dogboy**) What about you?

Dogboy I like this room. I like the way it smells.

Colin *laughs.*

Colin Jo used to joke. About me and trees. You're a bit of dead wood selling trees. It was a joke. But look Rosa, look. It's no joke. I was right. Things are dead. Hell is coming. When people left those words behind things started slipping. Slipping into the sea. One of your relatives is bound hand and foot on the living room carpet and he fucking likes it. Because without those words people swallow shit. Jo went just in time. And Jo was wrong. Sometimes there is no point in trying. No point because things have slipped too far. And you know what? The lot of you get what you bloody deserve.

Pause.

Goodbye Rosa.

Colin *exits.*

Rosa   Lectures. He always gave lectures.

Louise   Jo's gone.

Rosa   Yes.

Louise   You're with me now. I won't desert you.

Louise *hugs* **Rosa**. **Dogboy** *whines.*

Scene Thirteen

The house.

Rosa *and* **Dogboy**. **Dogboy** *as before.* **Rosa** *is sitting still on the sofa.*

Dogboy *edges closer to her. He rubs his head against her leg. Makes a soft growl.*

Rosa   What?

Dogboy *sits in a begging attitude.*

Rosa   What do you want?

He pants.

Rosa   I said I wouldn't.

He whines.

Rosa   Alright then.

Dogboy *pants enthusiastically. She unties his hands. He immediately unties his feet. He is free. He's excited. He bounds about.*

Rosa   You're showing off all your bits.

Dogboy   Pardonnez-moi.

Pause. He pulls the blanket round him.

I threw my clothes into the sea.

Rosa   Why did you do that?

Dogboy   I dunno. It was there.

Rosa   It's a good thing not everyone's like you. We'd all be running round naked.

Dogboy   Being naked. It's natural. It's an instinct. Dogs have instincts and they act on them. Quick. Pow. Like that. That's how they get by. They don't have thoughts. People love them. They love a dog's big furry face, its wet mouth, the way saliva suspension bridges between its teeth, the noise its paws make on lino. And their bark. A dog's bark keeps things away. Right away. It keeps things away. That's the point.

Rosa How can it?

Dogboy Come here.

Rosa Why?

Dogboy Come on?

She approaches. He growls. She slows her approach. He barks fiercely. She stops.

Dogboy See.

Rosa Stupid. We used to play this game.

Dogboy *listens to* **Rosa**.

You look at someone.

She looks at **Dogboy**.

You look at them hard and then you close your eyes.

She closes her eyes.

You count to ten.

She counts silently.

And then you open them.

She opens her eyes.

And you see if the face you have in your head is exactly the same as the one that's in front of you.

She looks at **Dogboy**.

It never is. Something is always different. Something, that means you can never know anything for sure. Nothing. But you have to keep looking because otherwise there's no chance of almost knowing something. The point of the game is not to stop looking.

Pause.

It doesn't work when the other person's gone. She never thought of that. When someone's gone it's hard to remember anything. She had a chipped tooth here.

She indicates.

I'll forget that soon. I'm glad. You don't need a bark to keep things away. Things go away on their own. Everything does. That's the point.

Pause.

He sniffs. He makes a sharp move towards the sofa. Pulls out **Jo**'s *old dressing gown from beneath the covers.*

Dogboy   What's that?

Rosa *snatches it back.*

Rosa   It's mine.

Pause.

I saved it. I didn't burn it.

Pause.

I might need it. For the hospital later.

She puts it on.

See.

She pulls it out at the stomach to demonstrate it fitting a pregnant woman.

Dogboy   It's quite nice.

Pause.

I itch. I long for a good scratch.

Rosa   Was it me?

Pause.

That did it to you. That made you like that.

Dogboy   Like what?

Rosa   Like you are.

Dogboy   What do you mean?

Pause.

Rosa   You're not a dog.

Dogboy   I wasn't born a dog, no. But something entered me. Something with teeth, fur and bone. I've never been so happy.

Pause.

Fur is itchy. Sometimes I feel like I'm on fire with it.

Rosa   You could roll on the floor. That's what dogs do.

Dogboy   Dogs rub against things, that's our nature.

Dogboy *begins to rub himself against the furniture.*

Rosa *watches.*

Rosa   Dirty old dog.

She joins in. They move over the furniture doing this.

Dogboy *makes small noises of appreciation.*

Tony *and* **Louise** *enter.* **Tony** *and* **Louise** *watch momentarily.* **Rosa** *stops.*

Rosa   He was whining. I let him go.

Louise   Tony's got some clothes.

Tony *places them on the sofa.*

Tony   There you are. Some clothes.

The clothes consist of plimsolls, overalls and an old white shirt.

Louise (to **Dogboy**)   Perhaps you'd better put them on.

Dogboy *gets up. Drops the blanket.* **Tony** *picks it up and tries to use it as a curtain.* **Louise** *looks away.* **Dogboy** *puts on the overalls.*

Tony   Not a bad fit.

Dogboy *puts on the plimsolls.*

Rosa   They're too big.

Dogboy *puts on the shirt. Examines his new clothes.*

Louise   Give him a tenner, Tony.

Tony   A tenner?

Louise   He may need it.

Tony   What for?

Louise   A bus or something.

Tony   He's not getting a bus.

Louise   He's not staying here.

Tony   I should imagine he is. For a bit.

Louise   That's out of the question, Tony.

Tony   What is?

Louise   He's not staying another night.

Tony   Why not?

Louise   Because if he does he may have even greater expectations of our assistance.

Tony   He could hardly have greater expectations. He spent the night tied up.

Louise   Yes. And you were the one that tied him up.

Tony   Under your instructions.

Louise   I didn't hold a gun to your head.

Tony   Not a gun exactly.

Pause.

Tony   I think we should all have some breakfast.

Louise   You can't go around helping people in a limp fashion Tony.

Tony   A limp fashion?

Louise   Do-gooding. It just makes things worse. Unless you want to form some kind of permanent relationship with this young man, some sort of long-term relationship, then I'm suggesting that your suggestion is more cruel than kind.

Tony   You're blowing this out of all proportion, Louise.

Louise   There's no need to raise your voice.

Pause.

I'm just looking clearly at the implications of your actions. It may be fun for a night or two but I'm talking about forever and if you can't face forever then I'd say you were being deeply irresponsible.

Tony   What sort of world would it be if we didn't hold out a helping hand to one another occasionally?

Louise   We did hold out a helping hand. That was yesterday.

Tony   Well, maybe that wasn't enough.

Louise   Enough for what?

Tony   For him.

Louise   And what is enough for him? We are not his parents Tony. There's nothing we can do. Putting him up one more night is a drop in the ocean. It's not caring, it's pretending to care. The less we pretend to care the better.

Tony   I care.

Louise   Tony is intent on repeating last night's fiasco indefinitely, Rosa. It seems he got some sort of kick out of it.

Tony   I did not get a kick out of it.

Pause.

What you seem to forget, Louise, is the inestimable value of the human creature. Quite simply we must provide opportunities for that value to express itself.

Louise   Ask him about his stone.

Tony   His stone?

Louise   Why he carries a sharpened stone.

Tony   I'm sure there's a perfectly reasonable explanation. Maybe it's a lucky stone.

Louise   For God's sake. Ask him. The stone.

Tony   In time. In time. I can't just blurt it out.

Tony *goes over to* **Dogboy**.

Pause.

Tony   Well.

Pause.

Ha.

Pause.

I was wondering. Do you always have a stone? A stone about your person.

Dogboy   Not always.

Tony   I see. You just like the look of this one.

Dogboy   It's sharp.

Tony   But you wouldn't want to hurt anyone with it?

Dogboy   I could. I could hurt someone.

Tony   But you wouldn't want to. You wouldn't like to hurt them?

Dogboy   Yes. I would. Some people.

Tony   But you'd stop yourself. You'd stop yourself when you realised it was a real live human being. With feelings.

Dogboy   It might be an animal.

Tony   Yes. Yes. It might be an animal.

Dogboy   In the old days that's what they had stones for. For cutting at the neck.

Tony   Cutting at the neck?

Dogboy *takes his stone and holds it to* **Tony**'s *neck.* **Tony** *is visibly startled.*

Dogboy   I works. I tried it.

Pause.

I had a dog. I had it and I cut it at the neck. I wouldn't have done it if it hadn't got on my nerves. It made a noise.

Tony   Oh.

Dogboy   It made a noise and it was like the noise was coming from inside me. It got on my nerves.

He takes the stone away from **Tony***'s neck.*

That was a fucking good dog too. She had a nice lick.

Tony *moves away.*

Louise   See. See.

Tony   Don't over-react Louise. It was a dog. Not a person.

Louise   I want him out. I'm sick of useless spouted ideals. They don't help anyone. They destroy things.

Tony   Just calm down.

Louise   Did you hear me?

Tony   I'm sorry. I'm not prepared to stand down on this one.

Louise   You're not?

Pause.

Tony   No.

Louise   Then I'm phoning the police. They can remove him.

Tony   Don't do that.

Louise   This is my house.

Tony   I'm perfectly aware of that.

Rosa   It's my house too.

Louise   Yes darling, I know.

Tony   Maybe Rosa wants him to stay.

Louise   She doesn't.

Tony   They were playing a game when we came in.

Louise   I think I'd know if they were friends.

Tony   They seemed quite close.

Louise   Close! What are you insinuating. I think Rosa can do better than an insane tramp.

Tony   He's right there. Louise!

Pause.

Perhaps it was the sort of thing Rosa was used to. People staying. When Jo was here.

Louise   Don't dare drag Jo into this.

Tony   I'm just saying. . .

Louise   What are you saying?

Tony   That whatever criticisms you may make of Jo she did have room for a notion of altruism.

Louise   Altruism. Do you think Jo did what she did out of altruism? Endless committees, secondary picketing, pinning nappies to the wire at Greenham. She did it because she liked the idea of telling people how to live. Because she liked the sound of her own voice, that's why she did it.

Tony   Well, we don't know. She isn't here to speak for herself.

Louise   No, she's got you to chirp up for her.

Tony   We're only talking about one night Louise. Actions like that they may be small but they're important. They may change something. I write books, it's the same thing. If I think those books go some small way towards changing something then I'm proud of that.

Louise   Fiction never changed the face of world history, Tony, neither did the odd meagre act of selflessness. Do you know how much it takes to change something? Have you any idea of the enormity of such an enterprise? Why do you think people are satisfied with giving a little here and a little there? Why don't they give more? Everything? Because deep down inside they know it's like throwing yourself into a bottomless pit. Because there's never enough you can do. That's what people know instinctively inside them. Its not selfishness. It's realism, survival. It's the people with the guts to face up to what they've got here and now, what's in their grasp. They're the people who have joy, they're the people who have normal decent lives. They're not hiding in useless dreams or compromising their intelligence with half-baked acts of atonement.

Tony   It is not half-baked.

Louise   It's all or nothing, Tony. If you take him on, you take him on full stop. There won't be much time for writing. You'll need to bath him, he stinks. You'll need to find out what he eats. Cook it. Be his therapist. Mop up his piss from the toilet seat. Don't expect me to do it for you. I don't want him interfering in my normal decent life in any way. And if he touches a hair on Rosa's head I'll kill you I swear. That's the deal.

Tony   You've lost your sense of perspective on this, Louise.

Louise   There are fifty-two weekends a year and you're just about to give up every one of them. A thoroughly decent act of altruism I must say. I imagine your contribution to the great post-modern novel will be the first thing on the list of sacrifices.

Pause.

Tony   I'm only talking about getting him on his feet, Louise. He'll have friends somewhere. Somewhere to return to.

Louise   Will he?

Tony   Naturally.

Rosa   He hasn't any friends. He's not very popular.

Tony   Usually, usually most people have friends somewhere, Rosa. Statistically he's likely to have friends.

Louise   Well no one's been clamouring at our door to find him so far. It's up to you. All or nothing.

Tony   I think you're being a bit extreme. About the writing.

Louise   I'm being practical.

Pause.

Tony   So that's how it is?

Louise   Yes. That's how it is.

Tony   You want me to be responsible for turning him out.

Louise   That's right.

Tony   Right.

Pause.

Tony *puts his hands into his pockets. He brings out a bunch of notes. He holds them out to* **Dogboy**.

Tony   Here. Take it.

Pause. **Dogboy** *does not take it.*

Take it.

He puts the money into **Dogboy**'s *hands.*

Don't worry about paying me back.

Pause.

You better go.

Pause.

Go and see social services on Monday morning. That's tomorrow. Monday.

Pause.

They're in the phone book. Where's the phone book, Louise?

Louise *gets and rifles through the phone book.*

If I were you I'd go to them first thing. Throw your weight about. Demand to see the manager.

Tony *gives a short laugh.*

Louise (*reads*)   060273

She tears the page out and gives it to **Tony** *who gives it to* **Dogboy**.

Pause.

Dogboy   Gull.

Tony   Pardon?

Dogboy   Smell gull.

Tony   Oh yes. I expect you'll remember someone. Some old friend.

Dogboy *doesn't move.*

Tony   He's not moving Louise.

Louise   I can see that, Tony.

Dogboy *pulls out his stone. This alerts everyone.*

They are all standing.

Tony   He's got that stone again.

Louise   We'll phone the police if you don't go quietly.

Dogboy *barks.*

Louise   Jesus.

Rosa   He doesn't want to go.

He barks.

Louise   He knows he's got to go. Tell him.

Tony   Go on, mate.

Louise   Don't be over forceful, Tony.

Tony   I'm sure if we all behave reasonably we can achieve a satisfactory resolution.

Louise   Little bastard.

Dogboy *barks. He backs himself against a wall holding out his stone.*

Tony He's tucked himself into a bit of a corner there, Louise.

Louise (*to* **Dogboy**) Just get out!

He barks.

Rosa You're making things worse.

Louise Things can't get any worse.

Rosa Much worse. (*To* **Dogboy**.) Why don't you go!

Dogboy *suddenly goes.*

Louise I have to do what I think is best.

Rosa You're fucking making things worse.

Pause.

Rosa Will he be alright?

Tony He's been alright up to now.

Rosa So he will be alright.

Tony Yes. I expect so.

Rosa He left his coat on the beach. Do you expect he'll find that?

Louise I should think so.

Pause.

What do you want to do? Because if you want him to live here I won't stop you. I'll go back to London with Tony, now, immediately. You can stay here as long as you like. Forever. Like Jo did. I don't know who'll look after you. I suppose you'll look after yourself. I looked after you like a daughter.

Pause.

Rosa *does not move.*

Rosa, why are you wearing that old thing?

Rosa What?

Louise That.

Rosa *takes off the dressing gown.*

Louise That's better.

Denise *enters. She is carrying a large rucksack. She has changed back into jeans etc.*

Denise This is about to split at the seams. You never know how much stuff you've got till you stick it all into a rucksack, do you?

Pause.

I'm off. I'm off. I've decided on the monks. Lovely calm spiritual bald monks. I knew this woman that went to Tibet and she had lunch with some. Well, she sat at their table and they included her. That's a very rare happening because on the whole monks think women are an unnecessary distraction. Like socks.

Pause.

I just decided. Why wait any longer? Why not go now? Instantly. Life's short.

Pause.

I hate men. Not you Tony. Men like·Colin. I thought his hair was ginger but it wasn't, it was sandy, like sand. I like travelling. When you're travelling you feel you're going somewhere terrific. Things go by so fast they disappear. Travelling is better than drinking and it's good for your health. This is my going away jumper. I've been saving it. Saving it for today.

Pause.

I've saved it so long that I've gone off it. I hate it when that happens. Still, I might like it again tomorrow. Do you like it?

Louise   It's very nice.

Denise   I wish I was a lesbian. That's what I wish. I'd save myself a lot of trouble. I'm going now. I hate goodbyes. Saying goodbyes. Don't say anything. I'm just going. Going now. I'm going to walk to the station. Walk by the sea. That'll be nice. Rosa, keep doing it to the power of seventeen. Don't anyone say anything. It's unlucky.

Silence. She picks up her rucksack. Goes.

Pause.

Louise   What a dreadful jumper.

Scene Fourteen

Rosa *on the beach.* **Dogboy** *is lying face down, curled up on the sand.* **Rosa** *looks at him.*

Rosa   I knew you wouldn't get far. I knew it. You're right back where you started.

Pause.

She approaches him. He doesn't move. She sees he has the stone in his hand. She prises it out.

Let me have a go. A go holding it.

Pause. She looks at the stone.

Blood.

She investigates closer. She puts her hand up to his throat which we cannot see. She draws it back and examines it. It is bloody.

I would have come. You don't know anything do you.

Pause.

It's grey today, the sea.

Pause.

She begins slowly to cover him in sand.

Some people spend time wondering what sort of mouth theirs will have. Or nose. Or eyes. They imagine the best features of themselves and their partners combined. They think what a good-looking child that would make. Only often that particular combination of features produces an extremely ugly child. A right dog. There's no rules for it.

Pause.

She continues to cover him.

You won't need a straw.

She stops when he is well covered. She holds the stone in her hand.

No rules for it.

She begins to hit herself repeatedly low down on her stomach with the hand in which she holds the stone.

No rules for it.

She crouches over.

Scene Fifteen

The house. **Tony** *and* **Louise.**

Tony   I had this thought today. I remembered this story. There's this magician and one day he goes out. And while he's out someone comes in. They come in and steal his book of spells. When the magician returns and discovers his book is missing he goes ape-shit. Suddenly he's just an ordinary guy in wacky clothes. He can't weave his magic. I remembered that today.

Pause.

Then I was thinking about the last thing my father said to me before he died,

'Please ensure these beds are made with corner tucks'. He used to be in the hotel trade. He believed in giving people good service. He didn't think any book of mine would do that. 'A refreshing look at famine'. That's what the *Sunday Times* said.

Pause.

You need people to believe in you. You need that in order to carry on.

Pause.

Louise   The things I said. About your book. I never meant anything bad. You knew that, didn't you?

Tony   Yes. Yes, I knew.

Pause

You still have faith in me?

Louise   Yes. Yes.

Tony   Good.

Pause.

He touches **Louise**'s *hair. Looks at her.*

We've had quite a weekend.

Louise *smiles. Puts her feet up.*

On the beach.

Rosa   There's blood. Where's it coming from. There's no rules. I did it just like you. Just like you. There's no rules.

Rosa *sits still.*

In the house.

Louise   God. I'm exhausted. I'm just glad it's over.

Tony   Poor Louise. You need to sleep.

Louise   It is over?

Tony   Don't worry. Hush hush. Louise needs to sleep.

On the beach.

Rosa   I did it just like you.

In the house.

Louise   This sofa could be a raft. If we keep our feet tucked up here they won't get wet. It doesn't matter how high the sea rises or how fierce the storm gets, we're safe here. Safe. Hidden. Safe.

Tony   Hush. Hush.

On the beach.

Denise *enters.*

Denise   Rosa? It's me. Denise. I've been wandering. Wandering. I never got to the station. I've gone off Tibet. I've gone off travelling. I looked in my book. It said 'The man with the scarlet knee bands is coming'. Brilliant, I thought.

Pause.

I can't really think of anything to do. What shall I do?

Pause.

Rosa *stays looking at the sea.*

Rosa   Jo? Mum. Jo?

She stands up shakily.

Lights down.

Hush

Hush was commissioned by the Royal Court for the Theatre Upstairs and was subsequently given a main stage production, directed by Max Stafford-Clark, in the summer of 1992.

In writing *Hush* I wanted to attempt something new for me. The past decade of women's writing had often dealt with what has come to be identified as 'women's issues'. I, too, had been working within this category. I now wanted to address subjects in which I felt less safe, to range wider, ask different questions, to explore my response to Britain today from outside the spectrum of the position of women in society.

The main question I began with in writing *Hush* was: What are the ideological alternatives available to us after a decade or more of radical free-market Toryism and the seeming demise of Socialism? This question seemed more pertinent when set against the background of, for example, the plight of the homeless. Each character in *Hush* in a sense represented a response to this dilemma. Dogboy retreats into madness, Denise into mysticism, Rosa into nihilism, Colin into pessimism, Louise into her personal relationships and pragmatisms and Tony into his so-called writing career. None of these positions help them to deal with the crises that confront them.

Stylistically I wanted to use a naturalistic form and to disrupt it with elements that were more surreal. The clash of these two formal realities I hoped would mirror my central preoccupation with our endemic disposition to carry on regardless until our problems are so overwhelming as to force us to look.

April De Angelis
April, 1993

April De Angelis' other plays include *Ironmistress*, 1988 (published by Methuen Drama in *Plays by Women: Eight*), *Crux*, 1989 for Paines Plough Theatre Company, *The Life and Times of Fanny Hill*, 1991 for Red Shift Theatre Company. Radio plays include *The Outlander*, winner of the Writers' Guild Best Children's Radio Programme, 1991.

Digging for Fire

Declan Hughes

Digging For Fire was first performed on 16 October, 1991 in a Rough Magic production at the Project Arts Centre, Dublin, with the following cast:

Clare	Jane Brennan
Brendan	Sean Kearns
Breda	Gina Moxley
Steve	Arthur Riordan
Rory	Peter Hanly
Emily	Pom Boyd
Danny	Darragh Kelly

Directed by Lynne Parker
Designed by Blaithin Sheerin
Lighting by Barbara Bradshaw
General Manager Siobhan Bourke

The play opened at the Bush Theatre, London, on 20 March 1992, with the same cast.

An oblique/stroke within a speech serves as the cue for the next speaker to overlap with the first.

Act One

Clare *and* **Brendan**'s *house, a roomy 'Artisan's Dwelling' a couple of miles south of the centre of Dublin.*

Action takes place in the living room.

A sunny afternoon in July.

Scene One

Music – Dig for Fire *– Pixies*

Brendan, *dressed in an apron and armed with a duster, is tidying up the room, fetching bowls from the kitchen etc.* **Clare**, *in a dressing gown and armed with a vodka, is riffling through old singles.*

Clare Shit. Ah *shit*, some fucker's gone and robbed it.

She finishes her drink and pours herself another.

Brendan Something the matter, love?

Clare Yes, some *fucker's* robbed one of my . . . can you remember what the flipside of *Pretty Vacant* was?

Brendan 'Fraid not. Can you remember how many vodkas you've had today?

Pause.

Clare 'Fraid not. But I bet you can, so we're laughing, aren't we? I wish we had a book.

Brendan We have plenty of books.

Clare He was known for his repartee, I mean one of those hit-single books. Course I'd be able to find out instantly if *somebody* hadn't thrown out my NME collection.

Brendan There were over five hundred of them, it was a fire hazard. (*Pause.*) Are you not a bit worried about being drunk by the time everyone arrives, love?

Clare No. 'Love'.

Brendan Oh?

Clare No, I'm not a bit worried about that, Brendan. But you are.

Brendan It's just that it *is* only –

Clare   Four in the afternoon, bit early in the day don't you think, no I don't think.

Pause.

Clare *finds a book*

Clare   Now this *should* have it.

She focuses on **Brendan** *for the first time.*

Arrah Jasus Brendan would you stop dusting, you look like a great big puff.

Brendan   If I said that, you'd call it homophobic.

Clare   If you said that, it would *be* homophobic. People our age don't dust.

Brendan   Is that right?

Clare   And people our age don't notice dust.

Brendan   Really.

Clare   And as the only people coming today are all our age, I say we strew the contents of the hoover bag about the room and prove my point.

Brendan   Fair enough, will you organise that then love? I'm just a bit busy here. Dusting.

Pause.

Clare   Bren where's your bleeper?

Brendan   I'm not on call. I took the weekend off.

Clare   You what the what *what*?

Brendan   I certainly did, I'm off all today and tomorrow.

Clare   How'd you manage that? You haven't taken a day off since you were in short trousers.

Brendan   I'm working the next six weekends in a row. I had to arrange it all months ago.

Clare   You arranged it all *months* ago?

Brendan   Yeah.

Clare   But . . . Jesus, we hardly know these people any more. Why is it all so important to you?

Brendan   I don't know. It just is.

Clare   But . . . God, last time you tried to make everyone stay the night, stay *up* all night, it was so embarrassing.

Brendan   No it wasn't. It was fun.

Clare   'Fun.' Everyone else has an arts degree, Brendan. All we ever did at college was stay up all night.

Brendan   Oh, whereas boring med here was in bed by eleven with his pathology books?

Clare   (Until you met me, yes.) *And* you kept saying 'Great to see you guys, how've you all been?', and of course nobody could think of anything to say to *that* until they were absolutely plastered.

Brendan   Which is why you're stealing a march on them all this time round?

Pause.

Clare, I really don't see what the big deal is. I remember vividly how happy you were the last time. We both were. We've been talking about Danny coming home for months, for fuck's sake.

Pause.

Clare   Brendan, why don't we just run away together?

Brendan   We already did, what're you –

Clare   I mean, run away for the weekend. Sky off somewhere, just the two of us, to, oh I don't know, Brittas Bay or something, somewhere really silly.

Brendan   What, now?

Clare   Now, this minute, this instant.

Brendan   But people are coming. They've been *invited*.

Clare   Danny and Emily aren't going back for another month, so we can see them again. And we can see the others any time. *Please*?

Brendan   But . . . what would we say?

Clare   Anything. Diseases. Dead aunts and uncles. Nobody will really mind, Bren. And we could be away for two whole days together, no calls, no bleeps, no essays to mark – we haven't done that in *ages*.

Pause.

Brendan   We can't. We can't just . . . I've bought all this food and everything. I can't just . . . let people down like that.

Clare   Okay, fine, it was just an idea.

Pause.

Brendan   I could try and arrange *another* weekend –

Clare   It's okay. Really, it is. Don't you have some booze to collect?

Brendan   Oh shit, I nearly forgot.

Clare Well you better go get it, they'll be here soon.

Brendan Right.

Clare And get another bottle of Stoli, will you? (*Pause.*) Danny drinks it too.

Brendan Right. I'll be back in a while then.

He makes to go out the door.

Clare Oh, and Brendan?

Brendan Yes love?

Clare Take the apron off.

Brendan Right. Are you sure you' re . . .?

Brendan *goes.*

Clare *snaps the book shut and flings it from her in disgust.* Pretty Vacant *begins, low. She gets up and pours herself another drink. Then, on the offchance, she goes to the albums and searches from the back of the pile. Within seconds, she's found it, picture sleeve and all.*

Clare Well hush my mouth. And the flipside is – of *course.* The old Iggy and the Stooges number – *No Fun.*

She takes a long, slow drink.

Now how'd I ever manage to forget that?

Blackout. Pretty Vacant *plays loud as the guests arrive for Scene Two.*

Scene Two

Brendan, Clare, Rory, Emily, Breda, Steve.

Everyone is sitting around drinking exotic beers, except **Clare,** *who is still on vodka.*

Silence.

Brendan Well, I have to say, it's great to see you here guys. How's everyone been?

Pause. **Clare** *raises her glass to* **Brendan** *and grins.*

Breda You've done a great job on the house, Clare. I wish I had the *time* to decorate.

Clare Oh it didn't take that much *time.* Flung it all together in an afternoon, actually.

Emily Funny, that's just what I was thinking.

Steve It's excellent Clare, like mondo serious visual scenario.

Pause.

Rory   It's so refreshing to see warm colours used again, after all that awful eighties coldness. You know, chrome and black floorboards and vast off-white walls.

Steve   Hey careful guy, you're talking about the apartment I love.

Breda   That's what Steve's bachelor pad looks like.

Steve   And it's still appearing at a screen near you.

Rory   How come?

Steve   We used it for the Techtron hi-fi ads.

Breda   No wonder, it's like *living* in a hi-fi ad . . .

Emily   Does he have a gin-still and a smoking jacket, Breda?

Breda   Not quite. But he did have one of those posters – you know, the airbrush things with the car and the girl?

Rory   Oh Steven.

Steve   Excuse me, it was a saxophone and a girl.

Breda   Well whoever they were, they went straight in the bin.

Steve   And it wasn't my poster anyway, some guy I sub-let it to left it behind.

Emily   Ah, that's what they all say. Like you only read *Playboy* for the interviews, right?

Breda   You know, it's still one good reason to live here. Maybe you can't get a divorce or an abortion, or even a decent late-night drink, but at least when you go to buy your paper in the morning, you don't have to run that nauseating gauntlet of porno wank mags.

Brendan   Absolutely.

Pause.

Breda   Does anyone else want the soap-box?

Emily   Park it in a corner, I'm sure Danny will need it.

Brendan   How's the show going, Breda, you still on Brian Reynolds?

Breda   Still in the driving seat, Bren. I nearly went to the Arts Show a while back, but I don't think they liked my attitude.

Clare   And knowing something about the arts wouldn't've helped.

Steve   Exactly what I said.

Pause.

Emily   Brian Reynolds. That wouldn't by any chance be . . .?

Rory   Bolshevik Brian? It certainly would.

Emily   You're kidding. The Students' Union guy?

Rory   Yes indeed. Comrade Brian got his *glasnost* out of the way early.

Brendan   Ah, he's great crack now, Emmo, and fair play to the guy, he's really opened things up.

Emily   He's a *DJ*?

Steve   He started out as your basic jock but he made the leap into talk-radio; now he's like a post-modernist Gay Byrne; he'll run this mega-heavy feature on like child sexual abuse or rape or something, then follow it up with a total spoof call from some guy who claims he's turning into like a *zebra*; it's mind fuck city.

Emily   *Jesus.*

Breda   That might sound tasteless but it's not; we're basically saying: let's have a completely open forum, right, let's not have any taboo subjects, but let's make it entertaining at the same time. (There's never been any zebras involved.)

Steve   (I thought there was –)

Breda   (Well there *wasn't*.) In many ways, we're in the business of shaping attitudes, it's quite subversive really.

Pause.

Clare   Really? How is the Brian Reynolds Show *subversive*, Breda?

Breda   By presenting your basic conservative punter with a totally radical agenda – it's already made some major waves.

Steve   Woman president's just the tip of the iceberg.

Breda   Next ten years is gonna see some serious social change in this country, and broadcasting like ours is gonna be the single most important cause of it. Just wait and see.

Clare   Brave new world. Sounds exciting.

Steve   Life in the fast lane. Everything, all the time. Rory knows what I'm talking about.

Rory   If only that were true, Steven.

Steve   Your new job.

Rory   My new job?

Steve   Yeah. By day, the anonymous solicitor – but at night, when the moon is high, Rory Jackson dons his scarlet cloak and becomes . . . Opera Man!

Rory   Oh *that*.

Emily   Oh what?

Rory   I review opera on the radio. Well, I reviewed two and they've asked me to do two more. It's utterly absurd, I don't even know that much about opera, and I certainly don't know what I like.

Breda   But you certainly like to row with your presenter.

Rory   Yes, well. He's so bland, isn't he? His problem is, he knows nothing about the arts, but he likes everything.

Brendan   Well this is gas, what a glittering array here assembled. I'd say myself and Clare must lead the most boring lives here, what would you say Clare?

Clare   I'd say that too, Brendan.

Pause.

Breda   How *is* the teaching, Clare?

Clare   It was doing fine 'til you reminded me of it. I wonder where Danny is.

Brendan   God, yeah. He is coming, isn't he Emily?

Emily   Don't look at me, I'm not his Mammy. I haven't seen him since we got back. But if you want me to hazard a wild guess, I'd say . . . oh, Mulligan's?

Steve   Or O'Neill's.

Breda   There's . . . The Norseman.

Clare   The International.

Brendan   The Stag's Head.

Rory   Or the Temple Bar.

Emily   So you see. He could be anywhere really.

Clare   Has he been writing, Em?

Emily   I think so. I think he had something in the *New Yorker*, yeah.

Rory   The *New Yorker*?

Emily   I think so, a short story.

Clare   But . . . but that's *incredible*, a story in the New Yorker . . . *Jesus*.

Breda   Did you read it Emily, was it any good?

Clare   It must've been good, otherwise it wouldn't've been published.

Rory   Are you sure it was the *New Yorker*?

Emily Yes I'm sure and no I didn't read it; I get enough of Danny whingeing down the phone about how he *can't* write without actually reading him when he *can*.

Steve I think this is gonna call for some celebration-type activity when the boy Daniel trots through the tunnel, eh Bren?

Brendan Fans to their feet, Steve. And let's not leave Emmo out.

Emily Oh let's.

Clare Em that was so brilliant, opening the *Irish Times* and seeing you glaring out.

Emily *Awful* photo.

Steve Irish Girl Takes Manhattan.

Rory How *did* it happen, Emily? Tell tell *tell*.

Emily Well . . . ah it's all so corny, it's like Lana Turner on the stool at Schwab's. I'm serving in the cafe one day, and of course the whole place is like some home for the deluded anyway – no-one *really* works there – here's a writer, there's an actress, hello you pair of poets – standard young hopeful stuff. So I'm serving, and this dapper little faggot is really hassling me . . .

Breda (I hate that word, faggot.)

Rory (I'm rather fond of it, actually.)

Emily Now I know this guy a little, I don't know who he is, but he knows I paint, and we'd made small talk about the scene before, bitchy stuff mostly. But suddenly he's being really obnoxious, like 'This glass is *not* clean', and 'I don't *believe* this oregano is fresh', and 'I really *need* a raspberry vinaigrette', and so on, and the cafe is *bunged* so we're all having a ball. Comes to the coffee, he wants a double expresso, decaff., which to me is like having sex with all your clothes on. Anyway, our owner being something of a coffee zealot, there isn't any decaff. on the premises, so he gets an ordinary expresso. Seconds later, these *squeals* suddenly go up, he's shrieking like a stuck pig, 'This is not decaff., this is caffienated, I wanted decaff.', and I have had it, I stand there 'till he's quietened down, and then I say 'Listen, you big fat baby, why don't you just suck my dick?'

Pause.

Rory Well what else *could* you have said, dear?

Emily Turns out this guy – Roland Michaels – owns the West 4th Street Gallery. Turns out also he's the kind of queen who keeps Bette Midler in diamonds, he loves a girl with a dirty mouth. I'm cleaning his table, he's left a $20 tip and his card, and written on the back of the card is 'If you paint as tough as you talk, I'm interested. Call me tomorrow.' I called, he saw, he offered. And four months later, I had my first show.

Rory   Is this the right moment to say 'Only in America'?

Steve   Fucking A it is, bubba.

Clare   Em, that's the third time I've heard that story, and I still don't believe a single word of it.

Emily   I know. I don't either Clare. But it's true.

Clare   Oh I don't doubt that it's true, I just don't believe it. *Jesus.*

Breda   Just goes to show, if you keep pushing, you're gonna get there.

Brendan   Absolutely.

Pause.

Emily   So. Anyone got any jokes?

Pause.

Steve   How many feminists –

Breda   That's not funny.

Pause.

Brendan   Well, guys . . . anyone for food?

Breda   Oh glorious words.

Emily   The best words of all.

A move to the kitchen, led by **Breda** *and* **Emily**. **Rory** *and* **Clare** *are left.*

Clare   You know, I bet Danny won't even bring that *New Yorker* with him.

Rory   You know, I bet you're right.

Blackout. Music – No Fun *–* Iggy and the Stooges.

Scene Three

Danny *has arrived.* **Breda**, **Emily** *and* **Clare** *are all still eating, passing things back and forth to each other.* **Steve** *is rolling a joint.*

Danny   I am deadly serious. For the purposes of research into the State of Deare Olde Irlande, I listened to Reynolds on the Radio every morning for the last week.

Breda   Well at least I get paid for it.

Danny   And my most treasured exchange runs as follows: (I quote from memory)

Danny   (*as Brian, inane mid-Atlantic DJ, voice*) Yes indeed, it's Reynolds on the Radio, it's right now, the subject is oral sex, let's take *Molly*, Molly, *talk* to me.

Breda I should've known it'd be this.

Danny (*as Molly, country*) Well Brian now, to be honest with you, I don't really like the taste.

Danny (*as Brian*) Right, now which taste don't you like, *Mollser*? The taste of the penis or the taste of the semen?

Danny (The time is 11.15 a.m., incidentally. I am eating toast and marmalade. I record this for what it's worth.)

Danny (*as Molly*) Well . . . I don't *really* like the taste of the penis . . . but I hate the taste of the semen.

Danny (*as Brian*) Okay *Mollso*, let me ask you this: do you like Camembert?

Danny (*as Molly*) Who's he now?

Danny (*as Brian*) Not a 'he', *ha ha ha*, it's a type of runny French cheese. Camembert – or Brie?

Danny (*as Molly*) Oh, I don't like the sound of that. Is it supposed to taste like . . . *semen*?

Danny (*as Brian*) Well, I'm *told* – *ha ha ha* – I'm told that it does, yes.

Danny (*as Molly*) Ah well I definitely wouldn't like it so. Yeucch!

Danny (*as Brian*) Okay, *Mollbo*, plenty to chew on there; Reynolds on the Radio, we're getting our mouths around oral sex; this is Mr Bruce Springsteen, and he's *Going Down*.

Breda He didn't play *Going Down* and he didn't say plenty to chew on and he certainly didn't –

Dan Alright, OK, bit of anecdotal licence here and there, but the thing I was wondering about, Breda, public's right to know and so on, and it's not that the item immediately preceding Mollso who won't go down, or who'll go down but won't stay down, was a woman who wept, on air, for half an hour while recounting the story of how she'd been sexually abused as a child by her father and two of her uncles; and it's not that the item immediately succeeding Mollbo who doesn't suck, or who sucks but doesn't swallow, was a bunch of actors pretending to be Cavan TDs/ discussing the new Condoms for Cattle bill, no, the question, the big question that really

Breda /We already discussed the composition of the show, Danny. If you bore the punters with too much grief, they'll just switch off.

Danny demands an answer is: Where does old Reynolds buy his cheese? What kind of camembert is he swallowing?

Emily This is what I was wondering.

Rory Mmm.

Breda   Oh I told him that.

Emily   Oh.

Pause.

Emily   But Breda . . . well, it doesn't taste *remotely* like . . .

Breda   Yes I'm aware of that, Emily. But he isn't. And . . . right, this is just pure badness on my part. You see, Reynolds loves to adopt this kind of 'Dr Sex' persona –

Danny   'The Erotic Oracle.'

Breda   Exactly, and he says things like 'I really *love* women, you know? I think women are really *great*.'

Emily   Whatever you're paid, they should double it.

Breda   Oh they have, they have. But you see, it means a woman can tell him almost anything to do with sex and he'll believe it. So I tell him loads of lies, and then he goes on air and makes a complete dick of himself.

Steve   And then the ratings go up again.

Breda   And he thinks it's all a great laugh, a great big game. Child.

Clare   So that's what you meant by subversive.

Pause.

Steve   Well what *does* it taste like?

Brendan   Oh come on, *guys* . . .

Rory   Salty.

Emily   Yup, very very salty.

Brendan   I don't *believe* we're having this conversation.

Danny   It's just standard State of the Nation stuff, Breno.

Clare   Brendan thinks we should be discussing the President or the Local Elections, like proper Grown-Ups.

Breda   Brendan has a point.

Pause.

Clare   So Danny, tell us more about the *New Yorker* story, you really should've brought along a copy.

Steve   Yeah Dan, like serious high-art puritan prose situation.

Danny   Nothing more to tell really.

Clare   But you haven't told us anything.

Danny   Alright – it's about a father who loses his child while they're out shopping in a department store – or thinks he does – and his life starts to unravel as a result. Turns out he didn't bring the kid along in the first place, but by the time he finds *that* out, he's lost his mind. That's all – a man goes mad in a big shop.

Breda   Weird stuff.

Steve   Sounds great, Dan. Make an amazing movie.

Clare   And are you now the Doyenne of the Smart Set? Are publishers and agents breaking down your door?

Danny   The door's still standing, but – well, yeah, things are beginning to happen at last. It's a start.

Clare   It's a great start. I can't wait to read it.

Brendan (*from kitchen*)   Absolutely, Danno, big cheers from the sidelines here.

Rory   Well done, Danny, congratulations.

There is a lengthy silence, finally broken by **Brendan**.

Brendan   So does anyone remember this day ten years ago, where we were?

Pause.

Clare   Were 'we' all in the one place?

Brendan   Very much so, we were at Julie-Anne Montgomery's parents' party –

Emily   Oh God, down in Greystones.

Breda   With us as the token peasants, invited to add some colour.

Rory   Which we seemed to supply rather effortlessly, remember Danny and Steve locking themselves in the bathroom?

Steve   That's right, the bath was full of ice and tonic, and we'd found a full bottle of gin we just had to drink.

Clare   Notwithstanding the fact that there was an ocean of booze for the taking, our boys figure, 'Rob some and drink the lot before you're caught.'

Emily   Complete tinkers.

Steve   And everyone was banging on the door for tonic.

Clare   And Danny was yelling, 'We're having a ride, go away.'

Emily   And the little Englanders were just wetting themselves with the wild Irishness of it all.

Clare   And Emily McAuliffe took her *bra* off in the living room in front of this, like, rake of stuffed-shirt crumblies –

Emily   I was hot –

Steve   Yeah, she kind of wriggled it out from beneath her top –

Rory   And she was clinging on to her bag the whole time like a madwoman, and some sweet old thing said, 'Oh do let me take your bag, my dear' and McAuliffe said, 'Oh no. I'd normally park it with the coats, but not here; rich people are such terrible *thieves*.'

Clare   And Danny was holding court with Mr and Mrs Montgomery and a clutch of aunts and uncles, feeding them some rare old times stuff about his father and Brendan Behan, the Montgomerys in a positive *rapture* of slumming –

Emily   Oh no, I remember this.

Clare   When suddenly Danny just picked up a wine-glass and puked in it – pfff – and then puked again into a second –

Steve   Dublin was like that in those days.

Clare   Each time without spilling a drop. *And then he continued his story.*

Danny   It was a good story.

Clare   I'll never forget the expressions on their faces, God it was brilliant.

Brendan   What a brilliant night.

Pause.

Breda   Sounds a bit pathetic at this stage, to me anyway. Puking for the revolution?

Emily   What revolution? It was just a bit of crack, Breda.

Danny   We were clowns – whores, bought in to reassure them of their superiority, their civilisation. And we complied. We tugged our forelocks and revelled in our muck. It *was* pathetic.

Emily   Oh hark at Dostoyevsky. Lighten up, *man*.

Clare   What's happened to all those Greystones West Brits anyway? Does anyone ever see them?

Breda   Rory still sees them.

Steve   Rory still sees *everyone*.

Rory   They're all married, all ensconced in incredibly expensive homes, all cleaning up making money out of money, all seeing each other *all* the time – round and round that tight little circle they go, all twenty-nine pushing sixty.

Danny   It's too weird, you know? It's as if they were all so eager to get their lives – well, *finished*, somehow, all their choices made, everything *decided* – do you know what I mean?

Clare   I know *exactly* what you mean.

Danny   As if the future was so terrifying, so uncertain, that the only course open to them was to imitate the past, imitate, and thus become, their parents.

Brendan   How's your Dad, Danny – still fond of the old sauce, is he?

Pause.

Danny   My old man's a character, Brendan – which means he'll drink with absolutely anyone who'll (a) buy the booze and (b) let him do all the talking.

Clare   So it's not off the floor you licked it.

Danny   Oh me da, me da, he's a terrible man and all that, yeah. Actually, the old man recently surpassed even himself. He was up the Rugby club with his cronies, hooting and blowing as usual; about half-twelve he decides to call it a night. Decants himself into the Volvo, rolls down the hill and straight into the arms of a Garda check point.

So 'Would you mind stepping out of the car, Sir', and 'Do you know who I am, Guard'? (I think that was a genuine inquiry) and 'You'll have to accompany us to the station, Sir', and off they go.

So in the station and mucho heaviousity 'cause there's about a quart of Jameson sluicing around in the old man's gut; so they're booking him and whatever else it is they do. Anyway, Dad suddenly has this flash of inspiration and asks for his statutory phone call, just like he's seen them do on *Hill Street Blues*. So fair enough, he picks up the phone, dials the Rugby Club, gets a hold of the lads and bellows into the receiver: 'Don't drive home guys, there's a fucking Garda checkpoint down the road.'

Emily   Oh brilliant!

Danny   So there's a fleet of taxis to the club that night, the Guards are seriously not amused and the old man's got his drinks free until Christmas.

Emily   Ah sure isn't it a great little country all the same.

Danny   I thought, this is the bit I really do miss.

Brendan *suddenly dashes to the kitchen.*

Clare   What's he up to now . . . oh my goodness.

Brendan *appears with a bottle of champagne and seven glasses.*

Rory   Well now, this is a bit more protestant.

Steve   Mondo exotic intake situation, guys.

Breda   This is great, Brendan.

Brendan   Ten years on and still around, guys – and we haven't killed each other yet – so a toast's in order. Emily, would you like to do the honours?

Emily   Who, me? But . . .

Brendan   You and Dan are the real guests, and since Danny's already spoken a *little* –

Breda   Ever the diplomat, Bren.

Brendan   I thought you should be top girl.

Pause.

Emily   Oh God, this is silly, it's all so *formal*.

Brendan   Come on, anything at all.

Emily   My mind's a blank, surprise surprise.

Brendan   And we'll have to hurry you.

Clare   Oh for fuck's sake Brendan, if she doesn't want to, just leave it –

Emily   It's alright Clare – I'm a big girl now. Hem hem – to us all – good luck . . . 'cause we need it . . . and let's hope we all make another ten years.

They drink. **Clare** *and* **Emily** *embrace. There is a lull.*

Danny   Right so, that's enough faffing around. Who's all going for a pint?

Blackout.

Music – Cecilia Ann *– Pixies.*

Act Two

The Pub. Groups weave in and out of each other, swelling and diminishing as necessary.

Brendan, **Steve**, **Danny**.

Brendan   Right, Sprake, Reaney, Cooper, Bremner . . . Charlton –

Steve   Yo Big Jack.

Brendan   . . . Madeley?

Steve   Sometimes, but more famously, He Who Was Born to Bite Your Legs –

Brendan   Hunter, Norman Hunter, right, ah – cannonball shot Peter Lorimer, Alan Clarke –

Danny   Sniffer, Sniffer Clarke.

Steve   That's right.

Brendan   Mick Jones, Johnny Giles and . . . aaaah. A clue, give us a clue.

Steve   Scottish, played on the wing –

Brendan   Gray, Eddie Gray. Yo! Don Revie's Dangermen.

Steve   The Leeds United Mean Machine, they should've won three trophies in 1970 – Everton pipped 'em for the league, Celtic knocked 'em out of the European Cup/and a totally crap . . .

Brendan   Proper order.

Steve   Chelsea team beat them in the FA Cup Final replay.

Danny   A season without silverware, well well well.

Brendan   They were never an attractive side though, Steve –

Steve   Compared to whom? The Arsenal team that won the double in '71?

Danny   Boring boring Arsenal . . . are they still boring?

Steve   They could cure insomnia, they're soccer's answer to Mogadon –

Brendan   They are, Dan, they're deadly.

Danny   'S weird about Leeds though, when I was a kid, I remember wishing our family *lived* in Leeds – then I'd be able to follow the team properly, I'd be . . . *authentic*, everything would fit. I even tried to speak in a Yorkshire accent.

Steve   'V you ever been in Leeds? We did a promotion there, man, the only thing that place has going for it is the airport.

Brendan   It's also bunged with loonies, it's like Connemara.

Danny   Yorkshire Ripper, was he from there?

Steve   Thereabouts, I think; Bren, it's your crack at the lightbulb.

Brendan   OK, OK, – How many . . . no, no, sorry, why does it take two women with PMT to screw in a lightbulb?

Danny *(beat)* Why?

Brendan *(ferocious)* IT JUST DOES, RIGHT?

Steve   Excellent, excellent, moving swiftly along, Danny, your first round qualifier –

Danny   Do it to me Bamber.

Steve   The Lisbon Lions.

Brendan   Good one, nice one.

Steve   Glasgow Celtic, May 25, 1967 – the European Cup winners – Danny, you are *on*.

Danny   Alright, Simpson, Craig, Gemmell, Murdoch, McNeill, aaaah . . . Hughes?

Steve   Hughes?

Brendan   No, Hughes was dropped – injured, I think.

Steve   And the crowds are hushed – can the boy Daniel live up to his early promise?

Danny   . . . Murdoch, McNeill . . . *Clark*. –

Brendan/Steve   Yo!

Danny   Wee Jimmy Johnstone, Willy Wallace, Stevie Chalmers, Bertie Auld and . . . and . . .

Brendan/Steve   Yes, yes . . .?

Danny   Bobby Lennox!

All   Yes!

Steve   Oh, and the corks will be popping out in Castleknock tonight.

Danny   Why is it always things from that far back you need to remember? Like Peter Glaze and Leslie Crowther on *Crackerjack*, or Bill and Ben –

Steve   *The Flowerpot Men*, and *Andy Pandy/* and *The Woodentops* –

Danny   Andy and Teddy.

Brendan   *The Woodentops* were rubbish, *Camberwick Green* –

Danny   *Camberwick Green*! God, Windy Miller –

Steve   And *Trumpton* and *Chigley*, but they were just pale imitations –

Brendan   *Watch With Mother*, when you were home sick from school, great stuff.

Danny   But why? I mean, we were just about old enough to see that Celtic game.

Steve   Well it's the earliest memories we have – TV programmes and TV soccer.

Brendan   And let's face it guys, the glory days of the game – Jock Stein's Celtic, Matt Busby's Man. United, Bill Shankley's Liverpool – great teams. Great days, guys.

Pause.

Danny   OK Steven, your big moment – lightbulb us.

Steve   OK, gotta keep this one low – how many feminists does it take to screw in a lightbulb?

Brendan   How many?

Steve   Two – one to screw in the lightbulb, and one to suck my dick.

And . . .

Danny, Clare.

Clare   Happy now?

Danny   Getting there. How're you?

Clare   Oh fine, you know. *Grand. (Pause.)*

Danny   It's good to see you.

Clare   Well it's good to see you too. Why didn't you write, you bastard?

Danny   I did – a bit.

Clare   What, 'hope you are well' postcards? Thanks a lot.

Danny   Well – 'I'm here, amn't I?' *(They laugh.)* Clare, do you know about Emily?

Clare   Yeah, she told me.

Danny   Right, good, just in case you . . . when did she . . .?

Clare   She came round last week when Brendan was at rugby training. She told me she was infected, then she told three really awful AIDS jokes, and then we cried for about an hour. Girls night in.

Danny   Shit, I didn't realise she was still so upset.

Clare   No, actually I cried, and that set her off. It was all arseways, she ended up consoling *me*.

Danny   I know, I was the same.

Clare   The weirdest thing though, is that . . . I mean, I still feel really upset and everything . . . but I also feel, I don't know, *alive* – like if everything's so fucking arbitrary, I've got to feel alive, it's like a duty – because there's suddenly no more time to waste. You understand me, Danny, don't you?

Danny   Oh yeah. I understand you perfectly.

Pause.

Clare   Well, I'd better bear these to their owners. Hey, later *dude*.

Danny   Yeah, later.

And . . .

Steve, Brendan

Steve   So you're doing it, right, and beforehand you were talking to them and they're like, 'I want to do this, or read that,' or 'Women get such a raw deal,' or they disagree with you over something . . . they're like, very together and independent and like that, yeah?

Brendan   Yeah.

Steve   But you're doing it, and they're into it, and you're like '*this* is what it's all about' and then they get really, they get going, and they're Oh yes and Don't Stop and everything . . . and then their face goes, their face . . . disappears.

Brendan   (*beat*)   What? It . . . their face . . .?

Steve   They were . . . she was, whoever she was, she was this . . . particular girl, with like this idea and that idea, but just when she's about to come, she's like . . . nothing, she becomes nobody, just pure fuck, you know? Like jelly, she can't *control* anything any more. You know what I mean, man?

Brendan   Ah, no, Steve. No, I can't say I do.

Steve   That moment is the greatest, it's absolutely . . . *excellent.* And the problem with someone you've known for years, been with for years – (the problem with Breda) – is . . . it's harder for her to disappear. You just always know it's her.

Pause.

Brendan   But that's what I love best, actually.

Steve   That you always know it's Clare?

Brendan   That you know it all – how everything is and is going to be. That we can all get together and, you know, *bond* again, that friendship survives like that – and that I do my job, and the patients respect me, and need me – and that Clare is there for me. Clare needs the stability, Steve, that sense of things being in their place, everything expected, everything in order. And okay, sometimes she might get . . . you know . . .

Steve   I know. They *all* get a bit . . .

Brendan   But it's fine really, great, actually. And when Danny was saying how all the Greystones gang had like finished their lives, well I could see another side to it, and I think it's called growing up, actually, accepting things in a certain way, saying: This is my life, I've got what I need to make it work, it trundles along, I'm not going to worry myself into the grave over . . . over what?

Steve   I know, like Danny man –

Brendan   I know Danny does, but Danny's special, he's got . . . something special. And that's great, I admire him./But that's not me. The only thing I can think of,

Steve   So do I, guy's a genius man.

Brendan   the only thing that would make it perfect, is if Clare would have a kid. I really don't think there's anything else I want.

Steve   How about a pint?

Pause.

Brendan   Steve, would you say you and Breda will have a family?

And . . .

Breda, **Clare**.

Breda   Clare, if you don't like your life, change it.

Clare   It's not really that simple –

Breda   But it *is*. For years men kept women out of the workplace by saying, 'Uh, it's not really that simple.' But it *is* that simple, you've just got to get focussed. You're a bright girl, Clare.

Clare   I know I am.

Breda   You got a first, for God's sake. You wrote all those revues, you and Danny, you were the ones who were gonna do it all. It must be Brendan, I bet things are simple for him.

Clare   Yes, but . . . he doesn't hold me back. He says exactly the same things you're saying. Exactly the same.

Breda   Have you thought of assertiveness training? I took a course in it –

Clare   You didn't.

Breda   I did, and it really works. Look, maybe you don't want to work in RTE, God knows the pace is too hectic for most people, but – life's too short,

Clare, you know? I know that's a cliche, but the thing about an awful lot of cliches is, they're true.

Pause.

Clare   So anyway, how are things with you and Steve?

Breda   Excellent. We work well together, you know? It may not last forever, but nothing does, what the hell. I try not to think about it too much, it's like too many parties you meet these women and all they want to talk about is how awful their relationships are, it's like they're complete *adjuncts*.

Clare   I imagine that would get on your nerves after a while.

Breda   Oh it does, believe me. Just remember – Brendan has his job, he's in there 100% – where are you? You owe it to yourself, Clare.

Clare   It's my duty.

Breda   Exactly.

And . . .

Rory, Danny

Rory   Oh, four nights a week, sometimes five.

Danny   Five dinner parties a *week*?

Rory   Sometimes. Always four: mine on a Tuesday, and then three others.

Danny   Jesus, and you *enjoy* them?

Rory   Oh yes, of course, even the awful ones. It's the perfect social gathering, second to none. But it must be carefully composed and delicately handled.

Danny   Yeah, like don't invite me; God I hate them. My memory of any dinner party I've ever been at is the sound of my own voice – chatting, talking, joking, ranting, harangueing – entertaining, even, but incessant. All I can think is: 'Why couldn't you just've shut up?'

Rory   Well you see that's the first rule. To get into my book of reliable call if you're stucks, you must understand that dinner party conversation isn't a competitive sport like football, where one brilliant individual can race away with the ball, leaving everyone else awestruck and admiring, but something more like, oh, Donkey I suppose – everyone catches, everyone throws, and if we all play well, the result is pleasure – delight, even.

Danny   And if someone can't catch –

Rory   Like you, yes, but worse are those who can't throw, or who think they're being fiendishly clever by throwing a spinning ball. That's a failure of manners, and therefore inexcusable. People who can't play very well are just slow, or dull, and these we will always have with us.

Danny You really are from another time, Rory. It's like you've recreated the eighteenth century for yourself, and happily dwell within it.

Rory Nothing of the sort. I've just made a selection, I've chosen things which please me, behaviour that suits me, a life I can live, in fact, and that gets me through. I don't like chaos, you see.

Danny But to live in the world, surely we must engage with chaos.

Rory (Oh Socrates.)

Danny (I know, I sound like a Platonic dialogue. Still, nobody's listening . . .) Must we not, oh Great One?

Rory I've never been convinced that the correct response to chaos is to embrace it with open arms. If you're caught up in a riot, do you pile in with gusto or try to find sanctuary?

Danny Does the riot not affect you directly? Shouldn't it always? And doesn't sanctuary sound a bit too much like running away for comfort?

Rory Does it? I should've thought finding sanctuary was what life's all about. But riddle me this, oh man in the eye of the storm. How does all this embracing of chaos square with the *New Yorker*, and with what Steve rightly dubbed 'a serious puritan prose situation?' I'd've thought that was all a bit minty for you.

Danny Well it was. So much so in fact that I haven't written anything since. I don't know why. There was that story, and then . . . nothing.

Rory Nothing at all?

Danny No. I can't . . . I just talk, I talk like a Trojan, if there was a Nobel Prize for Talk I'd walk it. Talk it. I can't . . . I can't select what I want. I'm just wide open, one day *this*, the next day *that* . . . I don't know how to choose . . . what to choose. Sorry, I'm not making much sense.

Rory You're making perfect sense. This evening could easily explode. That's what you want, isn't it?

Danny What?

Rory You want to destroy this, your place in this, so you can begin again.

Danny Do I?

Rory Natural Social Selection, you might call it. We're a dinosaur, you're not the only one to think so. But you're probably the only one who can do something about it. It being your character, after all.

Danny And what about sanctuary?

Rory Well there's certainly none of that here.

Danny I thought you were against embracing the chaos.

Rory But I won't be embracing it. You will.

And . . .

Emily, **Clare**, **Steve**.

Clare . . . then there was Helen O'Rourke, Orla Fitzgibbon, Deborah and Clodagh Jordan.

Emily At the same time?

Clare During the same weekend. I'm telling you, he's a total dog.

Emily Clare, how do you know all this? Does he have a press agent? Stick it in Saturday's *Irish Times*: Stephen Woods, BA, and Clodagh Jordan together with their parents, are delighted to announce their illicit bonk in a toilet in Bad Bob's during the week.

Clare Brendan told me.

Emily Brendan knows?

Clare Oh yeah, Boy's Club. It's alright 'cause it's Steve.

Emily God, I'd've thought Brendan'd be shocked.

Clare Oh Brendan *adores* gossip, I think 'cause his own life is so dreary.

Emily And just how exciting has *your* life been lately?

Steve (*aproaching*) Hey Emmo!

Clare (Not nearly as exciting as yours, pet.)

Steve (*arrived*) How's the groove?

Clare (*on her way*) ('Bye.)

Emily Oh mondo, Steve, mondo.

Steve Must say babe, you look amazing, totally –

Emily Don't. Just . . . don't. Alright?

Pause.

Steve Alright. Excellent stuff about the exhibition though –

Emily How can someone be so utterly insensitive? Is there a course you can take? Some kind of patent medicine? Or do you mug up on textbooks so you can hone your skills in hurting other people's feelings?

Pause.

Steve Sorry if I appear a complete moron, but . . . what, exactly, have I done?

Emily Nothing, Steve, that's what you've done – absolutely nothing.

Steve   You said to treat you as if nothing was amiss –

Emily   You said, I said, Jesus; one postcard, with the fascinating information that you had been promoted and that Leeds United are once again a force to be reckoned with. It's not as if I told half the world, you know, I only told Clare last week.

Steve   Oh look, I took you at your word, Emmo, I'm sorry, I never thought . . . God, I would've . . . like a shot.

Emily   Like a *big* shot.

Steve   Em, I *would've* . . . I felt terrible for you, honest.

Emily   Stop. I don't want that.

Pause.

Steve   I don't know what to say, Emily.

Emily   What're you doing with Breda, Steve? You don't love her. Life's too short for that kind of rubbish, when're you gonna dump her? When one of your bimbos turns out to have a brain?

Steve   Whoah, I'm not sure that this is the time or the place –

Emily   So what're you waiting for? The time she finally goes grey she's so miserable? The place she eventually catches you at it?

Steve   Breda isn't miserable, she doesn't have time. And since when've you been so concerned about her anyway?

Emily   I don't give a fuck about Breda, you know that. But then, that makes two of us.

Steve   I'd really appreciate if it you went easy on the insults, you know; you really don't know anything about it . . . it's all very well for people to get self-righteous, but nobody knows what really goes on between two people.

Emily   You're right, you're absolutely right, it's none of my business, shouldn't've opened my mouth.

Pause.

Steve   Look . . . I know in New York, when we . . . well, after, we said we'd be friends, and I didn't bother to write or anything –

Emily   Just forget it, alright?

Steve   But I'd like to. I . . . seriously, Emmo, if I haven't been too much of a creep already.

Emily   Well you have. But . . . only if you talk total rubbish and stop playing sincere, it really doesn't suit you.

Steve   So I should like, maximise the poly-communicational seriously laid-back vibe?

Emily   Affirmative. And Step One is . . .

Steve   Lay it on me, hit me with it.

Emily   Buy me a pint.

Steve   I'm on my way.

And . . .

All.

Danny   An *integrated* sense of community.

Breda   A *greater* sense than in other countries.

Danny   But I don't know what that's supposed to *mean*, it's just . . . alright, look at it this way. I grew up with the TV on, (and I'm not unique in this) with England and America beaming into my brain; I never had a single moment of, I don't know, 'cultural purity'. I didn't know where I was from. And the other big thing when I was a kid –

Emily   Was *Wanderly Wagon*.

Danny   Was the Writings of Enid Blyton.

Emily   Sure that explains everything.

Danny   In these books, seemingly parentless children stayed with mysteriously distant uncles during things they called 'the hols', solved mysteries and were generally free to create their own world. And I grew up longing for a similar freedom – from parents, locality, history – from roots of any kind – and especially from *community*.

Breda   Well I hardly think that can be described as *normal* –

Danny   No it's not normal, but it's certainly typical, there's hundreds of thousands in the same boat – no great 'shared vision', no sense of solidarity or common purpose.

Steve   But there never has been, Danny, that's just one of the lies the sixties tried to cash in on.

Danny   Well Jesus, they're certainly cashing in now, they're running everything. Anywhere you look – ad agencies, film companies, business, law, you name it – in charge there's an ageing hippy with a Paul Smith suit and his act together. And they have the nerve to condemn our generation for being cynical and apathetic and only interested in money – what wonder, with scum-bag example like that before us.

Clare   No wonder, Danny, none at all.

Danny   What have we got? What have we got, Bren? At least they have a summer of love to look back on; all we've got is a well-spring of cynicism.

Brendan   I don't know that people change that much over the years.

Danny   Don't you? Don't you though? Look at this fucking radio stuff then. People calling in from all over the contry, telling this jumped-up cretin with no qualifications for anything other than voracious self-promotion and demented egotism, telling *that* their intimate secrets. Whatever happened to talking to your friends? Whatever happened to privacy, to dignity?

Rory   I thought you were busy embracing the chaos in the biggest burgh in burgerdom, Danny, what's wrong, does it scare you when you see it in your cherished little homeland?

Danny   No, what I'm saying is: the chaos *is* here – wannabees and weirdoes on the airwaves, brains fried from TV and video and information overload – so acknowledge it, don't pretend there's some unique sense of community, that Ireland's some special little enclave – things are breaking down as fast here as anywhere else.

Breda   You just don't understand, talk-radio here – even if people feel isolated, lost in the suburbs or something, they can tune in and feel a part of what's going on – it's like they're living in a village, and they want to keep up with the gossip.

Danny   And what about the people who don't want to live in a village? The people who left before their village suffocated them? Is village life supposed to be the most authentic, the most Irish?

Breda   It's also about having a sense of place –

Danny   And what happens when you don't have a sense of place? When I arrived in New York for the first time –

Emily   (I think this is the eighth time I've heard this.)

Steve   (Get a tune and we could sing it.)

Danny   And as the cab swung past that graveyard and around the corner, and I got my first glimpse of the Manhattan skyline, I felt like I was coming home. The landscape was alive in my dreams, the streets were memories from a thousand movies, the city was mine.

Rory   Well you have a sense of place, Danny. It just happens to be somebody else's place.

Danny   No it doesn't, it's as much Ireland as Dublin is; millions of Irish went out and invented it, invented it as much, probably more than any ever invented this poxy post-colonial backwater.

Breda   So what's the problem? You don't like it here, fine, you don't live here; you feel at home there, great, you live there. What's the big deal?

Danny   The big deal, the big deal is, that *there* is as much *here* as *here* is . . . and I don't believe the *here* you're describing exists here. To me, *here* is more like . . . *there*.

Pause.

Emily Danny, are you on drugs?

Danny (Beam me up *now*)

Emily Because if you are, it was majorly mean of you not to spread 'em around.

Clare It's a fake though, this village idea, Breda. It doesn't solve any problems, it just uses them as entertainment.

Breda Is that what you think? That all I do is entertainment?

Clare I think that's what gets done; I think that's the way it ends up getting used.

Breda We expose social problems –

Clare But they don't go away. Nothing changes. People – all your As and Bs – swish past the beggars and the bricked-up streets, dart home to their little cubes, and then plug into Reynolds on the Radio – for what, to expand their consciences? No, to *assuage* them. A little squalor and heartbreak, a little zest to their complacency. That isn't community, Breda, it's slumming. And you can't go slumming in a village.

Pause

Brendan I don't know guys, Clare . . . but that's all far too cynical, I really can't agree. Even if things aren't perfect, they're better now, even than they were ten years ago. And the radio's just the radio – you can always turn it off, right? And the feeling that we can make a difference, our generation – we're not going to make the same mistakes the others did. Because we won't settle for the same rubbish they had to put up with.

Clare I thought you said people don't change that much over the years.

Brendan Deep down. Deep down people are the same, sure. They want the same things. But things are changing, they're definitely getting better, I don't know. More positive.

Clare Yeah. Go print it on a T-shirt, Brendan.

Pause.

Steve In advertising, if you want to get anywhere at all, there are two myths you've got to encounter, two sides to yourself you've got to develop. One is Faust, yeah? You've got to say, 'I am not a Great Artist, my creativity is important only insofar as it can sell this car, or these cornflakes, or whatever.' And then, two is Mephistopheles – you've got to convince everyone else that whatever it is in life they want, they can get it simply by consuming, by paying for it. That all there is in life, love and sex and happiness – it's all just goods and services. And you start off aware that these are two fictions you're purveying, purely in order to succeed. But pretty soon, you can't remember what the real things underneath them actually were. And then it's easier to decide that there aren't any real things, no way things really are. You can have whatever you want, if you can pay for it. Ireland as folksy little village or as fifty-first state in terminal stages of urban breakdown – all it is, is goods and services. One today, the other tomorrow, both at the same time. Look at the range that's available, look at all these things happening, turn them on, turn them off. It's a movie.

Pause

Do you know what I mean?

Silence

And. . .

Danny, **Clare**.

Clare   The year Brendan was on nights? I remember that Christmas, yes.

Danny   Alright, so there was one night I was coming down your street, it was late, and so was I. I got near to your house, and as I approached, I heard music, loud dance music – I forget what it was. Anyway, I stopped opposite your front door, you know the laneway, I stopped and I stood there in the dark. All the lights in the front room were out, there was just the red glow of the fire – and there you were in the window, dancing. Just dancing away on your own. I stood there, I don't know how long, song after song, and your face . . . you looked like you were in heaven. So abandoned, so . . . elated. And I stood there in the dark, cigarette after cigarette, just watching you.

Clare   I haven't danced on my own for ages.

Danny   You were the woman in the window. But then I blew it by knocking on the door.

Clare   You didn't blow it, Danny. You know that.

Danny   Good. That's good to know. (*Pause.*) Ah Jesus Clare, it's great to see you. (*He hugs her.*)

Clare   It's great to see you too.

Danny   It was good, wasn't it – that Christmas?

Clare   It was great.

Danny   I've thought about it a lot, what you said . . . have you kept writing?

Clare   For a while, I . . . I was full when you left, full to the brim, I was going to do everything. Do everything, see everything, feel everything, be everything. But then I sort of lost it somewhere. Somewhere between the house and school, it . . . went astray. I don't know. It's all so bland here now. Everyone wants to be a part of everything, to belong – there's no dissent, no opposition – no *passion* any more. There's just talk – endless, pointless talk, on the radio, in the pubs –

Danny That's it – Ireland as a massive pub – The Gael Inn. A year-long drink-fuelled talk-fest. Why do you think I got out, for fuck's sake? It wasn't money or jobs or me da or any of that, it was to get shot of the torpor, to feel the weight of all that garbage lifted off my back, that's why.

Clare And look at you now. Look at *you*. You've got your story published, you're on your way, it was worth it.

Danny Yeah, but . . . you can really do it, Clare, you were always better than I was anyway, I was just good at hogging the limelight.

Clare But I don't even know that I *want* to write . . .

Danny Whatever, whatever it is . . . it's important that you're able to do this, Clare, important to me. I . . . this sounds weird, but it's true, I . . . I believe in you. I really do.

Clare And I think I'm probably in love with you.

Pause.

Danny You are?

Clare Yes, and I swore I wouldn't say it, but suddenly everything's so simple: I look at you and I think, 'He hasn't stopped fighting, he hasn't given up, he's still possessed by passion,' and I think, 'He's just like me, we're the same, do something about it,' and I think, 'Say it. Act. Your life is a joke, but you can change it.' Suddenly it's all so simple.

Danny Simple . . .

Clare And I should never've married Brendan, it was always you, Dan, you know that, even at college – but I was such a little girl then, so scared – of you, of life, of everything. And Brendan made me feel safe. But I don't want to feel safe any more.

Danny Clare –

Clare And practically, there'd be no problem, I have a job in New York any time I want one, and I got a visa last year, so *that's* alright –

Danny Clare, wait a second . . . you're saying you're going to split up with Brendan, and move to New York, and . . . be with me?

Clare Be with you. Yes. (*Beat.*) No. Oh God, what a fool. I've made a mistake.

Pause.

Danny I'm sorry?

Clare I've made a mistake, haven't I? I thought you . . . felt something. But you don't.

Danny   I *do*, I just . . . I do feel something, it's just not what *you*   . . . It's very complicated –

Clare   Isn't it? What did you . . . you said, 'I believe in you.' What does that *mean?* 'I believe in you.'

Danny   That you've got something special, you've got to . . .

Clare   'I believe in you.' What is it, Dan? Is it like believing in Santa Claus?

Danny   I'm trying to explain –

Clare   And what about that Christmas, Dan? Was that all Santa Claus too?

Danny   No, it wasn't, it was special – then. But now – well, now, it's just . . . something that happened. There's a lot I haven't told you . . .

Clare   'Something that happened.'

Danny   Jesus, I've hardly written to you since. Surely that . . .

Clare   But I wrote to you. I thought you knew.

Danny   But you didn't tell me. You never said anything . . . like this. Jesus Clare.

Clare   And now you're not . . . you're not . . . something that happened. 'These things happen.' God, why am I such a fool? Why am I such a fucking fool?

Clare *is crying, but angry with it.*

You said I was the woman in the window. Why did you say that?

Danny   Clare, come on.

Clare   Why did you say it?

Danny   I just . . . oh God, I just said it.

Clare   Was it something for a story? Was it *art?* Was that it?

Danny   Oh Jesus, we're causing a . . . look, I'll get Brendan. Or Emily? And I'll talk to you later. OK, Clare? Clare?

Danny *makes to go.*

Clare   Danny?

Danny   Yeah?

Clare   Make sure everyone comes back tonight, won't you?

Danny   To the house? Do you not think –

Clare   It's pretty obvious I don't think. Just do that much, alright? I'll look after myself.

The light spreads to show the others. It's nearly closing time.

Clare   Brendan, I've become the Drunkest Lady in Ireland, take me home, will you?

Brendan   God Clare. Right, sure. I guess the others –

Clare   Will want a last pint. Now listen folks, I will accept no excuses and I will brook no fading – seven went out, and seven will return. Right?

Danny   Right.

Clare   I can't hear you, right?

All   RIGHT.

Clare   That's the way. Hey, later.

Brendan   See you guys.

They leave.

Emily   Ah, tears before closing time, takes me right back.

Breda   Maybe we should just give it a miss, you know? Looks like a pretty grim night ahead.

Steve   (*sings*) 'I think I'm going back, to the place I remember from my youth . . .'

Rory   Oh Breda, life in the fast lane hasn't made you a fader, now has it?

Danny   I think we should go back.

Emily   *Danny* thinks we should go back.

Steve   'I can recall a time, when I wasn't afraid to reach out to a friend . . .'

Breda   It just looks like it might get messy, you know? Get ugly.

Rory   Oh I'm sure it'll be nothing but beauty, Breda. Beauty all the way.

Emily   Hey Dan, half eleven, give the man high five.

Danny   Five have another pint.

Breda   Oh God, I haven't been this drunk in ages.

Rory   Beauty beauty everywhere, and plenty more to drink.

Blackout.

Music – Near Wild Heaven – *REM*.

Act Three

Clare *is sitting, drinking.* **Brendan** *potters about, tidying up plates and glasses.*

Clare The point is, not *that* I went to sleep, but when I went to sleep. I think it was 'round the time of the 1987 election. I certainly wasn't awake for the so-called fall of socialism, that was just images on a TV screen. No, it was definitely 1987, and I think I can remember why. Everyone was banging on about how disastrous the Coalition had been, (which it had), and how we were just imitating Thatcher in dismantling the Welfare State, (except we didn't really have one to dismantle), and Fianna Fail ran election posters with 'Health Cuts Hurt the Poor, the Sick and the Elderly', (which they do). Remember those posters?

And I was so disgusted at the pathetic excuse for a socialist party Labour had become that I actually voted for Fianna Fail. Oh yeah. And they were elected. And they proceeded, not to reverse the health cuts, but to increase them, thereby hurting the poor, the sick and the elderly more than ever. They had lied. And the thing was, it didn't matter. It was no problem. They'd lied through their teeth, and they hadn't apologised, and nobody cared. Nobody gave a fuck.

And I thought, this is unreal. There's such a blatant gap between what people say and what they do, and nobody gives a fuck about it. And . . . and then, how can you live in a country that doesn't care about lies? What's the point of speech, if no one values the truth? And then of course I felt like an infant, 'cause people just turned 'round and said, 'They're all crooks anyway, what did you expect?'

Well, I expected more, is the answer. I expected a lot more.

Still with me, Bren?

Brendan The country *was* in a terrible mess, Clare –

Clare I'm not talking about the country, I'm talking about myself. So . . . so I went to sleep. And then . . . something happened. Something happened to wake me, to remind me that things mattered, that you didn't have to be cynical to survive. Reminded me what all those records meant. But then I forgot it again. And slept on. Until tonight. Until now. And so . . . I've begun to realise that the thing that happened was telling me something serious about myself, it wasn't an aberration, it was truer than anything else in my life, not because of what it was in itself, but because of . . . the state from which it woke me.

Pause. **Brendan** *is staring at* **Clare**.

Aren't you going to ask me what the thing was, the thing that happened?

Brendan   Aren't you going to tell me?

Pause.

Clare   I had . . . two Christmases ago, for a fortnight, I . . . 'had an affair'. I had an affair. With Danny. That's why I was crying in the pub. Because I'm . . . I think I'm . . . still in love with him.

Pause.

Brendan?

Brendan   I'm here, I . . . just give me a minute on this, will you? You had an affair . . . Jesus, with *Danny* . . . and the reason was . . . because Fianna Fail won an election?

Clare   No, I . . . oh God, I don't know what I'm talking about.

Brendan   'Cause by that logic, there wouldn't be a marriage left in Ireland, the whole place'd be . . . Jesus, Clare, you had an affair? You're in love with someone else? (Someone else, with Danny?)

Clare   I don't know, I think . . . I know it was two years ago. I was close to walking out of here. But then I lost my nerve.

Brendan   So you were going to leave me two years ago but you lost your nerve?

Clare   I'm sorry if this sounds awful, Brendan, I know it does, but the only chance I've got now is to tell the truth. The only chance we've both got.

Brendan   Don't start preaching to me about my chances, don't start telling me this is better for both of us. Jesus, Danny? You fucked Danny . . . here? When? When I . . . when I was on nights, that Christmas? (**Clare** *nods.*) Oh choice. Class act Clare, in my own fucking house. And with *Danny* . . . he was supposed to be my *friend*. And you . . . I don't know what you're supposed to be, you . . . you . . . oh fuck . . .

Brendan *can't speak, he's gasping for breath.* **Clare** *approaches him.*

Get away from me. Don't you fucking touch me, I . . . you filthy fucking *bitch*, I . . . I . . . oh. Oh.

He composes himself.

Clare   I'm sorry Brendan, I –

Brendan   Why?

Clare   I don't know *why*, it just . . . happened.

Brendan   Give me a fucking break here Clare, why? Why did it just happen? And spare me the political science lecture will you, if I want to know about Fianna Fail I'll go to a fucking Ard Fheis.

Clare   I don't think I married for the right reason.

Brendan   You mean, you didn't love me?

Clare   No, I did – do – love you – but I don't think in the right way. Look – you know I went out with Danny before I met you – for about six months. Well those six months terrified me. It was like being on acid all the time, everything was . . . heightened, somehow. You never knew what would happen next. And I remember saying to myself, you're seeing it now. This is what you always wanted, what the small-town lads could never show you, what you dreamt of every night, playing your records alone in your room. But I was still a small-town girl. And it was too much for me. It was too close to . . . *chaos*. And Danny was past chaos and out the other side. And I got scared. And so I ended up doing exactly what I swore I wouldn't do, what my mother and the nuns prayed I would do – the H fucking Dip. And as bad luck would have it, I actually got a teaching job. And then suddenly everyone seemed to be going to New York, and we'd been going out for ages –

Brendan   So you thought, get married, you've nothing else to do.

Clare   So I thought, this is my life, I can only expect to change so much, settle down and accept it. And I did. And I thought I was happy. I suppose you don't realise how unhappy you actually are until something puts it in perspective for you.

Brendan   What, like fucking someone?

Clare   And it's not just me, you're not happy either, not happy with me.

Brendan   Yes I am. Well, I was until five minutes ago.

Clare   You're not, how could you have been? You just never have time to realise it, you're working ninety hour weeks, I could be anyone really.

Brendan   For fuck's sake Clare –

Clare   Well I could. We've nothing to say to each other, we don't like each other's friends, we disagree about everything and the only reason you don't know this is because it's been impossible to have a row with you!

Brendan   I really don't know you when you're like this.

Clare   That's what you say, exactly, and that proves my point, Bren, because I am like this. This is truly what I'm like. I tried to be someone else, the one who was married to you. But I'm not her. So if you don't know me like this, you don't know me at all.

Brendan   I don't believe that. I don't believe that.

Clare   I know you don't, 'cause you just see things the way you want them to be. Like me, like our marriage, like this ridiculous fucking reunion . . . I wanted to run away to Brittas because I could feel this coming on, Bren, and I was still scared. I didn't want to wake up. But each reunion, each memory, each time the past comes hurtling back, all it does is make me realise what a coward I've been to stay here, and that I can't do it any more.

Brendan I can't believe the way you're turning this around so that I'm to blame. You betrayed me –

Clare Oh spare me, 'betrayed'.

Brendan You have some scummy affair, you get drunk and talk a load of bollocks about elections and being asleep and telling the truth . . . the *truth* . . . and now it's all supposed to be my fault?

Clare It wasn't a scummy affair.

Pause.

Brendan What?

Clare It wasn't a scummy affair. It was not a scummy affair.

Brendan Oh what was it then, was it 'brilliant'? Was it 'beautiful'?

Clare Yes it was. It was brilliant. It was beautiful. And I'm not going to lie and say it wasn't.

Brendan You fucking *whore*.

He hits her across the face. She hits him back. There is a scuffle.

Clare *Oh*, is *this* what you want? Is this the kind of class act you're looking for, Brendan?

Brendan Stop.

Clare You haven't a clue, have you, not a notion why I'd be unhappy, you're too busy thinking about your*self*.

Brendan Clare stop it, I'm warning you.

Clare Oh warn me, go on Brendan, warn me before you what, kill me? You've got what you *want* – you've always got what you wanted – but you couldn't see that both of us were living your life. There were some days I couldn't even remember my own name –

Brendan And which days were those now, the half-a-bottle of vodka days? You could've stopped teaching, you could've done anything you wanted to. But you never bothered, you preferred to sit around drinking and feeling sorry for yourself.

Clare What anything? What other thing can I do, Brendan?

Brendan You could've had a kid.

Clare Oh brilliant. 'You could've had a kid.' Don't remember the page in the careers booklet on *that*. Yeah, I could've had a baby, and delayed this conversation by twenty years.

Brendan You did the house up yourself, you designed it.

Clare Yes, and there's another thing I can't do Brendan. Look at the place, it's a joke. It's the pages of magazines, it's the inside of Steve's brain, there isn't an ounce of originality in the whole house, it's ersatz designer tat, I *hate* it.

She starts breaking ornaments and throwing stuff about.

Brendan Clare, come on.

Clare Come on yourself, it's fun, Brendan, *fun*.

Brendan Clare don't, please.

Clare No no Bren, I'm confident here, destroying stuff is one thing I'm a dab hand at.

She breaks something else. He catches hold of her.

Brendan Stop it. Please stop it, love. I'm . . . I'm sorry I hit you.

There is a pause, and then **Clare** *starts to cry.*

Clare Oh Bren, I'm sorry. I'm so sorry.

Brendan Shhhhh. It's alright. It's gonna be alright.

They hold each other for a while. Then –

Brendan That was some smack you gave me though. (*Pause.*)

Clare You're lucky I didn't hit you with my left.

Brendan Right. (*Pause.*) Would you like a cup of tea?

Clare What? Oh. Yeah. Here, I'll make it.

Clare *doesn't move.*

Pause.

Brendan So, ah, what do you want to do?

Clare Well I suppose . . . I suppose I'd better move out.

Brendan Right.

Clare What do you want to do?

Brendan I want everything to be like it was ten minutes ago, before the sky caved in. I wish we *had* gone to Brittas. (*Pause.*) Clare?

Clare Uh huh?

Brendan What if we . . . do you think we could . . . well, look, try again. I don't mind about Danny, well I do, but I'm sure I'll get over it . . . I just don't want to lose you.

Pause.

Clare   I don't think, Bren – that I'll be able to . . . Christ, we've never even had a row before.

Brendan   Well maybe that was the problem, I didn't realise . . . haven't understood how unhappy you've been. That's my fault.

Clare   No –

Brendan   Yes, it is, and I'll . . . I'll be able to see more clearly now. I will. Say you'll give it another go. Please.

Pause.

Clare   I don't know.

Brendan   *Please.*

Clare   Oh no, the others are coming back. I wish they weren't now. Maybe they won't.

Brendan   Maybe they won't come back, and we can be here on our own, just the two of us, and we can work something out. We can make our own world again.

Clare   I feel under a lot of pressure here Bren, you're backing me into a corner –

Brendan   But it's a good corner. It'll be good for both of us. Please?

Doorbell.

Clare   Oh shit.

Brendan   We don't answer the door 'til we answer the question.

Pause.

Clare   I'll try.

Brendan   Attagirl. I'll get the door.

Clare   Bren . . .

Brendan   Just watch me. Everything's gonna be fine.

He goes out to answer the door.

Clare   Oh God, I just wish it was all over.

Brendan   (*off*) Amazing, guys, amazing.

The five come on, each brandishing a bottle of tequila.

Danny   Hey honey, we're home.

Clare   Holy fuck.

Steve   Holy fuck is right, what happened here?

Clare   Oh. I thought the decor needed a few post-modernist touches.

Emily   Big improvement. (You okay?)

Clare   (Tell you later.)

Brendan   Great stuff Danno, this is very definitely the business.

Danny   Medical opinion doesn't frown?

Brendan   It always frowns, so fuck it.

Brendan *and* **Danny** *are setting up the tequila on a coffee table.*

Steve   Let me take your wrap, Ma'am.

Emily   Why thank you, boy.

Breda   Clare, where's the loo?

Clare   One through there. Is this an entirely wise enterprise?

Rory   Of course it's not, that's precisely why Danny suggested it.

Clare   Oh it's Danny's idea.

Danny   Great Ideas of Western Thought, Volume Five. It comes between Schopenhaer and Thoreau – Tequila Run.

Brendan   Where's the ginger ale?

Emily   That's slammers, this is shots.

Steve   The salt on the crook of finger and thumb, the rush of the tequila, and the serious suck on the lime . . .

Emily   And it's Astral Plane In-Flight Activity, right Steve?

Steve   You got it babe.

Breda   *reappears.*

Clare   How's Breda?

Breda   Not wisely but too well, I think I'm gonna fade. Steve?

Steve   Yeah. Soon. Just need a couple of these to crank things up.

Emily   Ah Breda, you can't fade now.

Breda   (*curling up on a couch*) I can fade any time I fucking want.

Emily   (Oh lordy. Nervous titters all round.)

Steve   Not many of us left with *staying* power.

Emily   But hey – you've got enough for two, right?

Steve   *Right.*

Danny   Places, pilgrims – kneeling at the altar.

Rory   This is why I hated sports at school.

Brendan   C'mon in Clare, it's fine.

Clare   (*It's fun.*)

Emily   Salt me, Danny Baby, salt me.

Danny   Got your lime, now it's time. Count of three, everyone ready? Haon, do, *tri*!

They knock them back. Noise. **Steve** *sets up the next one.*

Rory   I can't help feeling this is just not *me*.

Emily   You should have your opera cloak on, Rory.

Danny   Yes, and heavenly choirs, 'Panis Angelicus . . .'

Rory   Such a fate – not just to be gay, but a gay cliche too.

Emily   Rory, Rory, how wonderful to be you, you've told us no secrets tonight, is there a boy on the leash?

Rory   No boys, Emily, sad to relate; the ones I seem to attract're never house-trained, for some reason. Or else they're too bloody house-trained, complete nellies, which is far worse.

Danny   Ah Rory, we'll just have to build you a boy.

Rory   Oh yes please, one I can programme myself.

Steve   'Build Me a Boy' – sounds like a Bronski Beat number.

Emily   I'm in need too, Ror – perhaps we could share him.

Rory   Mmmm, send him back and forth by parcel post, so we wouldn't get bored.

Steve   All right, *ready*.

Emily   (With an enormous willy.)

Rory   (But of course dear, like a baseball bat.)

Steve   (*simultaneous with 'baseball bat'*) Un, deux, trois.

They drink. Noise. **Emily** *sets up the next one.*

Emily   Un, deux, trois?

Steve   I know, and so effortless, yeah?

Danny   So quiz-time, guys – who remembers the Four Marys?

Emily   From the *Bunty*?

Clare   Oh God, hang on, there's something I *do* know.

Breda   (*half asleep*) Mary . . . Mary . . .

Rory   Look, it's a talking statue.

Breda   Mary . . . Mary . . .

Steve   I bet this is an RTE canteen joke, she's going to say Mary Banotti, Mary Kenny, Mary Holland and Mary Harney. (*Pause.*)

Emily   Is the thing about RTE canteen jokes that they're not funny?

Steve   Got it in one.

Danny   Give up?

Clare   *No.* Mary Cotter, Mary Field, Mary Simpson and . . . ah shit, I always forget one.

Emily   I got *June* and *School Friend*.

Danny   Give you a clue?

Clare   Yes please.

Danny   Her first name was Mary.

Clare   Oh fuck off.

Danny   Mary *Radleigh*.

Steve   How do you know this stuff man?

Clare   'Cause he had four sisters.

Rory   But were they all called Mary?

Danny   I don't remember. They called me Notice-Box, and I called them Sir.

Emily   Rock 'n' Roll High School, wan, too, tree, faw!

They drink. Noise. **Rory** *next.*

Steve   Like Last Train to Gonesville guys, Mondo Madness Mexicano.

Danny   Steve do you speak that way 'cause you can't help it, or 'cause the ad-world's addled your brain?

Steve   I do it for fun, Danny; what else is there?

Danny   Um . . . the English Language?

Steve   Like mega-overhyped conversational matrix vibe, Dan.

Danny   (*beat*) Now you've got me.

Emily   He means – shut the fuck up, you pompous wanker.

Danny   Oh, I *see*. Well that's *alright* then, I never listen when people say *that*.

Clare   You must play deaf a lot so.

Brendan   Oh I just feel like, so *elated*!

Rory   (What did he say?)

Danny   He feels like we're all related.

Rory   Oh dear. Alright then, ready, steady, go.

They drink. Noise. Everyone is completely drunk.

Danny   Ah now. *Now* we're getting somewhere. Gotta have some music.

Clare   Oh yeah. Something really noisy.

Brendan   Great night Rory, what do you say?

Rory   I find myself pretty incapable of speech at this time, Brendan.

Steve (to **Emily**)   You want some more?

Emily   Ah yeah, fill her up.

Danny (*his own tape*)   This should do it.

It's All Over the World *by the Pixies.*

Clare   We should dance.

Danny   Clare, listen, something I've gotta tell you –

Clare   Nothing I need to hear. Forget it. Never happened. Memory Lane. Let's just dance.

Danny   But it's not about *that* –

Clare   Ah ah. Do as you're told, and no lip. C'mon you shower of fuckers, *dance*.

Steve   So hey babe, how about it?

Emily   Ha! I thought you would've improved your line by now.

Steve   Oh right, sorry, how's this: 'Actually, I'm a feminist.'

Emily   I think I prefer 'Hey babe'. How about what?

Steve   You and me – we could slip off somewhere, nobody would notice.

Emily   You're not joking, are you?

Steve   No.

Emily   But . . . Breda's just over there.

Steve   She won't wake up now, she's out for the count.

Emily   And anyway – *no*.

Brendan   And fair enough, I know it was awkward, a bit awkward, for everyone initially, but people soon fall back into the old ways. I mean, look at all this!

Rory   I'm looking.

Brendan   I believe . . . you know, that friendship, love, even, that . . . once you establish it, forge that strong strong bond with another person . . . I, you know, don't really believe it can ever be broken. Not really.

Rory   Brendan, you are without any doubt the stupidest person I've ever met.

Brendan   I'm sorry?

Clare   We should've done this as soon as everyone arrived, you know, just turned up the music and danced.

Danny   I don't know that it's gonna help much now.

Clare   Well it's certainly helping *me*.

Steve   Why not?

Emily   Steve, Modern Man follows 'no' with 'cool enough' or 'what the fuck', not 'why not?'

Steve   Well meet Post-Modern man.

Emily   Piltdown Man.

Steve   Why not, babe?

Emily   Well, how to put this so you'll understand: one, because I'd quite like to, which is always a bad sign, two because I'm too drunk to be careful (that's safe), and so are you . . .

Rory   Stupid. Utterly, irredeemably stupid. You look at all this, Bren. Breda passed out, Steve trying to bed Emily, rows and envy and bad blood everywhere, and I would be dying of boredom were it not for the fact that I'm actually dying of acute alcoholic poisoning.

Brendan   But –

Rory   But nothing. It's dead, Bren, long dead, all we're doing is burying it. Dance on its grave and forget about it. We've nothing for each other any more. Everyone knows it but you.

Danny   There's just this one thing, Clare –

Clare   There's too many things, Danny. But they'll all go away. Everything will be the same as it was again. Nothing is going to happen.

Steve   And three?

Emily   And three, because you really are such a comprehensively epic *ass*hole that if I slept with you, I'd surely have to kill myself afterwards.

Danny   Right, now this bit we've got to have *loud*.

He turns the music up. Change partners.

Emily   How was I ever dumb enough to think I could be friends with that . . . prick with ears.

Clare   Steven?

Emily   Fuck, with Breda here and everything. I thought he was sending himself up. And how I ever . . . ohhh!

Clare   Yes, how *did* you ever?

Emily   I must've been desperate. And he did a better impersonation of a human being back then. God.

Clare   I think Steve's idea of friendship with a woman is pretty narrow.

Emily (*indicating* **Breda**)   But look how happy it makes them!

Steve   I tell you this man, I get so close sometimes to giving them a good solid smack, I get *this fucking close*. Fucking bitch . . .

Brendan   Steve I found something out tonight. About Clare.

Steve   All this flirty shit, and then 'drop dead, asshole'. What did she think I wanted, a fucking *conversation*?

Brendan   Steve.

Steve   I don't care what she's got, you should never treat a person like that, no way.

Brendan   *Steve*.

Steve   What?

Rory   Looks like you won't be needed after all, Danny?

Danny   What do you mean?

Rory I mean you won't need to push anyone towards chaos, they're all rushing headlong, they don't need any help.

Danny The tequila was my idea, remember? Sweet chaos, don't you love it? Listen to this.

Danny *turns up the music.*

Rory This is horrible, what is it?

Danny It's a nightmare.

Emily But that was useless anyway, all you were doing was swopping one man for another. What do *you* want, for yourself?

Clare I don't want anything, I was being an idiot, a teenager.

Emily What?

Clare You're all going to leave, and Brendan and I will be together, and everything will be just as it was.

Steve Bren, what is it?

Brendan Steve, I found out that Clare had an affair . . . with Danny.

Steve Yeah, that Christmas you were on nights, I know. I tell you what really gets me, okay I didn't write to her, but *I* had to go and get a fucking *test* –

Brendan You knew?

Steve Sure. Everyone knew. What . . . did you only find out *now*?

Brendan *Everyone knew.*

Clare Everything will be exactly as it was.

Danny It's the sound of a fucking nightmare.

The music has built and built. Suddenly **Breda** *shouts out in her sleep.*

Breda WHEN THE LIGHT GOES GREEN, YOU'RE ON THE AIR.

Music ends.

Blackout.

Act Four

Music to cover the scene change – Rainbirds – *Tom Waits*

All except **Brendan**.

A slow, careful breakfast is in progress. Coffee, juice, rolls and fruit.

Silence reigns.

After a while . . .

Danny If you think about it, there are twenty-five Famous Five books, each dealing with a holiday, so if you say three hol's a year, Christmas, Easter and Summer, then that's eight years, so if Julian is, say, fourteen in the first one, then he must be twenty two in the last; *but* he's still at school *and* going around in short trousers. So he can't be as clever as he thinks, what does anyone reckon?

Pause. **Danny** *is pointedly ignored.*

Then there's Dublin rhyming slang. What's that all about? 'I don't feel the Mae West, spent all me rock'n'roll on some lethal Bob Hope.' It's not the same as the cockney stuff at all. But maybe it was once. Maybe it came back from the trenches, a pernicious linguistic import, a foreign game. Maybe that's it. Oh yes, oh yes, oh yes indeed.

Pause. As above.

And then, we all know that Albert Camus and Humphrey Bogart were never photographed together, this being because they were in actual fact one and the same person, but what does anyone reckon on Lee Dunne and Sonny Knowles?

Emily/Clare Danny, Shut Up!

Pause

Breda Some girls with sore heads this morning?

Emily Sore everythings, thanks to Mr Brains Trust here. Never again.

Rory Never tequila again certainly, it's like liquid plutonium.

Emily I cannot believe we all crashed out here, Jesus, like freshers at our first party.

Clare No one was in a fit state to drive.

Danny No one was in a fit state to walk.

Rory We decided we'd see in the dawn. Then everyone else fell asleep, so I called a cab. But it never came. Or it came but I was asleep. Or . . . some combination of the above.

Pause.

Danny   Where's Bren, still in bed?

Clare   No, he's off out somewhere, I don't know.

Emily   Probably gone to work.

Breda   He wouldn't just go off to work like that.

Rory   Not without issuing Official Farewells.

Emily   Look, if you worked in a hospital, isn't that where you'd want to be right now? Ohhh.

Pause.

Breda   Well, time we made a move. Steve?

Steve   Yeah, we'd better hit the road alright.

Breda   Brunch with Steve's parents, mustn't be late.

Rory   Are you heading southside, Breda?

Breda   Killiney, yeah.

Danny   Where did you *think* Steve's folks lived, Darndale?

Steve   So speaks the working-class hero from Castleknock.

Breda   Do you want a lift, Rory?

Rory   I certainly do, my bathroom pines for me.

Breda   Anyone else? Right so. Clare, thanks a million pet; I know I crashed awful early, but by the looks of the rest of you I really can't say I'm sorry.

Clare   Don't be. You're lucky. Mind yourself. (*Front door opens.*) Ah, there's Brendan now.

Steve   Secret of good comedy.

Brendan *comes on.*

Breda   Glad you caught us, Bren, we're just about to go.

*But **Brendan** is silent, having walked as far away as possible from the others.*

Brendan?

Clare   Bren, are you really bad? Everyone's in the same sick boat. Have some breakfast why don't you, there's coffee here, and bagels.

Pause.

Steve   Well, we'd really better be moving anyway; sorry about your head Bren –

Brendan   Just hold on a minute, would you. I just . . . there's something I want to say to you, all of you.

Rory   (I do hope it's uplifting, after we all missed Mass and everything.)

Danny   I think we all agree that things have to get better, Bren, more positive, if it's *that* speech, if only, 'cause the way we all feel now, they can hardly get much worse.

Brendan   Well you can shut up for a start, you little shit. *(Pause.)* It's so strange – looking 'round, seeing all these faces I thought I knew, and realising I don't really know them at all.

Clare   Brendan, be careful, please. Be very careful.

Brendan   Careful how, Clare, do you mean *discreet?*   Do you mean smirks and jokes and knowing looks at the big fool's expense? Or do you mean full of cares, bursting into tears in public when the little shit you're actually in love with doesn't want to know? Guess you must mean discretion, 'cause that's what my old friends are expert at. My good, old friends. I've been out walking, I must've walked for miles, and I've had just the one thought to keep me company – the thought of my friends, who wouldn't even see each other if it wasn't for me, whom I've met at airports and moved to flats when I was the only one with a car, whom I've lent money to and pretended to forget when it was due back and genuinely didn't mind, was glad to do it – my good, old friends, so discreet that not one of you had the *guts*, or the decency, to tell me that my wife had an affair two-and-a-half years ago with this little shithead here. Not one of you. And you all knew.

Rory   (Oh my goodness.)

Clare   Brendan, what do you think you're *doing?*

Brendan   I'm rounding things up, Clare. You know, the way I usually do, with a sentimental speech about what great friends we all are. And everyone thinks, what a big fool, and laughs behind their hands. Well, I'm not going to play the fool any more.

Danny   So what do you think this is, you self-righteous maniac?

Brendan   If I were you I'd be too ashamed to open my mouth, you little *shit*.

Danny   Well you're not me, so –

Emily   Danny, shut the fuck up. Brendan, you're so big on friendship; you've known for ages that Steve works his way through women like most people use Kleenex. How come you've never had the 'guts' or the 'decency' to tell Breda?

Pause.

Breda   *What?*

Clare   (Oh Emily.)

Steve   (Oh man, this is just unreal.)

Brendan   I'm not talking about Breda and Steve, I'm talking about ingratitude.

Emily   Ingratitude?

Brendan   I'm the one who kept this whole thing going, kept us all together –

Rory   And now you see what a super idea that was.

Breda   Emily McAuliffe, what are you saying?

Pause.

Emily   Oh shit, that he cheats on you. He cheats on you all the time. He tried to get me into bed last night when you were crashed out.

Steve   In your dreams, you lying . . . I don't have to listen to this.

Emily   And it wasn't just the drink, he does it all the time. Brendan knows. He probably just thinks it's different 'cause you're a woman.

Breda   Brendan? Is this true?

Pause.

Brendan   I don't know what she's talking about, Breda.

Steve   You see? Thank you Brendan, I feel like I'm on fucking *trial* here. You see?

Emily   Oh Brendan, full of little surprises.

Clare   (God, what a fucking nightmare.)

Breda   Just what was this supposed to be, Emily, some kind of schoolgirl vendetta? Do you think this is the playground? Do you think we're all kids?

Emily   (I don't know what we all are.)

Breda   It's no surprise to me that you'd try and stir some shit anyway. I know you've always wanted Steve, that you did your best to get him when he was in New York; I saw you last night . . . flirting with him like a schoolgirl –

Emily   You saw *what*?

Clare   Brendan's lying, Breda –

Breda   And you don't really expect me to believe *you* either, do you? Look at the pair of you. You were so fucking smart in college, weren't you, you were gonna get to the top of the heap no problem, you were a cut above the likes of me – Breda the stage manager, Breda the clueless hick, don't tell *Breda* where the party is, she'll bore us all to death. So fucking *smart*, look at you now, you're *nothing*; drowning in self-pity or sneering at anyone who actually gets something *done*; incapable of controlling your messy, pathetic lives. People like you bore me to death now, you're *nowhere*.

Danny   And producing a radio show for people with the mental age of a potato is *somewhere*, is it?

Breda   Compared to what? Painting? The *Visual Arts*? Some exhibition that might be seen by ten thousand people if you're lucky. The whole art world is run by about ten thousand people anyway, it's irrelevant, it belongs to the last century. We talk to hundreds of thousands, to millions, every day of the week. *That's* what's happening. That's somewhere.

Danny   You're actually worse than Steve. He's completely corrupt, but that's what his job's all about. But you . . . you don't *need* to be like this. You're this way 'cause you like it. You like the power, you like the public in thrall . . . you think you mean something.

Breda   I know I mean something. And I know Steve does too. But I've got to be honest here, maybe it's that you can't roll out the old socialist shibboleths any more, maybe it's that you still aren't earning any real money . . . but I don't know *what* you mean, Danny. And I don't know that you do either.

Danny   I uh . . .

Breda   I mean, for someone who's had such a big break, you don't exactly come across like you know what you're doing. Why is that, Danny?

Danny   Because – (there isn't any story.)

Emily   (Danny *don't*.)

Pause.

Clare   *What?*

Danny   There isn't any story. In the *New Yorker*. Or anywhere else, for that matter.

Brendan   You lying shit.

Emily   (Don't tell them, Jesus.)

Danny   I haven't written a word for years. (Did you *know?*)

Emily   (Of course I knew.)

Danny   Rory knew too, I think. You read the *New Yorker*, don't you Rory?

Rory   There are eleven Irish subscribers, and I confess to being one of them.

Danny   Why didn't you say anything?

Rory   It hardly seemed a hanging matter. The only person you were harming was yourself.

Danny   I don't know about that.

Steve   You fucking prick. You patronising little prick. You come back here, oh how's Mr Advertising, Mr Crass, Mr Sell-Out, why don't you do something *important*, Steve, you owe it to yourself, you don't really want to sell your soul, to degrade yourself, for *money*, do you? And I'm thinking, at least Danny is writing, at least that's something . . . and all this time . . . what are you *doing*?

Danny   Nothing. Sub-editing. Drinking. Talking.

Steve   You fucking fraud, I thought you were doing it. We all did. And .. and . . . and if you don't write, if you're not a fucking writer, then what's the *point* of you?

Danny   Uh . . . as Eric Morcambe used to say, 'there's no answer to that'.

Pause.

Rory   You didn't really 'round things up' terribly successfully, did you Brendan? Probably because you don't seem very *familiar* with any of the people you call your friends.

Brendan   You don't know anything about me –

Rory   Yes well perhaps that's true too, but I do know that if friendship's an *investment*, as you seem to think, then it's a very dodgy one, and you really can't depend on getting the return you expect. Now, I hate to be the blushing eunuch at this little orgy of self-exposure, but I'm afraid I *am* a solicitor, I *am* gay, I *do* review opera on the radio and I'm now going home, before someone remembers how I once said boo to them at a drinks party. If any good comes of all this, it's surely that the seven of us need never sit in the same room again.

Goodbye.

Oh, and *hey* – it's been far too real.

Rory *goes*.

Brendan   Yeah, well. Good riddance.

Clare   (Oh my God.)

Steve   Man I need a drink

Brendan   So do I, this place is beginning to make me sick.

Breda (*to* **Steve**)   C'mon, let's go.

Steve   Bren, like to come for a drink?

Pause.

Brendan   Thanks Steve, I'd like that a lot. Danny, you really are the scum of the earth.

Danny Ah stop.

Clare Brendan, you go off and have a drink with what's left of your good old friends. I won't be here when you get back.

Pause.

Brendan This is the way you want it then?

Clare This is the way it *is*.

Pause.

Brendan Uh, Emily –

Emily Fuck off Brendan.

Pause.

Brendan *goes out quickly.*

Steve Right then. Ready to rock?

Breda Ready to roll.

Breda *and* **Steve** *go off.*

Emily I suppose it's just that they have so much in common.

Clare Emily, if you knew Danny hadn't written the story, hadn't written a *word*, why did you say he had?

Danny Yeah, I've been sort of wondering that myself.

Emily Oh, you know. Why not? (*Pause.*) Alright, 'cause I still sort of hoped he *had* written it, and 'cause I wanted him to look well in front of everybody and . . . and fuck it, just 'cause Brendan believed some bizarre late-sixties fantasy about us all being friends forever, it doesn't destroy the whole thing, does it? It doesn't for me anyway. And incidentally, why the *New Yorker*? It's got to be the dullest magazine in the universe.

Danny I know, it makes Jane Austen look like Erica Jong.

Pause.

Clare You really should've told me, Danny.

Danny I tried to tell you last night.

Clare You should've told me two years ago, I thought you *stood* for something –

Emily 'Bye.

Clare Oh Em, don't go.

Emily I really don't have time for this kind of stuff any more, Clare, I'm tired of it all: things standing for other things, dreams of what you might've been, what you could still be. It's not healthy.

Pause.

And for God's sake don't look at me like that, with those 'Poor Emily' expressions. Jesus, every time I tell someone I don't have time or I'm feeling tired, they're booking the plot and buying the flowers before I can blink. It's a disease, not a metaphor. It doesn't *mean* anything, it's just bad luck.

And now, before this hangover starts deluding me into thinking I have Great Truths to tell about Life and How to Live It, I'd better *frapper*.

'Bye Clare. Call me tonight?

Clare   Yeah. 'Bye love.

Emily   See ya Dan.

Danny   Em. See you soon?

Emily   Sure. But in Bewley's, right? We meet in a pub, you'll have two novels and a play talked away by closing time. Talked away to *me*.

Danny   Bewley's it is.

Emily   And *hey* –

Emily/Danny   *Get a job.*

Emily   Right so. I feel like a bit of a jerk having told Breda about Steve. I don't think I was acting from the purest of motives.

Clare   It was no harm. It was highly educational, in fact.

Emily   It certainly was. And sure where would you be without your education? 'Bye now.

Emily *goes.*

Clare   I think you'd better go too, Danny.

Danny   Right. (*He gets his jacket.*) Look, Clare, the reason I didn't tell you before – two years ago –

Clare   It doesn't matter.

Danny   It matters to me –

Clare   Then live with it. I don't have the fucking room, Danny, understand? Not now.

Danny   But the thing is, I was deluding myself all the time; I thought I was what I claimed to be –

Clare   Well that makes two of us.

Danny   And then –

Clare   Danny, I don't know if you noticed, but my marriage just broke up.

It may not've been a very good marriage, but it's the only one I've ever had; and I don't know how it's all supposed to make me feel, and I don't know how I do feel, but I certainly don't feel like listening to you talk about yourself any more. Got me?

Danny   Got you. I'm sorry. I . . . do you know what you're gonna do?

Clare   What's it to you? Or have you still got big plans for me, high hopes, seeing as how you *believe* in me and everything?

Danny   Always high hopes.

Clare   Well keep 'em to yourself. If you're really interested, I reckon I'll go and stay with Em a while. Get the fuck out of here anyway. And . . . oh, hang out, get drunk, you know. Do what you do. Nothing.

Pause.

Danny   Look Clare, this is not entirely my fault, you know.

Clare   It's not at all your fault, it's mine. All my own work. (*Pause.*) What're you going to 'do' now? Keep 'writing'?

Danny   I'm gonna stay here, actually.

Clare   You're what? In Ireland?

Danny   Yeah.

Clare   But . . . why?

Danny   Well, 'cause of Breda. (*Pause.*) This weekend, right . . . I couldn't even argue with her the way I used to, I didn't feel as sure of the ground. Didn't know the ground. I just knew she was wrong. And when she said she didn't know what I meant any more, I thought . . . sitting on your own in a beat-up apartment in Manhattan reading Don DeLillo and Thomas Pynchon and not writing a word and deluding yourself you're in the thick of the modern maelstrom is certainly pretty meaningless.

Clare   Whereas coming back here is meaningful?

Danny   It's all I ever thought about while I was away. I brought my village with me –

Clare   This is just words, Danny, what're you going to *do?*

Danny   See if I can start a fire . . . or dredge one out of the wreckage . . . *I don't know.*

Clare   Just words.

Pause.

Danny   Remember that stuff about you dancing on your own, being the woman in the window, all that?

Clare   You made that up too? I'd begun to remember it myself.

Danny   No, I said I couldn't remember the music you were dancing to. But I could.

He gives her a tape.

Clare   I'm not sure I want to listen to this.

Danny   Oh go on. Look, you'll be there, and I'll be here –

Clare   And if *here* is *there* and *there* is *here* –

Danny   And it's your memory. Brendan doesn't have the franchise on sentiment.

Clare   Not while you're around, no.

Clare *takes the tape.*

Danny   Right so, 'bye 'bye.

Clare   'Bye Danny. 'Keep the faith.'

Danny   What else is there to do with it? See you.

Clare *stands for a moment, then goes off and comes back with a bag. She begins to load records and books into it, then stops, and sits a while. She remembers the tape, picks it up and puts it in the machine. The sun is streaming into the room. The tape is* True Faith *by New Order.*

The music starts.

Clare   Oh *no*.

She holds her head in her hands. Then she begins to sway. By the time the singing starts, she is dancing.

The light fades slowly on the chorus. The music swells.

Digging for Fire

Set in contemporary Ireland, Declan Hughes's play was the toast of the Dublin Theatre Festival last autumn. It is an acute black comedy that sucks the audience into a reunion of seven college friends, now on the brink of turning thirty. The party starts off with shared memories, tipsy philosophy and the occasional barbed exchange but gradually slides into a nightmare. Beneath the comedy, the play is intentionally bleak about friendship. Declan:

> I hate the *Big Chill/thirtysomething* sentimentality and I've always been intrigued by the kind of spiritual investment they make in friendship. I've always felt that notion to be bogus.

The play is more than a riposte to the marshmallow relationships drawn in the treaclier soaps however, it also shows a cross-section of young middle-class Ireland, the adults who grew up during the eighties. Declan:

> I guess the bleakness was also to do with a sense that everything's getting worse. That seems to me to be true and it informs the writing. I think the people in this play don't really look to the future, it's something they've got out of the habit of doing. It seems almost impossible to have faith even in simple things any more. Everything seems tarnished or compromised.

Despite its bleakness *Digging for Fire* was a hot ticket in Dublin and Hughes points out that it is a natural successor to the sort of work the company was formed to do – plays that had nothing to do with the traditional idea of Irish theatre. Rough Magic was founded in 1984 by Hughes and Lynne Parker:

> We wanted to do new plays that weren't being done in Ireland. The kind of 'Royal Court plays' by people like Caryl Churchill, Howard Barker, Howard Brenton. In the last couple of years we have started to do new work which has fed, to a certain degree, off that kind of play. I guess it was stuff which was a little bit out of the usual mould of 'Irish theatre', in that they were modern plays from an urban experience with an international context, influenced by TV. And there wasn't that rural or rooted emphasis that people associate with Irish theatre.
>
> I expected someone else to write this play, or a play something like this. But I couldn't find one, so as nobody else was writing it, I thought I may as well.
>
> There's this terrible feeling in Irish theatre of trying to make things classics. It's as if there is the pantheon of great Irish plays and playwrights, so people will look at a play and try and decide almost overnight if it is a classic. We've got to have the canon; we've got to prove this is good. The fifties have been done to death in Ireland in recent times, between people doing plays from the fifties and writing new plays set in the fifties. It seems as though that was the last decade of what you might call cultural purity – pre-TV, pre-rock'n'roll – there isn't any modern world to clutter it up. You know, a play can't be art if it's got crisps in it. But that only acknowledges one kind of Ireland which is rural and rooted in the past. It doesn't acknowledge the new Dublin.
>
> I don't want to sound grandiloquent, but when it was staged in Dublin there was a sense of people having waited for a play like this – certainly people my age. The response was, 'At last here is an Irish play that just takes for granted the fact

that people have grown up with British TV in their homes and they don't have some unique sense of what it is to be Irish.'

Taken from 'Digging for Dirt' by Sarah Hemming
published in the *Independent* newspaper on 28 March 1992
Copyright © *Independent* 1992

Declan Hughes was born in Dublin. He is writer in residence with the Dublin theatre company Rough Magic. His other plays include, *I Can't Get Started*, on the lives and fiction of Dashiel Hammett and Lillian Hellman, (Dublin Festival, 1991 and International Festival, Stoney Brook, New York, 1992), *Love and a Bottle*, his adaptation of George Farquhar's play of the same name, (Project Arts Centre, Dublin 1991, Mayfest, Glasgow and Tricycle, London 1992), *New Morning* (Bush Theatre, London and Project Arts Centre, Dublin 1993). He was joint winner of the 1990 Stewart Parker New Playwright Bursary and the BBC (Northern Ireland) TV Drama Award.

Somewhere

Judith Johnson

Somewhere was commissioned by the Royal National Theatre Studio, where workshop presentations of an earlier version of the play were shown on Friday, 10 and Saturday, 11 April 1992 with the following cast:

Lee Kelly	Stephen McGann
Dawn	Katrina Levon
Jonno/Punter 1	Andrew Ballington
Clare	Melissa Wilks
Kev/Punter 3	Matthew Wait
Linda/Martini	Emma Amos
Barry	Ian Dunn
Shaun/Punter 2	Shaun French
Campbell	Callum Dixon
Val/Kaz	Joanna Bacon

It was given its first public performance on 30 March 1993 at the Liverpool Playhouse Studio in association with the Royal National Theatre Studio and was subsequently seen at the Cottesloe Theatre (as part of the *Springboards* festival), with the following cast:

Lee Kelly	John Hannah
Dawn	Katrina Levon
Jonno	Mickey Poppins
Clare	Elizabeth Chadwick
Kev	Karl Draper
Linda/Martini	Nicola White
Barry	Ian Dunn
Shaun	Matthew Crompton
Campbell	Callum Dixon
Val/Kaz	Joanna Bacon

Both productions were directed by Polly Teale and designed by Stephen Brimson Lewis.

With the exception of the opening speech, the first part of the play is set in 1981. All the characters (except Val) are sixteen-year-old school-leavers who live in the North West of England. Val is Dawn's mother. She is in her mid-to late-thirties.

In the second part, set in 1991, Kaz, Dawn and Martini are 'window girls'. Prostitutes working the windows of Amsterdam. Martini is Dutch (perfect English with a slight accent). Kaz is British. Barry is now a barman and Lee is on leave after his experiences in the Gulf.

Act One

Lee Kelly, *dressed in combat gear and holding a firearm, crouches down very close to the audience. He is near the border of Iraq and Kuwait. It is January, the week before the UN deadline and* **Lee** *is alone. It is night.*

Lee   It's funny sitting here like this, just sitting here waiting, 'cos your mind starts playing tricks on you after a while. Not like the Falklands. Dashing in, fighting, bam bam bam, then dashing out again. No. It's like border patrol. Ireland. A bomb about to go off. A clock tick ticking away inside your heart.

I'm thinking. If I die, if I get me head blown off by a mine or a grenade or a bomb or a fuckin' Kalashnikov rifle who the hell is going to give a shit? Who cares about Lee Kelly? Lee Kelly, the hard knock, the quiet one till you get him drunk. The violent one who's always ready for a fight.

He laughs.

And then she comes into me head like a shining star. A girl I haven't seen for ten years. Ten years. And there's her face. Still there. Me and Dawn. Still there. Clear as a vision in my mind.

A pause then Going Underground *by The Jam. Full blast. The lights fade on* **Lee**.

Part One

A small town in the North West of England.

The action take place in three places: **Barry**'s *flat, the park, the kitchen of* **Val**'s *flat.*

Barry's *flat.*

A get-together is in progress to celebrate the end of school for a group of sixteen-year-olds. **Barry**'s *parents are away. The flat is nicely done out in MFP's best. A cocktail bar. A smoked-glass table. A shag pile carpet and a velveteen settee. (Or the suggestion of these things.)* **Barry**, *wearing a pair of black strip sunglasses, has taken up residence behind the bar and is mixing cocktails from his parents' collection of spirits and the bottles of cider, pomagne, Babysham and cheapo lager brought along by his mates. The Jam play us into the party and a selection of records continues to play throughout this scene. The Beat, The Specials, The Clash, Madness, Sham 69, etc. There is a nouveau-mod feel to the clothing of the party guests. Fred Perry T-shirts, drainie jeans, ski-jumpers. Some of the lads have suedehead haircuts. The girls tend towards shortish denim or canvas skirts in pastel colours, Fred Perrys, big sweatshirts, bare legs and white court shoes. Wedge haircuts.* **Dawn** *is the only girl with a shaved head.* **Kev** *and* **Campbell** *are doing some speed on* **Barry**'s *Mum's smoked-glass table.* **Linda** *and* **Shaun** *are snogging on the settee. A spliff is being passed round.* **Clare** *lies flat out on the floor. Everybody is off their heads or on the way there.* **Dawn** *and* **Jonno** *sit on the floor centre stage.* **Jonno** *is pricking at* **Dawn**'s *arm with a sewing needle.*

Dawn (*after a bit*)   You sure that needle's sterilised?

Jonno   Course it fuckin' is.

Dawn   It better fuckin' had be.

Jonno   It fuckin' is alright?

Jonno *carries on. After a second.*

Jonno   Have I spelt it right?

Dawn *tuts, pulling her arm away.*

Dawn   You better not make a mess of it Jonno.

Jonno   I'm not. Gis your arm back.

Dawn *does so reluctantly*

Jonno   Go head.

Dawn (*checking it*)   S-P-E-C-I-A-L-S

Jonno *continues.* **Dawn** *looks round and spots* **Clare**.

Dawn (*shouting over*) You still with us Clare?

Clare (*without moving or opening her eyes*) Yeah.

Dawn You been on the Cider Shakers?

Clare Yeah.

Dawn Helicopters?

Clare Fuckin' whirlpools.

Dawn (*to* **Jonno**) Ay! You're hands are shaking.

Jonno No they're not.

Dawn They are. I don't want a mess like when you done Shaun's.

Jonno That was Shaun's fault not mine. He jumped every time I come near him. (*Putting the ink on* **Dawn***'s tattoo.*) There you go. The Specials. Now give it a few days for the scabs to heal and don't scratch it.

Dawn Alright. Ta Jonno.

Jonno My pleasure.

She moves away and sits down next to **Clare**. **Jonno** *goes to talk to* **Barry**.

Dawn Got any fags left Clare?

Clare No.

Dawn Barry!

Barry Yes, beautiful?

Dawn Give us a ciggy.

Barry (*chucking her a No.6*) Anything for you gorgeous.

Dawn Thanks fuckface.

Clare *cracks up.* **Barry** *pulls tongues at* **Dawn**.

Jonno Ay Dawn. Lee Kelly's coming later.

Dawn (*lighting her fag*) You don't say.

Jonno What was it you was saying about him at school today?

Dawn Nothing.

Jonno You remember Dawn. When Miss Perry was giving us her goodbye speech? You were sticking up for him.

Dawn Shurrup Jonno.

Jonno I'm surprised they never expelled you an' all.

Dawn How could they expel me you soft get? It was the last day.

Jonno   Alright smart arse.

Dawn   Anyway. You have to do more than that to get expelled. You have to hurt somebody like Lee did.

Everyone listens. **Clare** *sits up and* **Shaun** *and* **Linda** *stop snogging for a minute.*

Kev   D'you remember his face when he did it? He looked like . . . like . . . I dunno, like he'd just won the FA cup or something. He was dead happy. All that blood runnin' down his chin and everything and there he was, grinning all over his face.

Linda   Poor Mr Scott.

Dawn   What d'you mean poor Mr Scott? He was a bastard.

Linda   I know but there was no need to bite half his ear off.

Kev   He called Lee Kelly a stupid brainless animal. That's what Lee said when they asked him why he done it. He said, 'I'm a stupid brainless animal, I couldn't help meself'.

Jonno   And Mr Scott's alright now isn't he? Lee Kelly got expelled. He nearly got put in Risley. If he hadn't been a juvenile he would've been done for GBH.

Kev   But I tell you what, I bet every time Mr Scott puts his hand to his ear and touches the skin where it's gone all crusty, I bet he thinks of Lee Kelly and I bet he thinks twice before he calls anyone an animal again.

Dawn   Does he fuck. Mr fuckin' Oxford University. He hates us. He wants to be teaching at one of them posh schools, one of them private fuckin' boarding schools, but they wouldn't have him 'cos he's crap, he can't teach. So he had to come to our school didn't he? He can't stand kids like us. He's been giving us GBH of the earholes for years but no one expels him do they?

General agreement. **Clare** *suddenly gets to her feet.*

Dawn   Where you going?

Clare   I'm having a dance.

Dawn   You what?

Clare   Yeah. To celebrate the end of school. No more Mr Scott. Come on Linda.

She grabs **Linda** *and pulls her away from* **Shaun** *and starts dancing with her. They waltz.* **Linda** *thinks it's dead funny.*

Clare   Don't laugh Lind, this is real dancing this is, me Granddad taught me this. Come on. One two three, one two three.

She twirls **Linda** *round faster and faster.*

Linda   Aw ay Clare! You're making me dizzy.

Clare   Best thing in the world, twirling a young lady round the dance floor. That's what he used to say to me.

They twirl and twirl until they fall over and **Clare** *starts to cry.*

Linda   You alright Clare? Dawn she's crying.

Dawn *goes to* **Clare**, *pulls her to her feet and supports her.*

Dawn   Come on you. Barry, can I lie her down in your Mum and Dad's room?

Barry   Is she alright?

Jonno   Is she gonna be sick?

Dawn   No. She just needs a little lie down.

Jonno   It's just, you know, the candlewick. On his Mum's bed.

Dawn   Yeah. Don't worry.

Barry   Ere'ya. I'll give you a hand.

They half carry **Clare** *off.* **Linda** *follows.* **Shaun** *goes to talk to* **Campbell** *and* **Kev** *who start smirking and so on as he joins them.* **Campbell** *starts skinning up.*

Shaun   Er . . . Kev?

Kev   Yeah.

Shaun   You know when you, em, when you're with a girl like.

Kev   Yeah?

Shaun   Where do you take them? I mean to do it and that?

Kev   Down the park if we can't go in their house. Where d'you take them?

Shaun   Er. Same place.

Kev   Yeah?

Shaun   Yeah.

Campbell *starts laughing.* **Kev** *joins in.*

Shaun   What yous laughing at?

Campbell   Nothing.

The doorbell goes. A merry little tune. **Dawn** *and* **Linda** *come back in. They join* **Shaun**, **Kev**, **Campbell**.

Campbell   What's up with Clare?

Dawn   Nothing. She's had too much to drink. Give us some speed Campbell.

Campbell (*cutting up some speed*)   Her Grandad died didn't he?

Dawn   Yeah.

Campbell   How old was he?

Dawn   I don't fuckin' know

Campbell   Alright. Don't get your knickers in a twist. I was only asking.

Dawn   Well don't.

Enter **Barry** *with* **Lee Kelly**. *Nothing is said but the atmosphere in the room changes with* **Lee**'s *presence.*

Kev   Hiya Lee.

Lee *nods at* **Kev**. *He joins* **Barry** *and* **Jonno** *at the bar. The others resume quiet conversation*

Jonno   Where've you been Lee? Down the pub?

Lee   No.

Jonno   Oh.

Barry   D'you wanna cocktail? I'm doing a roaring trade on the Cider Shake Ups. Me own secret recipe. That's cider with Babysham and whiskey.

Lee   Barry. I'm gonna crash here tonight OK.

Barry   Yeah alright.

Jonno   Have you had some trouble at home then Lee?

Lee   Something like that. Where's your Mum and Dad gone Barry?

Barry   Me Dad took the wagon on a long haul. Germany. He took me Mam and our Jan with him.

Lee   You should've gone with them. Get away from this fuckin' place.

Barry   Na, its boring. Stuck on the autobahn, hour after hour. I've done it before.

Lee   You don't fancy following in your old man's footsteps then?

Barry (*half joking*)   Na. I'm gonna be an entrepreneur me. You know. Clubs, bars. I fancy a nice place somewhere abroad.

Jonno   He's gonna have a blues club aren't you Baz? In Amsterdam. D'you wanna see the brochure Lee? You can smoke drugs in public and everything.

Barry   Yeah. Amsterdam. Or Jamaica maybe.

Lee   In your dreams mate.

Barry   I'm gonna get a job and save up.

Lee You reckon?

Barry Might be some cleaning jobs going down the swimming pool. Are you working yet Lee?

Lee You're jokin' aren't you. No jobs worth doing round here. You wouldn't get me cleaning out no swimming pool.

Over to the other group.

Linda What time is it Shaun?

Shaun Two o'clock.

Linda I'm gonna have to get home soon.

Shaun Oh. Right. Er . . .

Linda You gonna walk me or what?

She pulls him to his feet.

Shaun Oh. Right then.

Campbell *starts whistling under his breath.* Puppy Love. *The others snigger*

Shaun Frig off Campbell!

Linda See yous then. I'll see you tomorrow Dawn.

Dawn Yeah alright.

They leave saying 'Tara' to everyone. **Dawn** *does her line of speed.*

Dawn I dunno what you're laughing at Campbell.

Campbell You what?

Dawn I can't remember you ever going out with anyone.

Campbell There's nobody round here worth going out with.

Dawn Nobody'd have you, you mean.

Campbell That's a quid you owe me for that line Dawn.

Dawn Is it?

Campbell Yeah.

Dawn You don't fuckin' need a quid. What's your Dad do again? Lawyer isn't it? Something stuck up anyway.

Campbell Are you gonna pay me or what?

Dawn Have you got a quid Kev?

Kev Might have.

Dawn Oh come on. Lend us a quid to keep this tight-arsed get quiet.

Kev What's it worth?

She looks at him defiantly. Pause. She gets up, leans over and gives **Kev** *an extremely sexy kiss. She holds her hand out. He puts his hand in his pocket and gives her a pound note. She slams it down in front of* **Campbell** *and goes to sit by herself on the settee. She rests her head on the back of the settee and closes her eyes.*

Campbell (*under his breath*) Tart.

At the bar, **Jonno** *quietly to* **Lee**

Jonno (*nodding towards* **Dawn**)   I reckon she fancies you.

Lee Do you.

Jonno You wanna get in there Lee. If she takes a liking to someone she doesn't mess about.

Lee Looks like she's going out with Kev to me.

Jonno No she's not. She doesn't actually go out with anyone does she Barry? She just . . . you know. I tell you, you wanna get in there mate. You should've heard her at school today. She was sticking up for you, wasn't she Barry?

Lee Ay?

Barry (*grudgingly. Not looking at* **Lee**)   Oh y'know. Miss Perry was coming out with some shit about you getting expelled and all that. Dawn was just putting her straight.

Jonno I'm telling you. She fancies you. Ay Dawn.

Dawn What?

Jonno Come here a minute.

Dawn What for?

Jonno Just for a minute.

Dawn I'm doing something.

Jonno You what?

Dawn I'm busy.

Jonno What d'you mean you're busy. You're just sitting there. She's just sitting there.

Dawn I'm thinking.

Jonno Thinking?

Dawn Yeah.

Jonno (*going to sit next to her*)   Just a sec Lee. (*Whispering.*) Dawn. Will you come over when I tell you? I'm getting you off with Lee Kelly here. You're gonna miss your chance.

Dawn *laughs.*

It's not funny. I thought you fancied him.

Dawn   You're sex mad you are.

Jonno   No I'm not. Come on. Come over and talk to him.

Dawn   No ta.

Jonno (*going back to the bar*)   Christ. Women eh? Mind you, there's always Clare. She's already in bed.

Lee   Why don't you just go and have a wank Jonno?

Jonno   You what?

Barry *Laughs.* **Dawn** *smiles.* **Jonno** *has to join in.*

Jonno   Oh yeah. Heh heh. Nice one Lee.

Kev *and* **Campbell** *get up to leave*

Kev   We're going Barry.

Barry   Oh. OK lads.

Kev   You coming Dawn?

Dawn   No. Barry said I could crash here.

Kev (*a second's pause*)   Please yourself then. See you Jonno, Lee.

They leave.

Barry   Look at the state of me Ma's table.

He gets a Duster from behind the bar and goes over to polish away the traces of speed

Jonno   That's the drugs gone then.

Barry   Yeah. Shame.

Jonno   He's always got drugs hasn't he Campbell? I dunno where he gets the money.

Barry   His Mum and Dad buy the weed for him.

Jonno   Frig off!

Barry   No. Honest. Don't they Dawn?

Dawn   So I'm told.

Barry   Yeah. They all smoke it together in the house. Couple of ageing hippies they are. I went round there once. He didn't want me to come in but I saw through the window. They've got carpets hanging on the walls. And loads of books.

Jonno   Christ! D'you think they do speed together an' all?

Barry   I dunno. God can you imagine? Speeding with your Mam and Dad?

They all laugh.

Jonno   So Dawn. You stopping here tonight are you?

Dawn   Yeah.

Jonno   Not going wiv Kev then?

Dawn   Very observant Jonno.

Jonno   So. You've gone off him then have you?

Dawn   Just 'cos I fucked him once doesn't mean I'm getting married to him y'know.

Jonno *double-takes.*

Jonno   Just a minute Dawn. What did you say? You fucked Kev? You didn't fuck Kev. Kev fucked you.

Dawn   We fucked each other, what does it matter.

Jonno   No no. Girls don't fuck lads. It's the other way round. Girls can't fuck lads can they Lee? Can they Barry? I mean. You haven't got, you know, you haven't got a dick Dawn.

Dawn   Alright. He fucked me and I engulfed him.

Silence.

Jonno   You did what?

Dawn   I engulfed him.

Jonno   Jesus. You don't half say some weird things Dawn.

Another pause.

Lee   What've you got to drink Barry?

Dawn   I think I'll have one an' all.

Barry   Two Cider Shakers coming up.

Barry *starts making them drinks, then begins to tidy up. He continues with the tidying through the rest of this scene.*

Barry   You're drinking a lot tonight Dawn.

Dawn   So what?

Jonno   Dawn can drink more than the rest of us put together.

Lee   I bet she can't drink as much as me.

Dawn   You what?

Lee   You heard.

Dawn   I bet I can.

Lee   Come head then. We'll have a contest.

Jonno   Aw yeah! Go on Dawn. Drink for drink and the last one standing wins.

Barry   Ay! You wanna be careful. You can die from doing things like that.

Jonno   No no. Yous'll be alright. Go on Dawn. You show him.

Dawn   Alright then.

Jonno   Good on you girl. Barry. D'you mind if we use your old fella's whiskey? We'll pay you back.

Barry   Er . . .

Dawn   Go on babes. It's just for a laugh.

Barry   Alright. But don't drink anything else.

Dawn   OK. Do the honours then Jonno.

Jonno   Hang on.

He reaches in his pocket and chucks 50p on the table.

I'm putting a 50p down on Dawn to win. If you beat her Lee it's all yours.

Lee   (*to* **Dawn**) He's a fuckin' head case isn't he?

Dawn   You're telling me.

Jonno   Barry. Come head. Put your money down.

Barry   No ta.

Jonno   What? Come on. It's a dead cert.

Barry   I said no.

Jonno   What's up with you?

Barry   Nothing.

Jonno   Please yourself then.

Jonno *sets up two glasses and pours out two whiskeys from a full bottle.*

Jonno   Right. Are you both ready?

Lee   Yeah.

Jonno   Dawn?

Dawn   Yeah. Get on with it.

Jonno   OK. One, two, three . . . Drink!!!

They both knock it back in one. **Jonno** *pours another. They do the same. And another. They knock it back, no problem.*

Jonno   OK Dawn?

Dawn   Fine.

Jonno   Lee.

Lee   Same.

Jonno   Right you are. Seconds out, round two.

He pours and they drink three more times. It gets a bit slower.

Jonno   Christ. Anyone had enough yet? We're getting a bit low here.

Dawn   Might as well finish the bottle off now.

Jonno   OK then. If you say so. On your marks, get set, go!

And they finish off the bottle, each taking a swig at a time. **Barry** *and* **Jonno** *watch,* **Jonno** *egging* **Dawn** *on all the way.* **Dawn** *takes the last swig and bangs the bottle down on the counter. She gives* **Lee** *a great big smile. Pause.*

Barry   Well that's it then. Finished. A draw.

Jonno   No no. We can't have a draw. Come on you two.

He takes them both by the elbows and moves them to the middle of the floor, away from the bar which was propping them up. They both look a little unsteady on their feet.

Dawn   What you doing Jonno?

Jonno   Tie break. I spin you both round, dead dead fast, and the one left standing after that wins.

Barry   Don't be stupid!

Jonno   No, we've got to have a winner Barry.

Barry   If either of these two spew up on me mother's carpet you're gonna be on your hands and knees cleaning it up lad!

Jonno   They won't spew up!

Dawn *starts giggling. She grabs hold of* **Lee** *and starts waltzing him round like* **Clare** *and* **Linda** *earlier on.*

Dawn   Just like Clare's Grandad. Real dancing. One two three, one two three, one two three.

*She goes faster and faster and faster until **Lee** spins off, falling onto the floor. They're both laughing their heads off then **Lee** suddenly goes quiet. He gets up carefully and exits. **Jonno** follows him. **Dawn** tumbles to the floor. She sits with her knees up and her head in her hands*

Barry (*sitting beside her*)   Dawn?

Dawn (*bit mussy*)   Yeah?

Barry *moves her hands away and lifts her head up. He looks into her eyes.*

Barry   You alright?

Dawn   Great.

Barry   You wanna be careful you know.

Dawn   With what?

Barry   With yourself.

We hear the toilet flushing. **Jonno** *comes back in.*

Jonno (*dead pleased*)   Lee's been sick!

Barry   Oh God.

Jonno   No you're alright. He made it to the bog. So that makes you the winner Dawn!

She gets on her hands and knees, crawls over to the settee and lies down on it.

Dawn   I'm going to go to sleep now.

She does so. **Barry** *and* **Jonno** *stare at each other.*

Jonno   One of the lads our Dawn. One of the lads!

Barry *shakes his head. He gets a blanket out and covers* **Dawn** *up then continues tidying.* **Jonno** *watches him.*

Barry   Turn the sounds off Jonno.

Jonno   Aw we're not crashing already are we Baz?

Barry   Well everyone else has.

Jonno   We don't have to. Aw come on Barry. I'm wide awake. Let's have another drink.

Barry (*looking towards* **Dawn**)   Shush. No. Me Dad'll go mad. We've drunk all his whiskey.

Jonno   Well let's go for a walk then.

Barry   Jonno!

Jonno   Go on. We can walk up to the refinery and watch the lights like when we had those mushrooms.

Barry   I'm too tired.

Jonno   You never had any speed, that's your problem. I'm going by meself.

Barry   We could look at some more brochures instead. I got Australia and the Far East today.

Jonno   Did you? Nice one.

Barry   Come on. I'll read to you from Amsterdam if you like.

Jonno   Oh alright then. As long as you don't fall asleep.

Barry   I won't. Come on.

They exit, switching the light out. **Barry** *pauses at the door for a second and watches* **Dawn** *sleeping. We see him silhouetted in the doorway. He exits, closing the living-room door behind him. After a moment* **Dawn** *shifts a bit in her sleep. There is a short pause then the door opens again.* **Clare** *stands silhouetted in the doorway. She is sleepwalking. The light streams in from the hall. She pauses a moment then sleepwalks over to the settee and gets under the covers with* **Dawn**.

Dawn   Clare. What you doing?

No answer. **Dawn** *sits up.*

Dawn   Clare? Clare?

Clare *starts to come round.*

Dawn   Ay sleepy head. What you doing?

Clare   Wha . . .? What's going . . .? Dawn.

Dawn   You've been sleepwalking again you daft cow.

Clare   Oh God.

She starts to cry.

Clare   Oh God Dawn I feel so awful.

She is very upset. **Dawn** *puts her arms around her and rocks her.*

Dawn   It's alright. It's alright.

This continues until **Clare's** *sobs subside and she calms down enough to speak.*

Clare   I had a nightmare about me Granddad.

Dawn   Did you?

Clare   He was sitting on the bench outside our flats. Like he used to. And, and me and you were there. Playing on the wall like when we were little. And I was dead happy. I was saying, 'Look, I told you he wasn't dead. There he is'. And then we went running over to him, and you fell over, Dawn, and you'd broken your leg. So, so I shouted for me Granddad and he come running over but when he got close up he was all sort of grey. And his lips were blue. You know. Like when I found him. Like a dead body. And he looked so sad. And as he got nearer he started to, you know . . . pieces started dropping off him. He started falling to pieces bit by bit. Until there was nothing left.

Dawn Jesus.

Clare Oh God Dawn she's in such a state. Me Grandma. She just sits there all day, staring at the wall and sometimes she looks at me. Like for ages, staring at me. She looks so lost Dawn. I don't know what to do.

Dawn Look. She's bound to be sad isn't she? Isn't she?

Clare I . . . I know but it's like she's blaming me. She just looks at me like she hates me.

Dawn She's just missing him. Same as you. She's an old lady.

Clare If it wasn't for me they would have had more time together.

Dawn Oh don't start that Clare.

Clare They would've.

Dawn They love you. Come on. Everyone dies. It's not your fault.

Clare She doesn't love me. It was him. He loved me. She had no choice. She just had to look after me. She doesn't even like me.

Dawne Clare, stop it.

Clare You know it's true. I don't know why you stick up for her. She's always said you're a bad influence. If it wasn't for me Granddad she would've stopped me coming down to your flat years ago.

Dawn I know.

Clare 'Cos of your Mum and that.

Dawn I know Clare.

Silence.

Clare I've got a terrible headache.

Dawn That'll be the drink.

Clare Yeah.

Dawn Come on. You'll be alright. Get some sleep. You'll feel better in the morning.

Clare I wish I was like you.

Dawn Like what?

Claire   You never cry.

Dawn   You have to keep going Clare. Don't let her get to you.

Clare   Yeah.

Dawn   Show her how strong you can be.

Clare   I'm not strong.

Dawn   You just have to keep going. Keep telling yourself you can take it and don't let anybody tell you any different. Then one day you'll turn round and it'll be true.

Clare   D'you think so?

Dawn   Yeah. Now come on. Get some sleep.

Dawn *puts her arms round* **Clare**. *They lie down.*

Dawn   That's it. Now go to sleep and no more nightmares.

Clare   OK.

Pause.

Clare   Dawn?

Dawn   Yeah?

Clare   You fancy Lee Kelly don't you?

Dawn   I might do.

Clare   You wanna be careful Dawn. He's got a right violent temper on him you know.

Dawn   Yeah. I know. Anyway. Go to sleep.

Clare   OK.

Pause.

Clare   Dawn?

Dawn   What!!

Clare   Me Mum phoned last night.

Pause

Dawn   Jesus Christ.

Clare   Yeah.

Dawn   What did she sound like?

Clare   She sounded tired. She sounded like me Grandma, but younger.

Dawn   Where was she phoning from?

Clare I dunno. Somewhere abroad.

Dawn Is she coming home?

Clare No. No. She's not coming home. She told me to be good and look after me Grandma. But who's gonna look after me Dawn? Who's gonna look after me?

Dawn Shush. Come on now. I'll look after you. Come on.

Dawn *strokes* **Clare's** *hair. She starts humming. A lullbaye.* **Clare** *shifts round to face* **Dawn**. *She starts touching her face, tries to kiss her.*

Dawn Go to sleep Clare.

Clare Dawn.

Dawn We don't do that any more Clare. We decided.

Clare Dawn I . . .

Dawn Come on. We're not kids anymore. Go to sleep.

Clare *turns away.* **Dawn** *carries on humming, stroking her hair. The lights fade.*

The park. A couple of days later.

A couple of swings. A grassy bank. **Campbell, Kev, Shaun** *and* **Linda**. **Linda** *and* **Shaun** *are arm in arm, very lovey-dovey.* **Kev** *and* **Campbell** *look bored.*

Kev I'm sick to death of this town. There's fuck all to do. No work, no money and no decent women.

Campbell The trouble is all the girls round here are thick as pigshit.

Linda Well none of them fancy you Campbell so I shouldn't worry.

Shaun Don't worry mate you'll be at college soon, doing your 'A' Levels, mixing with all the other clever bastards. You can get yourself a nice girl and you can both talk about books together.

Kev I wouldn't mind going to college.

Linda Only 'cos you've run out of girls to go out with.

Kev No no. I wouldn't mind doing something. You know. Mechanics or something.

Linda You what? You didn't even manage to turn up for your CSE Physics exam. Too busy polishing your scooter.

Shaun You could go on the YOP scheme. They have mechanics jobs.

Kev Frig off! I'm no fucking slave.

Linda Where is your scooter Kev?

Kev It's dead.

Linda Oh no, what happened to it? Polish it away to nothing did you?

Kev No. It's just knackered and I can't fix it.

Linda Shame really. All nice and shiny on the outside and falling to bits on the inside.

Kev What?

Pause. **Kev** *kicks the wall rhythmically.* **Campbell** *sighs. Enter* **Barry** *and* **Jonno**.

Jonno Evening all!

Kev Oh. Here come the workers! How was your first day then lads?

Jonno It was ace. There's some dead fit women working there.

Barry Jonno's in love.

Jonno Ah honest to God Kev you wanna see her. A lifeguard she is. She looks just like Raquel Welch. She smiled at me didn't she Barry?

Barry I think she might have been laughing actually.

Jonno No. It was definitely a smile. Looked me straight in the eye she did.

Barry She's 21 Jonno. You don't stand a chance.

Jonno She likes me I'm telling you.

Kev Any more jobs going at the pool?

Jonno No. They only had work for a couple of people. It's just for the summer like. Keeping it clean while it's busy. We're saving up aren't we Barry?

Barry Yeah.

Jonno We're gonna go to France after we've finished this job. Fruit picking.

Kev Is it easy to get work in France then?

Barry So we're told. There's this lad working at the pool for the summer, a student he is. He said he took a year off like and went travelling. Fruit picking in France, bar work in Greece, he even went to Australia. Slept on the beaches he said. Under the stars. You could do it if you wanted. You could come with us.

Kev I haven't got any money.

Linda You could sell your scooter.

Kev No I couldn't.

Shaun Why not?

Kev I just couldn't.

Linda   'Cos he's a lazy bastard that's why. Can you see him picking grapes all day?

Enter **Dawn** *and* **Clare**.

Dawn   Anyone got any fags?

Kev   Dawn never says hello does she?

Campbell   No. She just starts scrounging.

Dawn *ignores him.* **Barry** *passes* **Dawn** *a cigarette.* **Clare** *is very quiet. She goes and sits on a swing.*

Barry   Here y'are. D'you want one Clare?

Clare   No ta.

Barry   Have you give up?

Clare   No. I just don't feel like one.

Barry   Oh. OK.

Jonno   Me and Barry started working today Dawn.

Dawn   Oh yeah?

Jonno   We're gonna save up all our money and go fruit picking in September, aren't we Barry?

Barry   That's the plan.

Dawn   Are you leaving us Barry?

Barry   'Fraid so babes.

Dawn   Oh no! What will I do without you?

Barry (*serious*)   You can come with us if you like.

Dawn   Well you know I would, but me and Clare have got our own plans, haven't we Clare?

Clare   Yeah.

Barry   Oh yeah? What's that?

Dawn   We're going to Manchester aren't we? To live with our Jane.

Barry   Manchester?

Dawn   Yeah. We're gonna make a load of money.

Barry   Doing what?

Dawn   Escort work. Me cousin Jane, she works for an escort agency.

Jonno   What's one of them?

Linda   Oh you just have to look after businessmen for an evening, don't you Dawn?

Shaun   What d'you mean look after them?

Dawn   You go for a meal with them or to a club or something. Talk to them you know. Keep them company.

Jonno   How d'you mean keep them company?

Linda   You don't have to have sex with them or anything Jonno. But sometimes they ask though, don't they Dawn?

Shaun   You seem to know an awful lot about this.

Linda   That's 'cos we done it last time we went to see Jane.

Shaun   You done what?!

Linda   Don't worry. We just went out for a meal with some blokes. Nothing else.

Shaun   Hang on. Let me get this right. You went out with two businessmen for a meal and they paid you just for being there?

Linda   That's right.

Shaun   Christ!

Dawn   Its just a bit of female company for them.

Kev   Can't they get women without paying for them?

Dawn   Not as nice as us.

Kev   Not as young as you, you mean.

Linda   We didn't go to bed with them you know.

Barry (*changing the subject sharpish*)   Well. It looks like we're all off somewhere anyway.

Linda   I'm not.

Shaun   Neither am I.

Linda   That's alright then!

They embrace.

Jonno   Christ. Will you put her down Shaun? You never stop you two.

Campbell   How you feeling anyway Dawn?

Dawn   Eh?

Campbell   I hear you and Lee Kelly had a drinking contest.

Kev   Oh yeah? Who won?

Campbell   Lee Kelly was sick, but not Dawn. Takes after her Mum, don't you?

Dawn   You what?

Campbell   You heard.

Dawn   Don't talk about my mother Campbell.

Campbell   You both like your drink don't you?

Dawn   I said don't fuckin' talk about my mother.

Campbell   Oh dear. Touched a sore spot have I?

Dawn *goes for him. She grabs him by his collar and pulls him down so he falls on the floor. She goes to kick him in the balls but* **Barry** *pulls her away. Enter* **Lee Kelly**.

Campbell   You fuckin' bitch.

Dawn   You're the bitch Campbell.

Kev (*to* **Campbell**)   Come on. Let's go.

He pulls **Campbell** *to his feet and they exit.*

Dawn (*shouting after him*)   Bastard!

Barry   Calm down Dawn.

Lee   What's up with him?

Dawn   He hates me, that's what.

Linda   I reckon he fancies you. That's why he's always getting at you.

Dawn   Oh I don't think it's me he fancies.

Shaun   He was getting at Linda before, wasn't he Lind?

Linda   Yeah. He was a bit like.

Dawn   It's 'cos we've both been out with Kev.

Shaun   You what?

Dawn   It's Kev. He loves Kev.

Jonno   What d'you mean?

Dawn   I mean he loves Kev.

Lee   Did he hit you Dawn?

Dawn   He was saying things about me Mum.

Lee   I'll have a word with him.

Dawn   No. You're alright. I think he got the message.

Dawn *and* **Lee** *focus all their conversation on each other forgetting the others who listen in.* **Barry** *moves away from* **Dawn**.

Lee   You should take no notice of him.

Dawn   Yeah. S'pose so. He just winds me up that's all. How are you anyway? Still feeling sick?

Lee (*smiling*)   Feeling a lot better ta. How about you?

Dawn   Oh. I'm fine.

She returns his smile. **Linda** *and* **Jonno** *exchange a knowing look*

Clare   Dawn. I'm gonna go home, I don't feel very well.

Dawn   Oh.

She glances at **Lee**.

Alright babes. I'll come with you.

Clare   No. You're alright, you stay here.

Dawn   No. I'll walk you home.

Clare   You don't have to.

Dawn   I want to.

Lee   Er. D'you mind if I come too?

Dawn   No. Come if you like.

Dawn *and* **Clare** *start to exit.*

Dawn   Come head then.

Lee *follows them. The others start to exit in the opposite direction.*

Linda   Christ. Did you hear that? (*putting on a posh voice*) 'D'you mind if I come too?' I've never heard Lee Kelly talk like that before.

Jonno   He's different isn't he? From when he was at school. He's quieter. Doesn't take the piss so much.

Shaun   I still wouldn't mess with him tho'.

Jonno   No. Neither would I.

Barry   He just fancies Dawn that's all.

Jonno   What difference does that make? We all fancy Dawn, Barry.

Barry   The difference Jonno, is that she fancies him back.

Jonno   Well she fancied Kev back didn't she. He didn't start saying nice things to her and all that.

Barry Well maybe he should have, he might have got more than a quick thrill out of her.

Jonno Eh? What d'you mean?

Barry Oh nothing.

Jonno You always have to stick up for her don't you?

Barry She sticks up for herself Jonno.

They exit. Enter **Kev** *and* **Campbell**. *They're halfway through a bottle of woodpecker cider.* **Campbell** *sits on a swing.* **Kev** *hands him the bottle and he finishes it off.*

Kev (*watching* **Campbell**) Better?

Campbell Yeah. Stupid cow.

Kev You shouldn't have gone on about her Mam y'know.

Campbell Why not? Everybody knows about it.

Kev Yeah but . . .

Campbell Yeah but what? She thinks she's the fuckin' Queen of Sheba.

Kev She's just a girl Campbell. Don't get yourself so worked up.

Campbell You're just the same as the rest of them. Creepin' round her like she's Debbie fuckin' Harry.

Kev No I'm not.

Campbell You shoulda seen your face when she necked you on Friday night. Like a little dog, and she'd just threw you a bone.

Kev (*grinning*) Bone's the right word mate. She can't half kiss.

Campbell That wasn't for you. That was for Lee Kelly's benefit. She fancies Lee, Kev. She's not interested in you.

Kev She was interested enough after the Specials concert. *She* made me take her to the park. She asked me Campbell.

Campbell Yeah but your Scooter was working then wasn't it? I'll give her six months and she'll be picking up kerb crawlers in Manchester just like her Jane.

Kev What you going on about?

Campbell Nothing.

Kev Nothing!

Campbell I'm not meant to say.

Kev Come head Campbell. You can't just say something like that then shut your mouth.

Campbell   It's something me Dad told me.

Kev   Come on!

Campbell   Well. He helped Dawn's cousin Jane. She come to see him at the Advice Bureau. She got picked up for soliciting and she reckons the bizzies knocked her about a bit.

Kev   Jesus! So that's what Dawn gets up to when she goes to Manchester.

Campbell   You mustn't tell anyone Kev.

Kev   Jesus. Shit!

Campbell   What?

Kev   I might have caught something off her.

Campbell   Eh?

Kev   After the Madness concert.

Campbell   Don't be stupid. Anyway she's just as likely to catch something off you.

Kev   You what?

Campbell   You heard.

Kev   What you trying to say? I'm not a fuckin' whore.

Campbell   Well you're not exactly Mr Monogamous are you?

Kev   What's that supposed to mean?

Campbell   Well, you know. You sleep around just as much as she does.

Kev   Don't fuckin' use your big college words on me mate.

Campbell   I didn't mean . . .

Kev   Girls like me. They just like me OK?

Campbell   OK.

Kev   They fancy me.

Campbell   Yes. OK. I only meant . . .

Kev   You're gonna have to stop getting so jealous you know.

A slight pause.

Campbell   Jealous of what?

Kev   You'll get yourself a girlfriend one day.

Campbell   Oh. I see.

Kev   Yeah. They're not your type round here that's all. There's nothing wrong with you or anything.

Campbell   I'm not jealous Kev.

Kev   Wait till you get to college mate, they'll be all over you then.

Campbell   Kev. I'm not jealous of you. You're me mate OK? Me best mate. I'm not fuckin' jealous!

Kev   Alright. Keep your hair on!

Pause. Embarrassment.

Campbell   Kev?

Kev   What?

Pause.

What!?

Campbell   Don't you ever . . .

Pause.

Don't you ever . . .

Pause.

Kev   Don't I ever what?

Campbell   Oh nothing. It doesn't matter.

Pause. They're both a bit embarrassed.

Kev   So. Did she win the case then?

Campbell   Eh?

Kev   Dawn's cousin.

Campbell   Oh. No. Not a chance. Her word against the bizzies weren't it? Me Dad told her not to bother.

Kev   Fuckin' tart.

Campbell   She was covered from head to toe in bruises.

Kev   What does she expect? Women like that. They deserve it.

Pause.

You got any weed?

Campbell   In the house.

Kev   Well, what we doing here then? Let's go and have a smoke.

Campbell   Yeah. Alright then Kev. Let's go and have a smoke.

They exit. Enter **Dawn***, followed by Lee.* **Dawn** *sits down.* **Lee** *sits beside her.*

Dawn   Did you used to come here when you were little Lee? Me and Clare did. There was a roundabout wasn't there? Remember when they built the wooden castle?

Lee   Yeah. We burnt it down.

Dawn   We didn't go in the playground much. We used to come to this bit 'cos we liked the trees. We'd lie down and look at the sky through the leaves and then we'd levitate.

Lee   You what?

Dawn   We used to rise out of our bodies and float up to the sky.

Lee   Fuck off!

Dawn   No honest. It works. You just have to think really hard in your head. And you have to really want to do it. Come on.

She lies down.

Lee   Er. What you doing?

Dawn   Levitating. Come on Lee.

Lee *lies down beside her. He looks a bit unsure.*

Dawn   Just look up at the stars and think about floating up through the trees.

Lee   I done this once when I was really stoned.

Dawn   You don't have to be stoned.

Lee   It might help.

Dawn   Shush!

They lie still and try to levitate.

Lee (*after a bit*)   Dawn?

Dawn   Shush!

He sits up.

Lee   I can't concentrate.

Dawn   It was just starting to work. You're not trying hard enough.

Lee *puts his hand out and touches* **Dawn***'s face. She pushes his hand away and sits up.*

Dawn   Don't Lee.

Pause. **Lee** *turns away from her.*

Dawn   Got any ciggies?

Lee What's this all about Dawn?

Dawn (*not looking at him*) What d'you mean?

Lee You know. This weird act. You ask me to come back to the park with you, I don't expect to be lying down trying to levitate.

Dawn What *do* you expect?

Lee I dunno, I . . .

Dawn A quick fuck, is that what you want? OK then. Come on.

She grabs hold of him. Starts trying to undo his fly. She is very angry. He tries to push her away.

Dawn Come on. I'll lie down on the grass shall I and open me legs for you so you can get inside me. Is that what you want to do 'cos I can do that for you Lee, that's easy.

He pushes her off.

Lee Stop it will you. Jesus. What's up with you?

Dawn (*getting up*) I'm going home.

Lee (*grabs her arm*) Don't.

Dawn Why not? 'Cos you haven't got your end away yet?

Lee No! Can't we just sit down and talk?

Pause. She looks hard at him. He still holds her arm.

Lee Come on Dawn.

Dawn Let go of me arm.

He does so. She sits down beside him.

Lee I just don't know what's going on that's all.

Dawn I wanted to levitate.

Lee I thought you were taking the piss.

Dawn No. No. I wasn't.

Pause.

Its just . . . I'm worried about Clare.

Lee She's alright.

Dawn She's not.

Lee She's just sad about her Grandad dying. She's bound to be.

Dawn She's so quiet. She gets really depressed sometimes. Even before he died.

Lee   She'll be alright.

Dawn   I don't know what's going on in her head.

Lee   She'll be alright Dawn. Don't worry about it.

Pause.

Dawn   You're quiet too.

Lee   I don't know what to say to you.

Dawn   No. I mean compared with how you used to be. Before they chucked you out of school.

Lee   Yeah well. I've been doing a lot of thinking since then.

Dawn   About what?

Lee   About life.

Dawn   Have you come up with anything?

Lee   Yeah.

Dawn   What?

Lee   I've decided to join the Army.

Pause.

Dawn   You don't have to do that.

Lee   What else can I do?

Dawn   Working on the bin wagons is better than that.

Lee   There aren't any jobs going on the bin wagons.

Pause.

Me Dad's kicked me out. He said he was sick of me hanging round the house doing nothing. Getting in the way. Causing trouble. We had a fight. He tried to hit me Mum again and I tried to stop him. It's always the same. He comes back, crawling on his hands and knees, begging for forgiveness. She puts her arms round him like he's a little baby or something. Fucking cunt.

Dawn   Where you living?

Lee   At Barry's till the end of this week. Till his Mum and Dad come back.

Dawn   What you gonna do after that?

Lee   Dunno. Kip in the park till I join the Army and get away from this fuckin' town.

Dawn   You don't have to be a hard case y'know Lee.

Lee   It's either that or be a nobody Dawn.

Silence. **Dawn** *moves towards him. She takes his hand and holds it against her face.*

Dawn   You can come and stay with me.

Lee   Your Mum'd love that.

Dawn   She won't mind.

Lee   Won't she?

Dawn   She's not sober very often but when she is she understands.

Lee   Understands what?

Dawn   Understands me.

Lee   What's that on your arm?

Dawn   It's a tattoo. Jonno did it for me.

Lee   It says Special.

Dawn   The Specials

Lee (*smiling*)   Oh yeah.

She takes **Lee**'s *hand and moves it slowly down her body till it rests between her legs*

Dawn (*whispers*)   Touch me Lee.

Lee *moves forward to do so. The lights fade out.*

Same evening, **Val**'s *flat.*

The kitchen. Cluttered, dirty, cramped. The wallpaper looks old and damp. A stack of library books piled up on a small table, mostly romantic classics, reading glasses folded on top of them. Also a nearly empty bottle of cheap sherry and two glasses. Forty Benson and Hedges, a lighter and an ashtray. Two chairs at the table. **Val** *is in her mid- to late-thirties. She looks rough, has spent too many years on the bottle. She stands holding* **Clare**'s *hair out of the way while she throws up.* **Clare** *lifts her head up, wipes her mouth and moves away.*

Val   You feeling a bit better now then?

Clare   A bit. Sorry.

Val   Too much sherry.

Clare   I was feeling a bit sick anyway.

Val   Yeah.

Clare   It's her. She makes me sick. She wishes it was me dead instead of him.

Val   Yeah. Well. She's feeling a bit down love. You'll just have to bear with her for a while.

Clare　She's always been like that. She hates me. She's been waiting all these years for me to grow up and go away so she could have him to herself, and now he's gone and I'm still there.

Pause. **Val** *sighs.*

Clare　Oh God. And . . . and . . . at night. I'm just lying there. I can hear her. She thinks I'm asleep. She's sitting in the kitchen, making a noise like . . . like . . . an animal. Not like crying. Whimpering. That's it. Like when a dog's been hit by a car. I don't know what to do. I feel like everything's spinning in the dark. I feel like I'm falling down a big hole.

Val　Come here love.

She puts her arms round **Clare**. **Clare** *is very tense.*

Val　You're shaking.

Clare　Yeah. . . . I can't stop.

Val *rocks* **Clare** *for a while. She starts to calm down.*

Clare　Val?

Val (*still rocking*)　Yes love?

Clare　Can you dance?

Val　Eh?

Clare　You know. Old Time dancing. The waltz and the foxtrot. Can you dance like that?

Val　I was more of a twist and shout girl meself.

Clare　Can you do it though? Can you dance with me?

Val　Yeah. OK. OK love.

Clare *puts* **Val**'s *arms into position for a waltz. They start to dance.*

Clare　'No need to explain when you're dancing with a lady.' That's what he used to say, 'Just move together and let the music talk'.

Val　Who said that? Your Granddad?

Clare　Yeah.

Val　He was right love. Just move together and let the music talk.

They dance for a while, **Clare** *resting her cheek on* **Val**'s *shoulder.*

Val　Listen. Why don't you come and stop with us eh? Give your Grandma some time to herself.

Clare　I dunno . . . I . . .

Val　Come on. Just for a couple of weeks.

Clare Until me and Dawn go to Manchester?

Val Manchester?

We hear the door go. **Dawn** *comes in.*

Dawn What's happened?

Val Nothing. Listen love. Clare's gonna come and stay with us for a bit.

Dawn What's happened?

Val She's had a little row with her Grandma, haven't you love?

Dawn What about?

Clare Nothing. I . . .

Dawn Fuckin' old bitch. Has she been upsetting you?

Val Dawn. It's alright.

Pause.

Clare Your Mum thinks I should stay here.

Dawn Oh . . . er . . .

Val What's the matter, don't you want Clare to stop with us?

Dawn It's not that it's just . . . Oh it'll probably be alright. We can all stay. It's just . . . Lee Kelly. His Dad's chucked him out and he's got nowhere to go so . . . He's just gone to get his stuff from Barry's.

Pause.

Clare It's alright, I'll go home.

Dawn No Clare. It'll be OK. There's the settee and . . . You don't mind do you Mum? He's got nowhere . . .

Clare No. I'll go home.

Dawn Clare don't.

Clare No. There's no room for me.

Dawn We can all fit in.

Clare No we can't.

Clare *jumps up to go.*

Dawn Clare!

She grabs her arm.

Clare (*screaming*) Fuckin' leave me alone!!!

Dawn Jesus. Alright, alright. I will.

Clare *runs out. We hear the door slamming.* **Dawn** *sits down at the table with her mum.*

Dawn   What's wrong with her? We could've all fitted.

Val   She's in a bit of a state love. When she come round earlier, she was hysterical. Her Grandma said some nasty things.

Dawn   What did she say?

Val   I'm not sure. Something about her Mum. She was really upset.

Dawn   Fuckin' bitch.

Val   Yeah well. You go and see her tomorrow eh? She'll have calmed down by then.

Dawn   I hope so.

Val   They've always rowed Dawn.

Dawn   Yeah. S'pose so.

Pause. **Dawn** *lets out a big sigh. She takes the glass off* **Val**, *takes a swig then gives it back. She takes a ciggy out and lights it.*

Val   So. You going out with Lee Kelly then are you?

Dawn   Dunno.

Val   Have you been down the park?

Dawn   Don't be nosey.

Val   That's where we used to go.

Dawn   You and me Dad?

Val   Yeah.

Dawn   Lee said I was special. Sort of.

Val   They all say that.

Dawn   Thanks.

Val   Oh. Well. You are special anyway. You're special to me. I was special to your Dad once but not for long. Remember that Dawn. You can be special to any man but you've only got one mother.

Dawn   Clare's not special to *her* mother.

Val   No. Well. Her mother had problems of her own.

Dawn   So did you but you didn't abandon me.

Val   It was a long time ago. It was worse then if you got pregnant and you weren't married.

Dawn I don't care. She shouldn't have fucked off and left Clare.

Val She didn't even know who the father was. At least I was married.

Dawn Not to anyone special.

Pause. **Val** *laughs.*

Val You're right love. But anyway. At least I've got you. We've got each other.

Dawn Oh yeah.

Pause.

Val Can I tell you something Dawn?

Dawn Sounds like you're going to.

Val He's dangerous.

Dawn Who is?

Val Lee Kelly.

Dawn What you going on about Mum?

Val Oh I know you're young, I know he's exciting. But you be careful with him Dawn. If he so much as raises his voice to you tell him goodbye. 'Cos once they start they never stop.

Dawn Once they start what?

Val You know what I'm talking about. That's why I chucked your father out. It's in their blood Dawn. Thank God you weren't a boy 'cos, God bless them, try as they might they always follow through. Like father like son Dawn. Like grandfather like father like son.

Pause.

Dawn You saying you don't want him staying here?

Val I'm not saying anything. I'm just telling you. Watch him.

She pours herself another drink. She watches **Dawn**.

Val What's he gonna do when you go to Manchester?

Dawn Eh?

Val Clare said.

Dawn Oh. . . . It was just an idea Mum.

Val You could've said something to me about it.

Dawn I'm not sure about it now . . .

Val Clare is.

Dawn I'll have to talk to her.

Val I don't think I could stand it if you left me Dawn.

Dawn I've got to leave some time.

Pause.

Lee says he wants to join the Army

Val Oh Christ.

Dawn I know. Daft bastard.

Val Ah well. Someone's got to do it I suppose.

Dawn Not if I've got anything to do with it.

Val Oh brilliant Dawn. You've been going out with him for five minutes, you're already trying to change his life.

Dawn Someone's got to do it.

Val Yeah, but its always got to be you hasn't it?

Dawn *smiles. The lights fade.* **Clare** *sits on the swing in the playground and sings the lullaby* **Dawn** *sang her in the first scene.*

A couple of weeks later, **Val***'s flat.*

Dawn *and* **Lee** *sit at the kitchen table. They are playing cards.* **Dawn** *is in a T-Shirt with 'Two Tone' written on it.* **Lee** *is in his shorts, no shirt. It is a hot summer night. They are half way through a big bottle of cider.*

Silence. **Lee** *studies his cards.*

Dawn Come on.

Lee Just a sec.

Dawn Lee!

Lee Just a sec.

Dawn *sighs. She waits. She starts tapping her fingers.*

Lee Oi, stop it. You know I hate that.

Dawn Ten minutes you've taken so far.

Lee Have I fuck!

Dawn You have.

Lee I haven't Dawn.

Dawn You fuckin' have I've been timing you.

Lee *chucks his cards down annoyed. He lights a ciggy.*

Dawn What you doing?

Lee You're getting on me nerves.

Dawn *I'm* getting on *your* nerves?

She chucks her cards down. Silence. She sighs.

Lee D'you wanna fag?

Dawn Yeah go on.

She takes one off him. She touches his hand as she does so. He smiles.

Dawn D'you wanna play the Truth game?

Lee What, again?

Dawn Yeah.

Lee Go on then.

Dawn I'll ask first . . . er . . . oh I know. Did you fancy any of the teachers at school?

Lee Did I fuck!

Dawn (*laughing*) Jonno did. When we asked him that question he said yeah, he fancied Miss Perry.

Lee Christ. She must be in her sixties.

Dawn He reckoned she'd be a right goer in the bedroom.

Lee He's desperate. He'd fancy anyone he would.

Dawn Would you?

Lee What?

Dawn Fancy anyone?

Lee No.

Dawn Who do you fancy?

Lee Who d'you think?

Dawn Don't you fancy anyone else?

Lee No.

Pause.

Do you?

Dawn *doesn't answer him. She touches his face.*

Dawn   D'you love me Lee?

Lee   D'you love me?

Dawn   Yeah. I do.

Pause.

D'you love me Lee?

We hear the door go. Enter **Val** *with a bagful of booze from the offy.* **Lee** *jumps away from* **Dawn**.

Val   God it's hot isn't it? The bloody lift's out again. I'm out of breath. I'll have to go the doctor's about me chest again you know.

Lee *gets up to give* **Val** *his chair.*

Lee   Here Val. Sit down.

Val   Oh no. You're alright. I'm going to have a bath. (*Taking her coat off.*) I'm sweating buckets.

She looks through her library books, taking her time. A tense atmosphere. She exits. Silence.

Lee   First time she's been out the flat since I moved in. Two weeks. Doesn't she like being outside?

Dawn   No.

Lee   She's stupid.

Dawn   What?

Lee   I mean, she's a nice woman, she should get herself down the club. She might meet someone.

Dawn   She might not want to.

Lee   Course she wants to.

Dawn   Why? She hasn't been with anyone since me Dad.

Lee   She might leave us alone for a minute then.

Dawn   Ay you! This is her flat. Don't start slagging her off.

Lee   I'm not I . . .

Dawn   She's spent money on you.

Lee   I was just saying she needs to have some fun.

Dawn   She could chuck you out like that. (*She clicks her fingers.*) Don't fuckin' slag my Mum.

Lee   I'm fuckin' not. Christ!

He gets up. Gets his glass. Pours more cider.

Dawn   You just can't slag me Mum that's all.

Lee   I wasn't.

Dawn   Alright.

Pause.

God. It is hot though isn't it.

Lee   Yeah.

Silence. **Lee** *sips his drink.* **Dawn** *stares at him. After a minute he turns to meet her gaze.*

Lee   I do you know Dawn.

Dawn   You do what?

Lee   I do love you.

Dawn   If you love me you won't join the Army.

Pause. **Lee** *leans towards* **Dawn** *and points his finger right in her face, punctuating his words by poking at her*

Lee   Don't you ever, ever, tell me what to do.

The lights fade.

Ghost Town *by* The Specials *fades up and plays for a while. A sense of time passing.*

Two months later, **Barry**'s *flat. Evening.*

A going away party for **Barry** *and* **Jonno**. **Barry** *in position behind the bar,* **Dawn** *and* **Lee** *very much together on the settee.* **Jonno** *is giving* **Kev** *a tattoo and* **Campbell** *is chopping up some speed on the smoked glass table.* **Kev** *nurses a half drunk bottle of Bell's Whiskey. Music as at previous party. As we join them, the gang are all singing along to the last bit of* Ghost Town.

Kev   Brilliant record that.

Jonno   Shall we have it on again?

Campbell   Oh God. How many times?

Kev   No. It's good. It's true as well isn't it? Just like this town. Everyone's leaving 'cos there's nothing happening.

Jonno   Just think. This time tomorrow, we'll be standing on foreign soil. Where is it again Barry?

Barry   Calais.

Jonno (*French accent*)   Calais!

Dawn (*to* **Kev**)   You're not leaving.

Kev   I know.

Dawn   I'm not leaving.

Kev   I know.

Dawn   Neither are Shaun and Linda.

Kev   I bet you any money them two'll be married this time next year. Either that or she'll be pregnant.

Dawn   So. What's wrong with that?

Kev (*sings The Specials song*)

'You've done too much, much too young, you know you're married with a kid when you should be having fun with me!'

Jonno   Ay. Keep still will you!

Dawn   You're just jealous you are.

Kev   And you'll be in the same state yourself if you're not careful.

Lee   Watch it Kev.

Kev   It's true. Two months ago it was 'Oh I'm leaving this town. I'm too good for this town. I'm going to live with my cousin in Manchester.'

Lee (*going up to* **Kev** *and poking at his mouth*)   It's none of your business Kev so shut that.

Lee *sits down again.*

Barry (*changing the subject*)   Er. . . . What's your tattoo Kev?

Kev   Sham '69. (*Bouncing up and down, singing Sham '69.*) 'Hersham boys, Hersham boys, lace-up boots and corduroys.'

Jonno   Keep still will you!

Barry   God. Since when've you been into them?

Kev   'They call us the cockney . . . cowboys!'

Dawn   Fuckin' cockney boot-boys more like.

Kev   What's wrong with them?

Dawn   They're fuckin' southerners aren't they? They think they're hard but they're not.

Campbell   The Jam are southerners.

Dawn   They don't count.

Campbell Why not?

Dawn 'Cos Paul Weller's a genius. It's not his fault he got born in the wrong place.

Campbell It's not anyone's fault where they get born.

Dawn Yeah, but at least he's got the guts to stand up and say something about it.

Kev So've Sham '69.

Dawn Have they fuck. All they're saying is look at us 'cos we're well fuckin' hard.

Kev What's wrong with that?

Dawn If you're so fond of them why don't you fuck off down to cockneyland and join them.

Kev I might do!

Jonno Oh I wouldn't if I was you Kev. Soon as they heard your accent you'd be dead.

Kev You and Barry are going down there.

Jonno Only passing through on the way to Dover. I'm not even gonna open me mouth.

Barry Oh great! What if we wanna cup of tea or something?

Jonno You can ask mate. I don't wanna risk it. And I tell you something else an' all, I'm keeping me money somewhere very safe 'cos they're all pocket divers down there you know.

Jonno *puts the ink onto* **Kev**'s *tattoo.* **Campbell** *does a line of speed leaving one line spare.*

Barry Did you get in touch with Clare, Dawn?

Dawn I tried. She still won't speak to me.

Barry Me Ma saw her in the Spa Shop.

Dawn (*sitting up*) Did she?

Barry Yeah. She wouldn't stop to talk though. Just said hello and rushed past.

Dawn (*disappointed*) Oh.

Campbell Dawn?

Dawn What?

Campbell D'you want a line?

Dawn   Not if you want paying for it.

Campbell   I don't want paying for it.

Dawn   Oh. OK. Ta.

She goes over to the table and does a line.

Jonno   There you go Kev. Sham '69.

Lee   You can always get it removed when you grow up.

Kev (*ignores* **Lee**)   Ta Jonno.

Kev *stumbles towards* **Campbell** *and sits down next to him.*

Jonno   Campbell, can I have a line?

Barry   Ay you. We've got to be up early tomorrow you know, me Dad's leaving at six.

Jonno   Well we might as well stay up all night then.

Barry   I'm not carrying your bag for you when you're half dead tomorrow night Jonno.

Jonno   I won't ask you to.

Barry   Too right you won't.

Lee   Listen to yous. You haven't even gone yet and you're already arguing.

Kev   I'll have a line.

Campbell   D'you think you should?

Kev   What?

Campbell   Well it doesn't mix too well with the whiskey does it?

Kev   I said I'll have a line.

Campbell   OK. Don't say I didn't warn you.

He starts to cut up more speed.

Dawn   When d'you start college Campbell?

Campbell   Next week.

Dawn   You looking forward to it?

Campbell   I dunno. S'pose so.

Kev   We'll never see him anymore. He'll be knocking around with his clever mates. He won't be bothering with us anymore.

Campbell   I'm only doing me 'A' Levels Kev.

Kev   How's it going with you anyway Lee. Any sign of work?

Lee (*glances at* **Dawn**)   Er. Not exactly.

Dawn   He's got an interview for the Army.

Jonno   That's good Lee. You can learn a good trade in the Army. When's the interview?

Lee   Day after tomorrow.

Dawn *gives him a look.*

Lee   I'm just gonna see what it's like that's all.

Dawn *gets up and goes to stand with* **Barry** *at the bar. We listen to their conversation. The others continue talking amongst themselves.*

Dawn   A drink please barman.

Barry   Certainly young lady. What's your poison?

Dawn   Whatever's on offer.

Barry   What could be beautiful enough for a gorgeous girl like you?

Dawn   Shurrup and get us a vodka you daft get.

Barry   And such a way with words too.

He pours her a drink.

Dawn   I won't half miss you, you know Barry.

Barry   I told you, you could come with us.

Dawn   Oh yeah.

Barry   I was serious.

Dawn   As if! You don't want me cramping your style.

Barry   Oh but I do.

Dawn   Everyone's leaving me. He's going in the Army. You're off travelling the world. Clare won't speak to me.

Barry   I'm not leaving you Dawn. I'll come back and get you if you like. Just say the word.

Dawn   I love you, you know Barry.

Barry   I love you too.

Dawn   You're like a big brother. Always keeping an eye on me.

Barry   Yeah. That's me.

Dawn   You are gonna write to me aren't you?

Barry   Try and stop me. You better write back an' all.

She moves away, back to **Lee**.

Barry Dawn.

Dawn What babes?

Barry If Lee . . . I'm serious . . . if you wanted to come.

Dawn I might just take you up on that one day.

She smiles at him and goes back to sit with **Lee**.

Jonno . . . Yeah, live sex shows and apparently they can take the tops off bottles with their, you know, with their . . .

Kev With their cunts Jonno.

Jonno Well. Yeah.

Kev They're all a bunch of cunts anyway if you ask me. Can you do that Dawn?

Dawn Do what?

Campbell Kev.

Kev No. It's very important for her future career. Can you Dawn?

Dawn What's he going on about?

Lee Nothing much. And if he doesn't shut his big stupid mouth he won't be going on about anything at all.

Kev Oooh! That's right. Be a good soldier Lee. Defend the lady.

Lee Shut it Kev.

Kev Aw shame. He's going off to war. Leaving our little Dawny-warny behind.

Dawn Fuckin' shut up you dickhead.

Kev And what are you gonna do when your beloved goes marching off then? Off to Manchester are we? Off to Manchester eh Dawn. To stay with cousin Jane.

Campbell Kev. Don't.

Kev You and Clare and your Jane. That'd be nice wouldn't it? You could open your own brothel.

Lee You what?

Kev Or is it easier walking the streets like Jane, picking up kerb crawlers?

Campbell Shut up Kev.

Kev But watch out for the bizzies though, or you'll end up running to Mr Campbell for help, same as your Jane had to.

Lee What's he talking about Dawn?

Dawn *is staring at* **Campbell**.

Dawn I don't know.

Lee WHAT THE FUCK ARE YOU TALKING ABOUT!!

Kev 'S just something Campbell told me, doesn't matt . . .

Lee (*shouting in* **Kev**'s *face*) WHAT? WHAT DID HE TELL YOU?!!!
WHAT DID HE TELL YOU KEVIN??

Kev Dawn's cousin, she got done for soliciting, he said he thought Dawn was
on the game.

Silence for a second then **Lee** *grabs* **Barry**'s *mum's smoked-glass table with all the speed
on and hurls it at* **Campbell** *and* **Kev**. *It misses, hits the wall behind them. A loud
crash, speed and smoked glass everywhere.* **Lee** *runs out, slamming the door behind him.
Silence for a moment then the door bell goes, a merry little tune. Everyone ignores it. It
goes again.*

Jonno Er. I'll get the door.

He exits. No one moves or speaks. He comes back in with **Shaun** *and* **Linda**.

Linda Dawn. Is Clare here?

Dawn What?

Linda We just came past your flats and there was an ambulance outside.

Shaun And we saw Clare's Gran. She was getting in the ambulance.

Dawn (*quiet*) No.

Linda It might be someone else, a neighbour or something.

Dawn No.

Shaun Have you seen Clare today?

Dawn *turns on her heel and runs out of the flat*

Linda They reckon someone jumped from the top floor.

Jonno Jesus.

Barry *runs after* **Dawn**. *No one speaks for a minute.*

Shaun It might be someone else.

Linda (*looking round*) Christ, what a mess. What's been going on here?

No one answers. The lights fade.

The next day. The park.

Lee *sits on the grass. After a moment* **Dawn** *enters. She sits down beside him. A strained atmosphere. Silence.*

Lee   (*After a bit*) I thought you weren't gonna come.

Dawn   I wasn't gonna come.

Pause.

Lee   D'you wanna fag?

Dawn   Yeah alright.

He gives her a No.6 and lights it and one for himself. They smoke in silence.

I hear you went back to Barry's.

Lee   Yeah. His Mam and Dad let me sleep on the settee. But I'm off for three days tomorrow. To the Army base.

Dawn   You got in then.

Lee   No. Not yet. This is a kind of interview thing. We've got to do tests and stuff.

Dawn   Oh.

They smoke.

Lee   Are you alright Dawn?

Dawn   What d'you think?

Pause.

Did you hear the post mortem results?

Lee   Yeah.

Dawn   Accidental death. Like she fell or something.

Lee   She might have.

Dawn   She didn't.

Lee   You don't know that.

Dawn   She phoned me that night you know. But I was out. I was fuckin' out with you.

Lee   It was Barry and Jonno's party. It's not your fault Dawn.

Dawn   Isn't it?

Lee   You said it yourself. She got depressed.

Dawn   I kept telling her to be tough. I said I'd look after her and I never.

Lee (*angry*)   For Christ's sake stop blaming yourself!

Pause.

Dawn   Did you hear? Her Mum came home. Pity she never fuckin' came home when her daughter was alive.

Lee   How's the Grandma?

Dawn   What do you fuckin' care?

Lee   Dawn.

Dawn   Don't pretend it matters to you Lee. You didn't even come to the funeral.

Lee   I just . . . I just had to think.

Dawn   About what? Barry and Jonno dropped everything. Helped us arrange the funeral. What was there to think about?

Lee   All that stuff that Kev said. About your Jane.

Dawn   What the fuck's that got to do with anything?

Lee   I need to know if it's true Dawn.

Dawn   You bastard.

Lee   Is it true?

Dawn   What difference does it make?

Lee   I don't want you going on the game.

Dawn   I can't believe you're saying this.

Lee   It's important.

Dawn   How can you even think about it now?

Lee   Listen. I know that Clare's dead. I know you're sad. We're all fuckin' sad. But you and me are still alive. And I need to know.

Dawn   Are you gonna kill people if you join the Army?

Lee   What?

Dawn   You heard. Are you gonna shoot people dead Lee? If they send you to Ireland will you be shooting young lads the same age as yourself dead.

Lee   What's that got . . .

Dawn   'Cos I need to know Lee.

Lee   I haven't joined up yet, I still don't know . . .

Dawn   But you might do.

Lee   I wanted to talk to you first.

Dawn   And I might do too Lee. While you're shooting people dead I might just be walking the streets. Walking the streets, waiting for a car to draw up slowly, for a man to lean out the window. An old man in a grey suit with beads of sweat on his forehead. And I'll lean down to him Lee and I'll say 'Looking for company?' and he'll lick his dry lips and he'll cough a dry cough and say 'Yes. How much?'

Lee   Don't Dawn.

Dawn   And then I'll say 'Let's discuss that in the car shall we?' And then I'll slip inside into the comfort of his soft grey seats and his push-button tinted windows. And then later he'll slip inside me. Quietly. Sadly. Ashamed. Without looking at me or saying a word.

Silence.

Lee   So it's true then?

Dawn   Is it?

Lee   How? How can you do that Dawn? How can you do it?

Dawn   I do it with you.

Lee   It's not like that with us.

Dawn   Oh yes that's right Lee. You always forget to pay me.

He hits her. A flash of violence like a firework going off. The force of it knocks her over. Silence. After a second **Dawn** *gets to her feet. She stands over* **Lee** *and stares at him with hatred in her eyes.*

Dawn   Like father like son Lee. Like grandfather like father like son.

Lee *gets to his feet. He puts his hand out to touch* **Dawn**'s *face where he hit her. She moves her head away but stands her ground.*

Dawn   Goodbye Lee.

Lee *exits, running as fast as he can.* **Dawn** *stares after him. After a long moment she lies down on the grass in levitation position. Pause. The lights fade.*

Act Two

1991

Lee, *still in his dugout in Kuwait, a little while later.*

Lee All this time sitting here, it's doing me head in. It's doing my head right in.

Ten years I've been doing this job. I wanted to go home the first night. That poor kid. Dead quiet he was. Sarge and the other lads, they filled a bath for him. They made me piss in it. Someone else stuck their fingers down their neck. They lowered him down till he was covered. Everybody's crap.

I was disgusted. I wanted to go back, tell Dawn she was right. But she would never've listened to me. No. Not after . . .

So I stayed. I forgot. I stopped. I stopped being disgusted. I stopped being disgusted with my life.

I've got things to do if I get through this. I've got people I wanna see. I've got unfinished business. Me and Dawn. Unfinished business. Waiting for me to turn up and finish it off.

Blackout.

Part Two

1991

The action takes place in three places: **Barry**'s *flat, 'the windows', the bar.*

Barry's *flat. The early hours of the morning.*

The modern equivalent of his parents' flat. Cocktail cabinet, settee, coffee table, etc. State of the art music centre. Lots of **Dawn**'s *books on the coffee table. Otherwise very tidy. The flat is above* **Barry**'s *bar in the red light district of Amsterdam.* **Dawn** *and* **Barry** *are now 26. The flat is in semi-darkness. Enter* **Dawn**. *She is wearing a T-shirt which she sleeps in. She is crying. She picks a bottle of rum up and takes a large swig. She lights a fag. She sits down on the settee taking the bottle with her. She shakes. After a moment* **Barry** *enters, very sleepy, also dressed for bed. He sits next to* **Dawn** *on the settee, puts his arms round her and rocks her. He has done this a thousand times before.* **Dawn** *begins to calm down.*

Barry (*after a while*)   You OK?

Dawn   I had a dream about Clare. She was standing in the doorway of me Mam's flat at home. And . . . and there was a sheer drop Barry. From me Mam's front door all the way down to the ground. And I pushed her. I pushed Clare and I watched her falling down till she hit the floor. Then I shut the door and I turned me back on her. Like I did in real life.

Barry   It's just a dream. Come on now. Come back to bed.

Dawn   It's not gonna work this you know Barry. I can't. I can't do it. I can't keep holding meself together.

Barry   Yes you can. Come on now. You'll feel better in the morning. You've just had a bad dream. It's all in the past all that stuff. You're with me now. You're alright.

Dawn   It's too hard. You should've left me at Kings Cross. I'm gonna fall apart again. I'm gonna fall . . .

Barry   You're not.

Dawn   I wish I was you, you know Barry.

Barry   Don't be daft.

Dawn   I do. I wish I was you. You're like the eye of the storm you are. The centre of the tornado. I get swept along by the wind and me feelings come crashing down on the hard ground but you, you just keep still until the storm's passed you by. Calm and still. I wish I was you.

He holds her face in his hands.

Barry Look at me. Come on. I love you Dawn. It's gonna be alright. Everything's sorted. You've got a new life now. A new life. Don't give up. OK? . . . OK?

Dawn I'm scared.

Barry What's there to be scared of?

Dawn I'm gonna fuck it up like I've always fucked everything up.

Barry You're not. You're not Dawn. You're gonna be OK.

Silence. She stares at him for a moment then throws her arms round him and holds him tight.

Dawn Oh God, Barry. What have I done to deserve you?

Barry Nothing. I'm just a daft bastard that's all.

Dawn No you're not.

Barry Well then. You must've done something right then. Eh?

She laughs.

Dawn Yeah. I guess so.

Pause.

I had another dream as well. About Lee Kelly.

Barry Bloody hell. You have been delving into the past haven't you?

Dawn He came to see me in me window. All dressed up in combat gear. Like a soldier.

Barry I thought you'd forgotten all about him.

Dawn No. He's still there. Tucked inside my heart. Tucked away like Clare and me Mum. Comes to haunt me in my sleep, the bastard.

Barry Come on Dawn. Come back to bed now. I'm tired.

Dawn Yeah. Yeah. OK.

They exit arm in arm.

Dawn (*exiting*) You're too good to me you know.

Barry I know. I'm your Guardian Angel babes. It's my job.

The lights fade as they exit.

The bar, next day.

Just before lunchtime. Shiney Happy People *by REM plays loud. Behind the bar is* **Barry**, *polishing glasses, wiping the bar down, singing along with REM. He looks happy. After a bit, enter* **Kaz** *and* **Martini**. *They enter laughing, two women sharing a* *dirty joke.* **Barry** *turns the music down a bit but the tape continues to play throughout this scene. A selection of* **Barry** *and* **Dawn**'s *current faves. REM, Stone Roses, The Farm, The Las, Primal Scream, Nirvana, etc, etc.*

The women take up position on stools in front of the bar.

Kaz   Give us a rum and coke Barry, it must be nearly 12 o'clock.

Barry *starts making drinks.*

Barry   Do you two fancy coming down the Milky Way tonight?

Martini   D'you want to go Kaz?

Kaz   If I can get a baby sitter. Are we on a freebie Barry?

Barry   Mick'll leave some tickets on the door for us.

Martini   Great. You know Kaz, Barry knows everybody in the Dam doesn't he? I don't think I've paid to get in anywhere since I met him.

Kaz   It's his charming pesonality and good looks Martini.

Martini   Don't I have a charming personality and good looks?

Kaz   Oh yeah. It's just a lot more rare in blokes. That's why everybody loves him.

Barry *laughs. Enter* **Dawn**.

Barry   Morning gorgeous.

Dawn   Morning.

She gives him a kiss. Sits on a stool. **Barry** *gets her a rum and Coke.*

Dawn   Morning girls.

Kaz (*looking at her watch*)   Afternoon.

Dawn   Who's turn is it to cook tea tonight Baz?

Barry   Mine. What d'you fancy?

Dawn   New potatoes and butter?

Barry   But of course. Would you like to try something new?

Dawn   Like what?

Kaz   Oh, sounds like his Mum's sent him a new recipe!

Barry   Squid with garlic and tomatoes and stuff. They done it at her cookery class last week.

Dawn   Can we still have new potatoes?

Barry   Anything for you babes.

The door goes. Enter **Lee** *in civvy clothes and carrying a holdall.*

They all look round.

Barry (*to* **Lee**)   Good afternoon sir. What's your poison?

Lee   Barry?

Barry (*looks at him properly*)   Bloody hell!

Barry *comes from behind the bar and gives* **Lee** *a pat on the back, etc.*

Barry   My God. I don't believe it. It's Lee Kelly, Dawn.

Dawn   So I see. Hello Lee.

She doesn't move from her bar stool.

Lee   Dawn.

A slight moment of awkward silence which **Barry** *hurriedly fills.*

Barry   So. Christ. Come and sit down mate, I'll get you a drink.

They move to the bar. **Kaz** *and* **Martini** *eye* **Lee** *curiously.* **Lee** *nods at them.* **Barry** *gets him a beer.*

Barry   God you know. It's so weird to see you. You on leave are you?

Lee   That's right. Thought I'd come and look up some old mates. Linda and Shaun give me the address. I've just been home for a few days.

Barry   Oh. How are they? They're meant to be coming over to see us soon.

Lee   Yeah. They said. When Shaun gets the time off.

Barry   Yeah. How's the kids?

Lee   Great. Three kids eh? I couldn't believe it.

Barry   Of course. You wouldn't have known would you? You haven't been back since . . .

Lee   Just the once. For me Mam's funeral.

Dawn   We'd better get going girls. We're wasting valuable time sat here.

Kaz   And time is money!

They get up and start to go.

Lee   How are you anyway Dawn?

Dawn   Fine. I'm fine.

Lee   Will you be around later?

Dawn   I don't know. Maybe.

She goes to exit.

Barry   Ay! Don't I get a kiss goodbye.

She pecks him on the cheek.

Dawn   See you later.

Kaz *and* **Martini** *speak simultaneously.*

Kaz   Ciao for now!

Martini   See you later Barry!

They leave.

Barry   So. How long you here for then Lee?

Lee   I'm not sure. A few days, maybe longer. I've just come back from the Gulf.

Barry   Serious?

Lee   Yeah. They're giving me a rest. Apparently I've got 'post-Gulf trauma'.

He laughs.

Barry   God. It must have been well-heavy like.

Lee   Yeah. Yeah it was. How are you anyway? Nice place you've got here.

Barry   Great eh? It's not mine yet. I'm buying it off me boss soon though. 'Cos he's retiring.

Lee   You always said you were gonna do something like this Barry.

Barry   Yep. And I always knew I would.

Silence.

Lee   Linda was telling me Dawn's a salesgirl.

Barry   Did she?

Lee   Yeah. What is it? Perfume counter or something?

Barry   Er. Yeah. Sales.

Lee   And her friends?

Barry   Yeah. They all work together, em, you know. Same department.

Lee   Right. She's lookin' well anyway.

Barry   Oh she is. Yeah.

Lee   I haven't seen her since Clare . . . died.

Barry   No. I know. Well. She's had a few rough patches but she's been alright since she came here.

Lee   How long she been here then?

Barry Six months. I went to see her in London. She wasn't in a very good state. She was drinking a lot. You know. So I made her come over here. She needed someone to look after her for a bit.

Lee *Her* Mum died too didn't she?

Barry Oh yeah. But that was years ago. Not long after Clare . . . Didn't you know?

Lee No. Linda and Shaun told me.

Barry Oh. God. You're well out of touch aren't you mate?

Lee Yeah.

Barry She's had a bit of a rough time Dawn. But she's better now. She likes it here.

Pause.

Lee So. Tell me all the news. D'you ever see Jonno?

Barry I haven't for a while. He writes to me now and again though. He got married you know. When we were working in Australia. Lives over there now.

Lee It's meant to be a great lifestyle.

Barry Oh it is. We got plenty of work and all that. But I wanted to come here. You know, it's nearer home. I met the bloke who owns this place so I was guaranteed work. He's been very good to me. I stand to make a lot of money when I take over here.

Lee Nice one Barry. I'm pleased for you. I saw Kev when I was home.

Barry Oh yeah. Is he working now?

Lee No. Says it's been five years now.

Barry Yeah. Sad eh?

Lee Yeah. He looked a right mess.

Barry He's been inside twice you know.

Lee What for?

Barry Fighting. He drinks too much.

Lee He was always a loser.

Barry Ay! Did he tell you about Campbell?

Lee No. What about him?

Barry Oh he's got his own company and everything apparently. Advertising. Lives in Brighton. Right whizz kid he is.

Lee Jammy bastard. D'you ever see him?

Barry   Na. He doesn't bother with his old mates now.

Lee   Well. He was always brainier than us wasn't he?

Barry   Yeah.

Pause.

God. It's been a long time Lee.

Lee   Yeah.

Barry   Ten years.

Lee   Yeah.

Pause.

Barry. D'you mind if I ask you something?

Barry   No. No. Fire away.

Lee   Are you and Dawn together?

Pause.

Barry   Yes. Yes we are.

Pause.

What about you Lee? Have you got someone?

Lee   No. No. It's difficult you know. Being in the Army. I mean you can always get a woman. They hang around and all that. But I've never wanted to marry anyone. It's not a very nice life, being married to a squaddie.

Barry   No. I guess not.

Lee   Listen. I need to get a place to stay sorted out.

Barry *writes something down on a bit of paper.*

Barry   Get the taxi bloke to take you there. The Frisco Hotel. If they're full just come back here and I'll phone round for you.

Lee   Will you be here all day?

Barry   Oh yeah. I've got a flat over the bar so I'm never far away! We're going to the Milky Way later if you fancy it. To see a band.

Lee   I'll see you later then.

Barry   Yeah. Tell Tony at the hotel that I've sent you down. He might knock a few bob off for you.

Lee   OK then. See you Barry.

Barry   See you.

Exit **Lee. Barry** *puts his head in his hands.*

Barry   Jesus. Lee Kelly.

The lights fade.

A little later.

Dawn, **Kaz** *and* **Martini** *at work in their windows in the Red Light District. The windows display the women for the men passing by. They wear their work gear. Stockings, suspenders, basques, etc. Business is very slow.* **Dawn** *is reading a book (* Postcards From the Edge *by Carrie Fisher) and listening to her personal stereo,* **Martini** *is doing her nails and* **Kaz** *is asleep.* **Dawn** *is in the middle window. The windows are accessible from the back and have a walkway in front of them. The women all have keys to each others' windows and move in and out via the back.*

Martini *stops doing her nails. She sighs a big sigh. She moves up to the window front and peers out. She sighs again. She goes to the wall that separates her from* **Dawn** *and bangs on it. No answer. She bangs again. Still no answer. She goes out the back and we see her coming in through the curtains at the back of* **Dawn**'s *window.* **Dawn** *doesn't notice her. She creeps up on* **Dawn** *and lifts the personal stereo off and kisses her on the ear.*

Dawn   What the . . .? Oh it's you! I thought someone had broke in you daft cow.

Martini   (*laughing*)   Only me. What's the book?

Dawn   I'll pass it on to you when I've finished.

Martini   Dawn, I haven't got through any of the others yet.

Dawn   Well get a move on then!

Martini   I wish I could read like you do, it might make the time pass quicker. I am so bored! Not one punter in two hours!

Dawn   That's Tuesdays for you.

Martini   I bet Kaz has fallen asleep again!

She bangs on the wall.

Martini   KAZ!!!

No answer.

Martini   Fast asleep! D'you think we should wake her?

Dawn   Na, let her sleep. They can fuckin' knock on the window if they want her.

Martini   Yeah.

Pause. **Dawn** *reads.* **Martini** *paces.*

Martini   So. Who was this man who came to the bar today.

Dawn   Which man?

Martini   You know. The one who made you go so quiet.

Dawn   Oh him. Just an old school friend of Barry's.

Martini   Barry's friend eh? Not yours.

Dawn   No. Not my friend.

Martini   I see.

She gives **Dawn** *a knowing look.*

Dawn   What?

Martini   I think he has some sort of effect on you this man.

Dawn   Don't talk shite Martini.

Martini   Yes. I think so.

Dawn   Leave it will you.

Martini   And you on him.

Dawn   Look, fuckin' drop it. I used to go out with him when I was a kid. End of story.

Martini   Aha, the first love comes back into her life! I see trouble brewing.

Dawn   Will you fuck off Martini. I'm trying to read.

A knock from the back of the windows.

Oh. Sounds like you're in business.

Martini *goes out.* **Dawn** *puts her book away, stretches and yawns then goes out the back. She comes into* **Kaz's** *window.*

Dawn   You awake?

Kaz (*waking up*)   Eh? Course I am! Anything doing?

Dawn   Well I had an easy job earlier. He threw up in the sink, gave me some money and left.

Kaz   The perfect punter!

Dawn   If he'd cleaned up after himself I might say that.

Kaz   Martini got a punter?

Dawn   Yeah.

Kaz   (*she yawns*)   God. What a day. If I'd known it was gonna be this slow I'd've stayed home with the littl'un. Given the minder a day off. (*She yawns again.*)

Dawn   Don't drop off your stool.

*Dawn goes out the back then comes back into her window. She picks her book up again and starts to read. **Martini** comes back. We see **Lee** giving her some money.*

Lee *walks past **Dawn**. He sees her. He stops in his tracks. She looks up. They stare at each other. **Lee** exits, slowly, staring at **Dawn**. The lights fade. Primal Scream's* Damaged *begins to play.*

Fade down Primal Scream.

Barry'*s flat, a while later.*

Barry *is sitting smoking a spliff. He looks troubled. Enter **Dawn**. **Barry** looks pleased*

Barry   Hiya babes.

Dawn (*quiet*)   Hiya.

She sits down and takes the spliff off him.

Barry   Drink?

Dawn   Yeah.

Barry   Coming up.

He makes her a rum and coke. Silence.

There you go.

Dawn   Ta.

Barry   You finished? It's early.

Dawn   I've had enough today.

Barry   Punter been hassling you?

Dawn   No.

Barry   Oh. Business a bit slow then?

Dawn (*quiet*)   Yes.

Barry   Pardon?

Dawn   Yes. Business is a bit slow.

Barry   Well never mind. We can spend the rest of the day together. Boss is coming later for a chat. We can talk about you coming in on the bar and that. You'll be able to give all this crap up soon Dawn.

Dawn   I'm going to sleep soon.

Barry   Oh.

Dawn   I'm tired.

Barry   Are you coming out tonight still?

Dawn   Dunno.

Pause.

Barry   Fancy Lee Kelly turning up eh?

Dawn   Fancy.

Barry   He seems well anyway. He's coming to the bar later. Thought we could show him the town tonight. Introduce him to a few people.

Dawn   Did you.

Pause.

Barry   It's upset you hasn't it?

Dawn   What?

Barry   Lee Kelly turning up.

No answer.

You'll never guess what Linda's told him.

Dawn   That's right.

Barry   Eh?

Dawn   I'll never guess. But you're gonna tell me anyway.

Barry   I don't have to tell you if you don't want me to.

Dawn *finishes her rum.*

Dawn   Can I have another drink?

Barry   OK.

He gets her one.

Dawn   So. What's Linda been saying?

Barry   She told Lee that you're a salesgirl.

Dawn   I am.

Barry   Yeah, but Lee thinks she means in a department store or something.

Dawn   Not any more he doesn't. He came past the windows this afternoon.

Barry   Oh. I thought that might happen. That's what this is all about.

Dawn   I'm just tired that's all.

Barry   You've got nothing to be ashamed of Dawn.

Dawn   I don't need you to tell me that.

Barry   No. I guess not.

Dawn   Anyway. He's a punter.

Barry   What?

Dawn   Yeah. He went with Martini.

Barry   Jesus.

Dawn   She reckons he didn't recognise her.

Barry   How could he do that with you next door and everything?

Dawn   I was with Kaz. He saw me afterwards.

Silence. She finishes her drink.

He's just a fuckin' punter like all the rest. I'm going to bed.

She gets up.

Barry   What d'you want me to tell the boss then?

Dawn   What?

Barry   About you coming into the bar with me.

Dawn   Barry. I haven't decided yet.

Barry   I thought you wanted to.

Dawn   I said I was thinking about it.

Barry   You can't work the windows for the rest of your life you know.

Dawn   Why not?

Barry   You have to think about when you're older.

Dawn   Oh. So you reckon it would be better for me to wash glasses and work me arse off behind the bar serving boring fuckin' tourists do you? I'm good at my job. I earn good money. I don't need you to change things for me.

Barry   I know. Christ. I thought you wanted to. The boss needs to know.

Dawn   I haven't decided Barry.

Barry   Well. It's up to you.

Dawn   That's right. I'm going to bed.

Barry   (*standing up. Touching her*)   I'll come with you.

Dawn   (*She pushes his hand away. A reflex action*)   No. I . . . I'm tired Barry.

She goes to exit.

Barry   Dawn?

Dawn   Yes.

Barry   Do you love me?

Dawn   (*She doesn't look at him*)   Yes.

Barry   Do you Dawn?

Dawn   I just said I did didn't I?

Barry   Then what's the problem?

Dawn   There isn't one.

Barry   Tell me the truth.

Dawn   It just feels a bit weird that's all.

Barry   I've done everything I can for you Dawn.

Dawn   I know.

Barry   You would have died if I hadn't brought you away from King's Cross.

Dawn   I didn't ask you to.

Barry   I spent ten years keeping track of you, finding you when you disappeared. I spent my fuckin' savings to pay your court fines for you when you were working Park Lane. My life savings Dawn. All the work, all the travelling from country to country getting more and more money so I could come to Amsterdam and make my dream come true. The fuckin' down payment Dawn, the down payment on my dream and I spent it all on you. I could've bought this bar by now.

Dawn   You can't blame me for . . .

Barry   I've stood by you time after time after time. And have I ever, once, asked you for anything more than friendship?

Dawn   No.

Barry   It was you that started this relationship Dawn.

Dawn   I know.

Barry   If you had left things as they were I would've been OK. But I . . . I don't think I could stand it if you changed again now.

Dawn   I haven't changed.

Barry   You dreamt about him.

Dawn   It was just a dream.

Barry   You still love him don't you?

Dawn   I hate him.

Barry   That's a strong emotion after all these years.

Dawn   If I dreamt about him it was a bad dream. He's just brought some memories back. That's all.

Barry   He's still there you said. Tucked inside your heart. Still there. After all this time.

Silence. After a moment **Dawn** *goes to* **Barry.** *She tries to kiss him but he won't let her.*

Dawn   Barry.

Barry *grabs hold of her, clumsily, and kisses her too hard.*

Dawn   Don't! It hurts.

He turns away from her. He is almost crying. She turns him back to face her and kisses him gently. He gives in. They begin to touch each other, sad and slow. Fade up Damaged *by Primal Scream.* **Barry** *and* **Dawn** *kiss. The lights fade slowly. We listen to* Damaged *for a while then the lights fade up again.* **Dawn** *is on her own. She sits in her dressing-gown on the settee, a glass of rum in her hand, listening to Primal Scream, staring into space. The door goes.* **Dawn** *answers it. It is* **Lee.** *Silence. They stare at each other.*

Dawn   What d'you want Lee?

Lee   Is Barry here?

Dawn   No.

Lee   Can I come in?

Dawn   No.

Lee   Come on Dawn.

Dawn   No.

Lee   Would you let me in if I came to see you in your window?

Slight pause.

Dawn   If you paid me well enough. How much did you pay Martini?

Lee   I can't believe it Dawn. I thought . . . I thought . . . things would be different for you. You're too smart for all this. I just can't believe it.

Dawn   Well don't then. Go somewhere else and pretend it's all dream.

Lee   A nightmare more like.

Dawn   Look. What the fuck's it got to do with you? What right have you got to make a judgement on my life. I don't even remember you.

Lee   It's my fault.

Dawn   What?

Lee   I should never've left you.

Dawn   You didn't leave me. I sent you away.

Lee   I thought you didn't remember.

Pause.

I can't believe you're with Barry.

Dawn   Oh. Jealous are you?

Lee   How can he let you . . .

Dawn   Oh so you're starting on him now as well.

Pause.

Lee   I shouldn't have joined the Army. I should've stayed home and stuck by you.

Dawn   I've done fine without you thank you.

Lee   It's just like you always said.

Dawn   What?

Lee   A bunch of morons led by a bunch of shitheads.

Dawn   Did I?

Lee   I wanted to come home Dawn. I wanted to come back to you. But it was too late. Because . . . because of what I did to you. I . . . you don't know what it was like . . . I don't want my life to be disgusting any more.

You're like a shining star in my life Dawn. Nobody's ever meant anything near what you meant to me. I was just too young and too fuckin' stupid to realise it.

Dawn   We're different people Lee. It was ten years ago.

Lee   Did you go and live with Jane after your Mum died?

Dawn   It's none of your business.

Lee   I guess you didn't know what you were doing. Same as me.

Dawn   Leave me alone Lee.

Lee   I can't. I still love you.

Dawn   You what?!

Lee   I do.

Dawn   You haven't got the faintest idea what love is. You bastard. I am the happiest I've been for . . . since my Mum died. My life is just . . . just coming together, just getting sorted and you turn up and you want to turn it all upside down again and you think that's love. That's not love. Where were you when my Mum died Lee? Where were you when I was arrested on Park Lane, when I was doing five minute jobs behind King's Cross station, when I was drinking a bottle of vodka a day? You weren't fuckin' there. You think what

I'm doing's bad? You haven't seen a thing. The times I've been punched and kicked and infiltrated and penetrated and ground down into the dust.

She has started crying. She is very angry

You haven't got a clue. You're just a fuckin' punter Lee. You're just a fuckin' punter. All you ever did was make me sad.

Lee   I would've been there if you'd let me. I would've made you happy. I can make you happy now.

Lee *goes to touch her. She slaps his hand away.*

Dawn   Fuck off. Just fuck off and leave me alone.

Lee   No. We've got unfinished business.

Dawn   No. No. NO!!

She slams the door in his face. She puts her face in her hands and cries her eyes out.

Blackout. In the blackout fade up Altogethernow *by The Farm.*

The bar, much later that night.

Altogethernow *plays in the background.* **Barry** *is just about to close up. He looks tired.* **Kaz** *and* **Martini** *are sitting at the bar, waiting to go to the Milky Way.* **Barry** *joins them at the door and pours himself a drink.* **Martini** *is chopping up some coke, getting a line ready for* **Barry**. **Kaz** *is in the middle of a story.*

Kaz   . . . so he opens up his bag and brings out . . . you'll never guess . . . a roll of clingfilm! Yeah. He's standing there stark bollock naked and he hands me the clingfilm and he goes . . . 'Would you mind wrapping me up in this!' ..

Martini   Wrapping him up?

Kaz   Yeah. He had a holdall full of the stuff. I covered him from head to toe in it. Like an Egyptian Mummy.

Martini   I hope he paid you extra!

Kaz   Course he did, I'm not complaining. Makes the day go quicker when you get someone like that. Just like doing a bit of cooking it was.

Martini   I don't like them. The weirdos. Weirdos and talkers. They get on my nerves.

Kaz   Oh talkers, yeah. Terrible.

Martini (*mimicking*)   'My wife doesn't enjoy it any more. I'm just an ordinary married bloke. It's just that she's lost interest.' As if we're interested!

Kaz   It's 'cos they feel guilty. They think it's better if they talk to you. They couldn't give a shit really.

Martini   Dawn was telling me, when she was working King's Cross she was threatened with knives every other week. Left right and centre. They used to do the business at knifepoint, then run off without paying.

Kaz   Well that's not business is it? That's rape.

Martini   She had a bad time at King's Cross eh Barry? But she's better now eh? She was in such a state when you first brought her here.

Barry   Yeah. Yeah she was.

Martini   Here. (*Passing him a rolled up note.*) A little pick me up. You deserve it.

Barry   Thanks Martini.

He takes the note and leans over to do the coke. Someone starts trying the bar door from outside.

Barry   Who's that?

He is walking towards the door when it is suddenly kicked through with an almighty crash and **Lee Kelly** *wades in. He is steaming drunk. Violent and belligerent.*

Barry   Jesus.

Lee (*shouting*)   GET ME A FUCKIN' DRINK, BARMAN!!!

Silence. **Lee** *stumbles towards the bar.* **Kaz** *and* **Martini** *move away, deftly.* **Lee** *leans on the bar.* **Barry** *doesn't move.* **Lee** *sweeps his arm across the bar, knocking off glasses, ashtrays, the mirror with the coke on and anything else that gets in his way.*

Lee   I said get me a fuckin' drink.

Pause.

Barry (*quietly*)   Get out Lee.

Lee   Make me.

Barry   I'm sure you can manage it by yourself.

Lee   You dirty little pimp.

Barry (*still quiet*)   What?

Lee   You heard me. You dirty little pimp. I thought you were a good lad Barry. I respected you. I was even nearly glad for you 'cos I thought you might have put her on the straight and narrow, but you're nothing but a dirty little pimp.

Kaz   We don't have pimps mate. We work for our . . .

Lee   SHUT UP!!

Kaz   Don't you tell me . . .

Lee   SHUT YOUR FUCKIN' FACE UP!!!

Kaz *goes for him but is held back by* **Martini**.

Barry (*to the women*)   Listen. You'd better go on. I'll follow you later.

Kaz   No! He's gonna . . .

Barry   It's alright. Go on now.

Martini   Come on Kaz.

Kaz   Are you sure you'll be . . . D'you want me to phone your boss up?

Barry   I'll be alright.

Kaz   Well, I . . .

Martini   Come on.

They pick their things up and exit.

Lee   Those two work for you an' all?

Barry   Nobody works for me. They work for themselves Lee.

Lee   How can you . . .? How can you let her. I don't get it. I don't get it.

Barry   It's not a case of letting her. She does what she likes.

Lee   She's a fuckin' dirty whore. Always was and always will be.

Barry   You still love her don't you?

Lee   A fuckin' dirty whore.

Barry   All these years and we both still love her.

Lee   Opening her legs for anyone.

Barry   I've waited all my life for her. These last few months have been the happiest time of my life.

Lee   I'm gonna take her away from this. This is no good Barry. You can't let her do this.

Barry   She does what she likes.

Lee   All these dirty old men fuckin' her day after day after day.

Barry   What about the dirty young men?

Lee   What?

Barry   What about yourself?

Pause.

Lee   I needed some company.

Barry   You needed a fuck.

Silence.

You wanted Dawn and you couldn't have her. So you went to a prostitute, you paid her 50 Gildas and she opened her legs and let you inside. And while you were banging away she closed her mind Lee. She didn't think of you, she thought of money, what she was doing tonight, what to have for her tea. She thought 'I hope he hurries up and comes the dirty little punter. I hope he hurries up and comes.'

A long pause.

You had your chance with Dawn and you fucked it up.

Lee   I was just a kid.

Barry   You hit her Lee.

Pause.

Lee   I thought she was on the game. I didn't know what to do.

Barry   So you had to come the big fuckin' man didn't you.

Lee   She was going over to Manchester and . . . Kev told me.

Barry   It doesn't matter whether she was on the game or not. She loved you and you fucked it up. Her best friend had killed herself and all you could think about was you.

Lee   I was in a bad state. I'm different now.

Barry   Leave her alone Lee.

Lee   Are you threatening me?

Barry   I'm telling you. She's happy. Don't wreck her life again.

Lee   You mean you're happy. She's not happy. She's a fuckin' prostitute for Christ's sake.

Barry   What have you got to offer her? Army wife? Not a chance.

Lee   I'm getting out of the Army.

Barry   Oh yeah? Life on the dole then. She'll love that.

Lee   I can make her happy. I've got money. You don't understand Barry. I need her. The war you see. It . . . I've got to sort my life out, otherwise what's the point? Love. That's the important thing. I want to love her. I want to love someone instead of hurting them. Instead of killing them. You don't understand. I feel like I'm falling down a great big hole. She's the only person who ever . . . ever . . . made me feel good. She's good Barry. And you're just letting her be . . . what she shouldn't be.

Barry   Leave her alone Lee.

Lee   You're worried aren't you?

Barry   I don't want her getting upset.

Lee   If she's so fuckin' happy why are you worried?

Barry   She's just getting her life back together.

Lee   She hasn't forgotten me has she?

Barry   She's coming into the bar with me. Giving up the windows.

Lee   Unfinished business.

Barry   Don't spoil it Lee.

Lee   There's unfinished business between us.

Barry   Please. Leave us alone.

Lee   No. I can't. I can't.

Barry *stares at him.*

Barry   Get out then. Get out of my bar.

Lee *gets up and moves to the door.* **Barry** *starts picking up glass and so on.* **Lee** *pauses in the doorway.*

Barry   (*still tidying, not looking at* **Lee**) Go on.

Exit **Lee.** *The lights fade as* **Barry** *tidies.*

The next day. **Dawn's** *window.*

The back bit of **Dawn's** *window. A small room. A basin and a narrow bed. Almost like a doctor's surgery.* **Dawn** *has just said goodbye to a punter and is cleaning her teeth. She goes to the door to lock it just as* **Lee Kelly** *comes in. She tries to push him out but he's too quick. He closes the door behind him. Silence.* **Lee** *is carrying a holdall, ready to leave.*

Dawn   Get out.

Lee   No.

She tries to get to the door but he blocks her.

Lee   I'm not here to hurt you Dawn. I need to talk to you.

Dawn   I don't want to talk to you.

Lee   Please Dawn.

Dawn   No.

He goes to her. Puts his arm round her, tries to kiss her, she pushes him away. Violently.

Dawn   NO!!!!!!!

Silence. After a minute **Lee** *gets his wallet out. He chucks money at her. It falls on the* *floor between them. Long pause.* **Dawn** *sits down on the bed. She goes into her patter. Very hard. Very cynical.*

Dawn   Well then. What would you like me to do for you? There's breast relief, that's 40 Gildas, hand relief French Polishing, that's a bit more expensive, that's 50 Gildas. Then we've got straight sex. Until you come or ten minutes if you don't. Then there's extras. Extras cost extra and include domination, submission, dressing-up of various kinds and golden rain. What will it be? What's your fancy? What do you want to do to me?

Lee   I want to make love to you.

Dawn   You can't pay for love.

Lee   You want to make love to me too.

Dawn   I don't.

Lee   Come on Dawn. It's me. It's Lee.

Dawn   It was ten years ago Lee. You can't just turn up and expect me to just . . .

Lee   Ten years. Ten years we've been apart and look at the state of us both.

Dawn   I told you. I'm alright.

Lee   Oh yeah? You enjoy your work do you?

Dawn   Do you enjoy killing people?

Lee   No. No. I don't. I've spent ten years in the Army, like a fuckin' zombie or something thinking I was OK but I wasn't. I was a dead man. I had nothing, nobody, emptiness. I thought I was going to die in the war Dawn. Without showing you how I love you. Without loving you properly, like you deserve. I was a kid before. I was stupid. I'm not stupid anymore.

Dawn   Just like that eh? You want me to drop my whole life just so you can prove you love me.

Lee   There's another way. It doesn't have to be like this.

Dawn   What other way?

Lee   Come with me and find out.

Dawn   Come where?

Lee   I don't know. Anywhere. Somewhere. Together.

Dawn   No.

Lee   Dawn.

Dawn   No.

Lee   Dawn.

Dawn No!

Silence. After a pause **Lee** *sits down on the floor.*

Dawn What are you doing?

Lee I'm going to levitate.

Dawn What?

Lee Come on. You remember. In the park, flat on our backs looking up at the sky. You said it was something you and Clare did. When you were little. I didn't understand it then but I do now. It was a way out wasn't it Dawn? An escape to another place. A safe place. Somewhere away from your life. Away from your Mum, away from school, away from our estate. Don't you want to escape any more? It doesn't have to be like this. I've got money. I'm getting out of the Army. I'm starting somewhere new. Come on Dawn. Let's start again. Let's escape.

Dawn Escape to where?

Lee Anywhere in the world you want to be. You don't have to settle for this Dawn. Life's too short. Come on.

Long pause. **Dawn** *is near to tears.*

You and me Dawn. Come on. Let's do it. Let's rise out of our bodies.

He lies down flat, in levitation position. After a moment **Dawn** *joins him. They lie very close. After a while he leans towards her and starts to kiss her. She tries to sit up, away from him, but he grabs her arm. He looks at it.*

Lee What happened to your tattoo?

Dawn I tried to burn it off when I was in London. I didn't feel special anymore.

Lee It didn't work.

Dawn No.

Lee You can still make it out.

Dawn Just about.

Lee It's clear as day to me.

She stares at him. After a moment she takes his hand and moves it down her body to rest between her legs. Tom Waite's Somewhere *begins to play.*

The lights fade.

Barry's *Flat.*

Barry *sits smoking a spliff, listening to Tom Waites. He is waiting.* **Dawn** *comes in.*

She sits next to **Barry** *on the settee, next to him but a space between them. Neither of them speaks or looks at each other. After a while* **Barry** *passes* **Dawn** *the spliff. She smokes.*

Dawn   I slept with him.

Barry   I know. I guessed you would.

Dawn   He wants me to go with him.

Barry   Yeah.

Dawn   I don't know what to do.

Pause.

Why don't you say something?

Barry   What's there to say?

Dawn   How about I love you, I beg you to stay, I'll kill him, I'll kill both of you?

Barry *(deadpan)*   I love you, I beg you to stay, I'll kill him, I'll kill both of you.

Dawn   You hate me.

Barry   Go with him if you want to.

Dawn   You want me to don't you?

Barry   Is that what you want me to say? Is that what you need from me? An excuse?

Pause.

Decide for yourself Dawn. I haven't got any fancy words for you. I just love you. I love you and I'm always here. Down here in the land of reality. I don't want to control your life for you. Decide for yourself.

He gets up

I've got to go back to work.

At the door

Dawn?

Dawn   Yeah?

Barry   If you go with Lee, I won't wait for you to come back crying to me with a broken heart. I've waited long enough for you. I've got me own life to lead.

He exits. Long pause. **Dawn** *listens to Tom. Lights come up on the three areas.* **Dawn** *on the settee in* **Barry's** *flat.* **Barry** *in his bar slowly and deliberately polishing glasses* *to a high shine. He places them on the bar shelf, high up where they catch the light.* **Lee** *with his luggage, waiting.*

Dawn   I've been dreaming lately. About Lee. He comes to see me in the window. All dressed up in combat gear like a soldier.

All those feelings, all those feelings we used to have, all those feelings have come rolling back to me. Still there. Me and Lee. Still there tucked inside my heart.

She watches **Lee**. *He looks at his watch. She turns towards* **Barry**. *The music becomes louder.*

But it's only a dream. And you can't build your life on dreams 'cos life won't let you. You have to find a safe place. A safe place inside a dangerous heart. The centre of the tornado, the eye of the storm.

She turns away from **Barry**.

You have to find it yourself 'cos no one else can do it for you. There has to be a tranquil place. Somewhere. Somewhere. Somewhere inside your heart.

Lee *is still waiting.* **Barry** *still polishing.*

Fade lights on the three characters.

Fade up Tom Waites and play right through to the end.

Somewhere

In the Spring of 1991 I was lucky enough to spend eight weeks in residency at the Royal National Theatre Studio, and to be commissioned by them to write a play. To be given time, money, and a quiet space in which to write is wonderful for any writer; but for me the most important thing was that I could write anything I liked. I had no restrictions on length or cast or subject matter.

Having spent a couple of years prior to this writing mainly with and for community groups and Young People's Theatre, I was now in seventh heaven. Much as I had enjoyed this work, I now welcomed the freedom from its restrictions. For the first time in a long while I could forget about budget, I could swear as much as I liked, I could write in detail about sex, and, most important of all, I could afford to make mistakes and still get paid! And if that wasn't enough for me, I was given a 'guru' to work with. The Studio's policy is to pair up new writers on residency with more experienced writers. My 'guru' was Winsome Pinnock, a writer I already knew and respected. Winsome visited me twice weekly at the Studio, read any work I had produced and discussed it with me. Then we would gossip indulgently for hours about 'our lives as writers'. It was great!

So I was ready. I sat down to write. I knew that I had four major preoccupations running around in my head at that time. Firstly, I was interested in people of my own age group, who had left school at the beginning of the 'Thatcher' years. What had happened to the people I grew up with and how had eleven years of continuing recession in the North West affected their lives? Secondly, I wanted to look at the sex industry, in prostitution in particular, and in the process that led to women becoming prostitutes. Thirdly, I wanted to write about a tough, fighting, well-hard, working-class girl. And finally, I wanted to write about love.

I sat down to write and the story just flowed out. By the end of my eight-week residency I had finished my first draft. And I felt better about it than anything I had ever written. Not only had I been able to pour my heart out, I had been helped along the way by Winsome's advice. Having somebody to discuss my play and help me shape it at such an early stage meant that my first draft was more like a second draft. I had saved myself a lot of lonely explorative work, wondering which direction to go in, wondering whether my instincts were right.

Of course that wasn't it. I've rewritten *Somewhere* at least twice since then and I expect I'll find yet more things to consider before its production at the Liverpool Playhouse and at the National in 1993. Last year *Somewhere* was workshopped at the National Studio. A group of actors, a brilliant director, a designer, stage manager and myself got together for three weeks to explore the text. Again I was able to learn a lot about the play and have a good look at how my ideas worked when tested in the arena for which they were intended. The live, 'workshopped' version was performed twice to invited audiences. The response was very positive. I hope that your response to the written version is the same.

Judith Johnson
January, 1993

Judith Johnson has been writing since 1987 when her first full length play, *Working Away*, won the Second Wave Young Women's Writing Festival at the Albany Empire (produced at the Soho Poly, 1989). Her one act play, *The Edge*, toured community venues during the East End Festival, 1988, and she was then commissioned by Tower Hamlets Arts Project to work with a Young Women's Drama Group on the Isle of Dogs. This collaboration produced *Le Camp*, which also toured in the East End. Her radio play, *Swiftlines and Sweetdreams*, was short-listed for the LBC/Crown FM 1990 London Radio Playwrights competition and she was commissioned by the Liverpool Everyman Theatre to devise and script *Death Party* with members of its "Acting Up" course (theatre training for unemployed 16–21 year olds). During this time she completed work on *Nowheresville* which was later shortlisted for the Verity Bargate Award 1991. She wrote *The Scrappie* for Red Ladder Theatre Company, which toured nationally in youth clubs (Spring 1991) and was also commissioned by the National's Education Department and Studio (where she completed an 8-week residency, Summer 1991). Her play *Los Escombros* (written for the National's Young People's Theatre Group) was performed in the Cottesloe in March 1992. Her radio play, *Octopus Boys* was broadcast on Radio 5 in January 1993.

East from the Gantry

Edward Thomas

East from the Gantry was first performed at Tramway, Glasgow on 10 October 1992, with the following cast:

Ronnie
Wymff
Mr Bratton   } Boyd Clack
Clint

Bella
Donna   } Ri Richards

Trampas
Martin Bratton   } Richard Lynch

Directed by Edward Thomas
Songs written by Boyd Clack and Clive Trevelyan.
Music written and performed by Gareth Whittock.

Setting and style

A hanging window frame and three door frames may suggest the interior/ exterior of a house. A disparate jumble of objects and memorabilia clutter the set underlying the fragile and dislocated nature of the play, its characters, their identities and memories. These may include photographs, fridge, chairs, table, train seat, food cartons, Christmas tree, TV, video, vacuum cleaner, pots, pans, arms, legs, knives, forks, rotting vegetables or whatever objects have a relevance to the actors performing the play.

At the beginning, most of these objects may be covered in white sheets and then uncovered during the performance suggesting the slow reclaiming of memory and self. They may also be re-arranged and re-organized. Perhaps a clothes rail can hang the various characters' costumes where they may change in front of a mirror in view of the audience or may not. If possible the 1942 film *The Silent Village*, directed by Humphrey Jennings for the Crown Film Unit, may be projected or seen on the TV. There may be sounds which can be heard during the play which suggest a strange, incomprehensible world outside and a playing style which suggests we are only party to some of the characters' fears, loves and memories. It is a play of possibilities where anything is possible.

Dean Martin's Memories *may play as* **Bella** *enters throwing bits of paper from her bag.* **Trampas** *watches her from the shadows before exiting.* **Ronnie** *enters with a gun.*

Ronnie   Bella.

She ignores him.

Bella.

She continues to ignore him.

Be-la!

Silence. She stops.

Bella   Can't you see I'm thinking.

Ronnie   With paper?

Bella   My mind is scrambled, my thoughts are scattered, my brain is fragmented to fuck.

Ronnie   That's because you're drunk.

Bella (*throwing paper at him*)   I am not fucking DRUNK, RON.

Ronnie   Don't you throw paper at me.

Bella   It's my paper.

Ronnie   How do I know that?

Bella   Look for yourself.

Ronnie   I'm not going to get down on my hands and knees to do that.

Bella   Here then, look, have one from my bag.

Ronnie *takes it, looks at it.*

Ronnie   This isn't mine.

Bella   Exactly.

Ronnie   Who's handwriting is this?

Bella   What?

Ronnie   This isn't yours, Bella.

Bella   It is.

Ronnie   It's not. Your handwriting slopes backwards.

Bella   Let me see.

Ronnie   It says 'I love . . .' Who the fuck's been writing you love letters, Bella?

Bella   You don't think . . .?

Ronnie   You could have . . .

Bella   Oh come on.

Ronnie   You're capable of anything when you're drunk.

Bella   I'm not drunk, Ronnie, smell my breath.

Ronnie   Pooh . . . whiskey.

Bella   Bollocks. It's definitely not whiskey, you know I don't drink whiskey.

Ronnie   Rum then, rum, it's definitely rum.

Bella   I had a tipple that's all.

Ronnie   You're drunk, Bella.

Bella   No way.

Ronnie   Prove it.

Bella   I'm not going to prove it to you. Why should I?

Ronnie   Here we go again, looking to start something, bit of a bundle, a shot in the dark.

Bella   You are deliberately provoking me.

Ronnie   Walk the line.

Bella   What?

Ronnie   If you're not fucking drunk, fucking walk.

Bella   You bastard, I . . .

Ronnie   THE LINE, THE LINE. WALK THE LINE!

Bella   What line?

Ronnie   That line over there will do.

Bella   I don't see it.

Ronnie   It's covered in crap, that's why.

Bella   It's your crap.

Ronnie   You put it there.

Bella   I was tidying up, that's all.

Ronnie   Is that what you call it?

Bella   Yes. I tidy as much as you.

Ronnie   Crap.

Bella   I defrosted the fridge, Ronnie.

Ronnie   I did it both times before that.

Bella   Impossible. We haven't had it that long.

Ronnie   It didn't defrost by itself, Bella.

Bella   I know.

Ronnie   So what are you saying?

Bella   I'm saying it's come to something when a man asks his wife to walk one fucking line for him.

Ronnie   It's a point of principle, Bella.

Bella   I will not walk the line, Ron.

Ronnie   Not ever?

Bella   No.

Ronnie   Not even in the interests of truth?

Bella   Not in this case, no.

Ronnie   This is very disappointing Bella, truth is the cornerstone of marriage.

Bella   I'm telling you truthfully, that I am not drunk, Ron.

Ronnie   I'd like to believe you but I'm afraid I just can't, Bella.

Bella   This is sad, Ron, this is really sad.

Both of them looking into the wilderness.

Ronnie   I know.

Bella   You realise what this could mean?

Pause.

Ronnie   I do.

Fade in the music of the TV series Mastermind *as the lights change.* **Ronnie** *exits and* **Trampas** *enters. As the music fades* **Trampas** *uncovers a black leather chair, identical to the one used in the TV series. The lights develop into two pools, one for* **Bella** *and one for* **Trampas**. *He sits in a chair. She sits behind a desk which she newly uncovers.*

Trampas   It was a Sunday night.

Bella   I see.

Trampas   There'd been some flooding down the valley, Uncle Jim had gone to see the damage for himself.

Bella   I don't think I know Uncle Jim.

Trampas   No?

Bella   No.

Trampas   Liked disasters he did. My mother told me not to be too hard on him because of the trauma he suffered as a boy. She was still in her cot when it happened, Uncle Jim was ten and my Uncle Ieu was fourteen.

Bella   Fourteen is a difficult age.

Trampas   My grandmother was making breakfast when Ieu picked up a loaded shotgun and shot her dead with both barrels.

Bella   No.

Trampas   Yes. It was an accident, he didn't know it was loaded, but it affected him and Uncle Jim, they were never the same again.

Bella   That's terrible.

Trampas   When he was out watching the valley flood, my mother turned to me just as Fred Housego, the taxi driver, was winning *Mastermind*.

'Can I let you into a secret?' she said.

And I said 'Sure thing ma, what's on your mind?'

'I'm in love with him' she said.

'With Fred Housego?' I said.

'No', she said, 'with Magnus Magnusson.'

Bella   Get away.

Trampas   It's the truth, she said she'd written him hundreds of letters.

Bella   Did he ever reply?

Trampas   Not personally, no, just a note from his office saying best wishes and a signed photo. She was very disappointed.

Bella   I can imagine.

Trampas   She was gutted.

Bella   I bet.

Trampas   She always thought she'd meet him somewhere see, perhaps share a drink in front of the fire, chew the cud. She thought Magnus would have told her fantastic tales of old Iceland long into the night.

Bella   She sounds a very nice person.

Trampas   She was. She got me to hire a sailing boat once, with a European skipper to take us to Iceland but we got lost in heavy fog off the Scottish coast and had to turn back.

Bella   That's a pity.

Trampas   I suppose it is.

Bella   They say Reykjavik's a really interesting place.

Trampas   Really?

Bella   Yes.

Trampas   Have you ever been there?

Bella   No. I just read about it once.

Trampas   Oh.

Pause.

She died not long after that, on the same day I saw Telly Savalas window shopping in the city.

Fade in music, lights change, **Ronnie** *enters in dark glasses and a hat with a lollipop in his mouth.*

Trampas   I was on a bus stuck in traffic, just staring out of the window when bingo, there he was, bald head, dark glasses, lollipop in his mouth, dark trousers and canary yellow shoes. I jumped out of my seat, taking a pen and an unpaid gas bill out of my pocket for an autograph and ran downstairs. I had to move fast, Telly was making his way to a smart black limo parked on double-yellows with a chauffeur holding on to the door. With my eyes fixed firmly on my prize, I stepped off the bus and smash, collided with an Australian cycle messenger, overtaking on the inside, who knocked me senseless to the floor.

Ronnie *exits*

Bella   And Telly?

Trampas   By the time I came round, Telly, the cyclist and everyone else was gone. When I got back to Johnny Greco's I got a phone call from Uncle Jim, saying I had to come home straight away because my mother wasn't well. 'But I've just seen Telly Savalas in the street', I said.

'Did you get his autograph?' asked Uncle Jim.

'No,' I said, 'I . . .', but before I had time to explain, Uncle Jim called me a stupid git and put down the phone and that was that.

Bella   How insensitive can you get.

Trampas   Exactly, I was gutted, when I got home I found Uncle Jim sitting with Mam looking sheepish. She was looking up at the ceiling with a Turkish delight on her chest, Uncle Jim said she'd been dead for two hours, but it was very peaceful.

Bella   It must have been a shock.

Trampas   It was.

Pause.

I loved her, I really loved her.

Trampas *begins to break down:* **Bella** *rummages around in her bag. She pulls out an apple and offers it to him.*

Bella   I'm sorry.

Trampas   Forget it.

Fade in music as **Trampas** *uncovers a photograph of his mother from under a sheet, then slowly disappears into the shadows.* **Ronnie** *enters suddenly.*

Ronnie   Have you got an apple?

Bella   An apple? What for?

Ronnie   To place on my head, after which you can take my shotgun, stand twelve paces away and shoot.

Bella   Shoot what?

Ronnie   The apple, woman, the apple.

Bella   And if I miss?

Ronnie   Then it proves you are drunk.

Bella   But . . .

Ronnie   No buts, Bella, this is important.

Bella   You are prepared to risk your life in order to prove to me I'm not drunk?

Ronnie   Yes.

Bella   Then I'm sorry.

Ronnie   For what?

Bella   I won't do it.

Ronnie   You must, Bella, you must.

Bella   I have only had one shot of rum, Ron, now why won't you believe me?

Ronnie   Because, Bella, I am after a higher truth.

Bella (*aiming gun at him*)   But I'm a lousy shot.

Ronnie   It's something I've already taken into account, Bella, but I think your love for me will bring you through.

Bella Love doesn't always shoot straight, Ronnie, look what happened to William Burroughs.

Ronnie Will you please not mention William Burroughs when you're contemplating shooting an apple off your spouse's head?

Bella But it's extremely relevant to the case, Ron.

Ronnie (*angry*) William Burroughs was drunk, doped and crazy when he tried it and so by all accounts was his wife, now either confirm that you are as well or continue with the test.

Bella I am neither drunk, doped or crazy and you know it.

Ronnie Then let's hope you won't William Burroughs me, now fetch me an apple while I get the gun.

Bella *laughs*.

Bella There's no apple.

Ronnie What?

Bella There's no apple, Ron.

Ronnie I don't believe you, Bella, you always carry apples in your bag. You have a well documented phobia of dentists.

Bella I ate my last one only this morning. We need to go into town to get more supplies.

Ronnie Show me your bag.

Bella I can't.

Ronnie You must.

Bella Impossible.

Ronnie Don't get obstinate with me, Bella, this is no time for obstinacy, now pass me your bag.

Bella No you can't. I don't want you looking in my bag, it's private.

Ronnie There are no secrets between a husband and a wife, Bella.

Bella I know, but this is a question of my preferring my independence, Ronnie.

Ronnie If your independence stands between me and your bag then God help this marriage that's what I say.

Bella You are missing the point altogether, Ronnie.

Ronnie Okay, okay, have it your way, fuck the apple, fuck truth.

Bella (*laughing*) Ronnie.

Ronnie   Fuck William Burroughs, fuck marriage, fuck trust, long live INDEPENDENCE. SHAG THE WORLD.

Bella   YOU ARE BEING COMPLETELY IRRATIONAL.

Ronnie   I don't know what else to say, Bella, but I'm gutted, you hear me, gutted. I've worked hard at our relationship as you well know, fraught as it's been with difficulties from the beginning. I have struggled to keep house and home together, endeavoured to keep our waning spirits high, while all you can do is stare at ceilings, rip up paper, deny me your most intimate secrets and fucking drink yourself stupid.

Bella   So would you if you had been married to a trigger happy has-been, who, if he isn't sitting in a corner, is basically blowing the brains out of neighbouring townsfolk's domestic pets.

Ronnie   (*uncovering a dead cat from the bag*)   I never meant to shoot that cat Bella, it was an accident, I . . .

Sudden sound of a ringing phone, fade in music as the lights change. **Ronnie** *and* **Bella** *look warily around them.*

Ronnie   It's the phone

Bella   I know.

Ronnie   Are you expecting a call?

Bella   No. Are you?

Ronnie   No.

Pause.

Bella   I think we should answer it.

Ronnie   No.

Bella   Why not?

Ronnie   It might be a crazy bastard. I hate crazy bastards.

Bella   You're a crazy bastard.

Ronnie   You think so.

Bella   I do.

Ronnie   That's interesting.

Pause.

Bella   I'm going to answer it.

Ronnie   No, let me, it may be obscene.

Bella   So.

Ronnie   I don't want you taking obscene calls, remember your pain is my pain, your perversion my perversion.

Bella   I'm a grown woman, I can handle it.

Ronnie   No.

Bella *picks up the phone quickly. Music fades.*

Bella   Hello?

Pause.

Did we order a pizza?

Ronnie   A pizza?

Bella   A dish of Italian origin consisting of a baked disc of dough covered with cheese and tomatoes, usually with the addition of mushroom, anchovies, sausage or ham.

Ronnie   No.

Bella   This woman says we did.

Ronnie (*victorious*)   We can't have. You know I hate anchovies.

Bella   You don't hate anchovies.

Ronnie   I do, ever since I had a sea food platter in Sorrento.

Bella   Sorrento?

Ronnie   A port in South West Italy between the Bay of Naples and the gulf of Palermo, we spent our honeymoon there.

Ronnie *grabs* **Bella** *and starts to dance, after uncovering a postcard of Sorrento.*

Bella   We went to Sorrento on our honeymoon?

Ronnie   Of course we did, Bella, we stayed in the Settimo Cielo! They double-booked. We spent our first night in a windowless room hewn from the rock, next to an Italian couple with a wailing child.

Bella   Ricardo!

Ronnie   That's the one.

Bella   And that's the last time you ate an anchovy?

Ronnie   Yes.

Bella   Jesus.

Ronnie   Tell her we'll have the pizza with artichoke instead of anchovy.

Bella   Hello? Yes we'll have a thin crust ten-inch pizza with artichoke instead of anchovy.

Pause.

No artichoke.

Ronnie   No artichoke? What sort of pizza joint is this.

Bella   Don't argue Ronnie, what else do you want with it?

Ronnie   Tell her we'll have pepperoni.

Bella   Pepperoni? Good . . . how long will it be? Good.

Pause

Do you want garlic bread with it?

Ronnie   No, do you?

Bella   No, soft drink?

Ronnie   Two soft drinks.

Bella   We'll have two soft drinks, thanks.

She puts the phone down.

Ronnie   I don't remember ordering a pizza do you?

Bella   No.

Ronnie   That's strange.

Bella   It is, but I suppose it's a strange and weird world out there, Ronnie.

Ronnie   I know.

Fade in music of the sixties western series The Virginian *as* **Ronnie** *exits and* **Trampas** *enters.* **Bella** *is rummaging around in a blood-spattered fridge. Music fades.*

Bella   My name is Bella.

Trampas   Pleased to meet you Bella.

Bella   And you?

Trampas   Trampas.

Bella   That's a funny name.

Trampas   From *The Virginian*.

Bella   The Western series?

Trampas   Yeah.

Bella   Six fifty-five till eight on a Friday night?

Trampas   Bingo.

Bella   Me and my brother used to watch that regular.

Trampas   So did I.

Bella   Instead of *Bonanza*.

Trampas   I never watched *Bonanza*. Not when *The Virginian* was on.

Bella   I suppose not.

Trampas   Trampas had a brown horse with a white patch.

Bella   Trampas was a drifter.

Trampas   Trampas was a good cowboy, ma'am.

Bella   You called me ma'am.

Trampas   Pardon me?

Bella   Ma'am. You said ma'am.

Trampas   Did I?

Bella   Yes.

Trampas   I'm sorry.

Bella   I'm no ma'am, mister.

Trampas   No, I know, it slipped out. What I mean is I didn't mean to . . . I
. . . it was a mistake. It's been a long time.

Bella   What has?

Trampas   I'm sorry.

Bella   It's a funny thing to say.

Trampas   I know.

Bella   In a derelict house.

Trampas   Yes.

Bella   In the middle of winter.

Trampas   Yes. I'm an idiot.

Bella   It's strange.

Trampas   Need my head read.

Bella   Weird even.

Trampas   I don't know what came over me.

Bella   Because I mean, it's not as if we were in Wyoming, is it?

Trampas   No.

Bella   Or Idaho.

Trampas   No.

Bella   Or Iowa.

Trampas   Dakota.

Bella   Minnesota.

Trampas   Utah.

Bella   Or any other mid-Western American State.

Trampas   Exactly.

Bella   We're in Southern Powys.

Fade in music, low level, suggesting slow discovery.

Trampas   Yes.

Bella   In Wales.

Trampas   Yes, Wales.

Bella   A country.

Trampas   On the west coast of Great Britain.

Bella   Conquered in 1282.

Trampas   Is it really that long ago?

Bella   It certainly is.

Trampas   Wow.

Bella   Its economy is mainly agricultural.

Trampas   Mainly, yes, but with an old industrial area down here in the south.

Bella   Yes.

Trampas   And old quarries and stuff in the north.

Bella   With holiday destinations.

Trampas   And holiday-makers.

Bella   Places to eat.

Trampas   Yeah? Eat what?

Pause.

Bella   (*hesitant*)   New season lamb on a Sunday with mint sauce, buttered new potatoes, honey-glazed carrots . . .

Trampas   . . . Cut into rings not strips!

Bella   With cabbage and a little gravy followed by . . .

Trampas   . . . Home-made rice pudding with the skin on top!

They laugh.

Bella   Afterwards we sit down together with coffee and chocolates.

Trampas   Yees!

Bella   Sometimes on summer afternoons, we go west as a family with children, parents and grandchildren in search of an afternoon tea, hoping to find a secluded farm house free of the Lambrettas and two strokes which our youths use to express their manly development.

Trampas   I never express my manly development with a Lambretta, ma'am.

Bella   Please don't call me Ma'am.

Trampas   I'm sorry.

Bella   Forget it.

Pause. They both look out the window.

Plenty of space here see, mister.

Trampas   There is.

Bella   I can see for miles.

Trampas   Could be a good place in the right hands.

Bella (*uncovering a pair of severed hands from her bag*)   I suppose you're right, but it's the hands you got to be choosy about.

Trampas   You're right. No point in having all this space if there's no hands to do something about it.

Bella   No.

Trampas   Do you know whose they are?

Bella   I did once.

Trampas   Oh . . .

Pause.

Bella   With these hands . . .

Trampas   I will sing to you.

Bella   TOM JONES.

Trampas   A legend.

Bella   I used to think so but not any more.

Trampas   Why's that?

Bella   I threw a pair of my best French underwear at him in a concert in Swansea but he never noticed.

Trampas   No.

Bella   Yes.

Trampas   That's a shame.

Bella   That's what I thought. I'm sorry I didn't throw him a pair of cheap ordinary ones now.

Trampas   Or not bothered at all.

Bella   Exactly. It affected me badly that did. Made me lose a lot of self-confidence.

Trampas   Superstars, even legends can be so thoughtless sometimes, so unpredictable.

Bella   I know. It was only a few days after that that I met my husband, Ronnie.

Fade in guitar. Lights change, **Trampas** *exits.* **Bella** *looks at herself in the mirror. During the next speech* **Trampas** *re-enters wrapped in a blood-stained sheet.*

Bella   It was a Saturday afternoon. It was raining. I was watching greyhounds chase a fake rabbit round a track in the name of sport on TV. I'd just had a bath. I felt warm and good. I felt horny. I dreamt I was in a hotel room with Martin Bratton in a large bed, champagne, sex, heat. He was stroking my breasts with long delicate fingers and kissing the back of my neck. I could feel the heat from the inside of his thigh and his breathing heavy. I wanted to fuck him there and then, on the bed, on the floor, on a chair, crazy, biting, clawing his back, making me come, again and again and again.

Pause. **Trampas** *exits.*

But I was alone in my room, with the rain and the greyhounds, the fake bunnies and a phone. I picked up the phone book and flicked through the pages. I picked a number, any number at random. I lit a cigarette, and dialled.

Ronnie *walks to another part of the stage and continues.*

Ronnie   I had some money on the 3.40 race, *Brief Encounter*; he came fourth after leading for three-quarters of the race. I felt empty and cheated, my mother said I was a fool for wasting my money. I was about to take her up on this when the phone rang. I don't know why but I decided to answer it upstairs.

Ronnie (*on phone*)   278063 . . . hello?

Bella   Can you say that again?

Ronnie   Sorry?

Bella   What's the number again?

Ronnie   What number do you want?

Bella   278063.

Ronnie   This is 278063, who's calling?

Pause.

Hello?

Bella   Bella, my name is Bella.

Ronnie   Bella.

Bella   Bella . . . Who am I speaking to?

Ronnie   My name is Ron, Ron John, but most people call me Scon.

Bella   Scon.

Ronnie   Yes, Scon, plain Scon.

Bella   Growing up around here as a plain Scon can't have been easy.

Ronnie   No, no, it wasn't, if you don't mind I'd rather you called me Ronnie.

Bella   Ronnie?

Ronnie   Yes. Ronnie.

Bella   I've just come in, I've been shopping. There was a note on the table by the phone with this number on it. It said that I should ring it.

Ronnie   I haven't spoken to anyone today. I'm sure I haven't . . . there must be a mistake.

Bella   Do you think so?

Ronnie   Probably didn't write the right number down.

Bella   Yes . . . yes . . . that's probably it . . . well I'm sorry to bother you. I didn't mean to take up your time.

Ronnie   Don't worry . . . it's just a mistake.

Bella   I . . .

Ronnie   Can I ask you a question, please?

Bella   If you like.

Ronnie   Are you . . . dressed?

Pause.

I'm sorry.

Bella   I didn't hear what you said.

Ronnie   Oh.

Pause.

I asked . . . if you had . . . any clothes on.

Pause.

Bella?

Bella   Yes, I have some, yes.

Ronnie   What exactly?

Bella   I'm wearing a black silk robe.

Pause.

Ronnie   Yes . . .

Bella   And some underwear.

Pause.

Ronnie   What kind of underwear?

Pause.

Bella?

Bella   Yes . . .?

Ronnie   What kind of underwear?

Bella   French . . .

Ronnie   French?

Bella   Yes, French . . . do you like French, Ronnie?

Pause.

Ronnie?

Ronnie   I love it, Bella, God I love it.

Bella *laughs.*

Bella   What are you wearing, Ronnie?

Ronnie   Me?

Bella   Yes.

Ronnie   Oh . . . (*looking at his filthy vest*) I'm . . . uh . . . wearing . . . a smoking jacket, just my old smoking jacket.

Bella   That's nice.

Ronnie   Yes . . . um . . . Bella?

Bella   Yes.

Ronnie   Could we meet somewhere?

Pause.

What I mean is . . . I have so much to say, I . . .

Pause.

I could love you, Bella.

Bella   Really, Ron?

Ronnie   Really, Bella.

Fade in music as **Ron** *begins to sing the following song, aided on the chorus by* **Bella***, as they uncover objects from under sheets, referring to the song. These may include photographs, a Christmas Tree, presents, etc.* **Trampas** *enters and turns on the TV set. He settles down to watch* A Silent Village. *This whole action should have a fragile, simply choreographed feel to it.*

Hate Street

I spoke to you on the phone last night after all these years.
And you asked me if I was alright and the years just disappeared.
And it was as if no time had passed and we were sitting once again.
In that room, where nothing seemed to last, listening to the rain.
And we were reading different books when you said you realised
That we had, for quite some time been leading separate lives
The clock was ticking loudly like an unexploded bomb
And I saw then for the first time that your love for me had gone.

I spoke to you on the phone last night and it seemed just like a dream.
Your voice was beautiful and light and it entered into me.
And we talked about how young we were, almost children when we met.
How we used to cling together in the darkness as we slept.
And we were playing 'Tell the Truth' when you looked at me and said.
That what we had was yesterday and what we had was dead.
The T.V. screen was flashing. I looked but could not see.
I sat there in the dying light as it washed all over me.

Chorus

Please don't walk away from me, I want to see your face.
I want to touch your body and I want to share your fate.
The shadows are all falling, I don't want to be alone.
I called around to see you, babe, but you were not at home.

Snow falls on Ynyscedwyn Road, it is written in the stars.
We kiss beneath the mistletoe in the House of Cards.
We kiss beneath the mistletoe by the light of Christmas trees.
By the dying light of innocence in the nineteen-seventies.
Then the miracle was happening and love was all aflame.
And the smoke rose up like angels and the Holy Spirit came.
And we laughed there in the darkness at the stars all peeping through.
It was twilight down on Hate Street, there was nothing we could do.

Chorus.

As the song ends, **Ronnie** *fades into the background and* **Bella** *looks at a bleeding heart in the fridge, closely watched by* **Trampas**.

Trampas   I was in love once.

Bella   Really?

Trampas   Yes. I met her on a busy city street three years last July. She was carrying groceries piled up to here. She couldn't see where she was going. I was on the other side of the street just coming out of the chemist's with a powerful concoction for curing cold sores when she stepped into the road and collided with an elderly cyclist who suffered a heart attack.

Bella   No.

Trampas   Yes. He never recovered and died on the spot leaving her with a badly twisted ankle that kept her off work for a week.

Bella   Was she compensated?

Trampas   No but the surviving family suggested she keep the bike.

Bella   That's nice.

Trampas   When the commotion was over I took her to a cafe for a coffee and a fine Danish pastry, which was a great stroke of luck because it's through pastries that she connects with her roots.

Bella   I don't follow you.

Trampas   Her grandfather came from Copenhagen.

Bella   Ah.

Trampas   Money was no problem to him either. He once paid for us to go on an exotic holiday in the tropics.

Bella   How lovely. They say the tropics are stunningly beautiful.

Trampas   They are, they are, do you know I once saw a manta a foot under the water twice the size of my duvet?

Bella   How big is your duvet?

Trampas That's a leading question.

Bella Size isn't everything, Trampas.

Trampas No, but it nevertheless is a very big duvet. A passing stranger with the flimsiest knowledge of duvets could tell you that.

Bella Are you saying you'd invite a passing stranger into your bedroom alone, to estimate the size of your duvet?

Trampas Why not?

Bella Because of the safety aspect.

Trampas A drifter is always reckless, Bella.

Bella That's as maybe, but in this day and age.

Trampas I harbour no grudge against the day but I'm not fond of our age.

Bella I agree with you. It is a most difficult one.

Trampas Especially for love.

Bella Love is strange, Trampas.

Trampas You can say that again.

Bella Love is a mystery too.

Trampas Love is a short-tempered baker and a Danish pastry, Bella.

Bella I'm sorry?

Trampas My love went away with a baker, Royston, a swarthy man with a short temper. I never know to this day what she saw in him.

Bella Some Danish girls like the swarthy short-tempered baker type, I suppose.

Trampas He had a windfall, won a lot of money on the pools. He was in a syndicate.

Bella They say it's the only way to win the pools.

Trampas But do you know what I think is odd, weird even, is that he never, as far as I know, ever wore a moustache.

Bella Do you think a moustache would have made a difference?

Trampas Definitely. She loved a moustache on a man, Bella.

Bella Really?

Trampas Yes. She was in love with Burt Reynolds.

Bella No kidding?

Trampas   That's why I grew one.

Bella   To make her fall in love with you.

Trampas   Exactly and pretend I was the man himself.

Bella   Did it work?

Trampas   What do you think?

Bella   It's hard to say, you haven't got a moustache.

Trampas   Yes, but you can imagine me with one.

He puts on a false moustache.

Bella   Yes, yes, I suppose you do look a bit like Burt Reynolds.

Trampas   His spitting image, I reckon.

Bella   But it didn't make any difference, did it?

Trampas   No. She ran away with Royston without so much as a note.

Bella   That's tough.

Trampas   It sure is.

Bella   And now?

Trampas   Now?

Bella   Is there anyone on the horizon?

Trampas   For me there is no horizon, man, only the indistinct meeting of the sea and sky.

Bella   That's sad Trampas, that's really sad.

Fade in Nina Simone's 'Everything Changes' *as* **Trampas** *starts to undress in front of the mirror. He is leaving his* **Trampas** *gear behind him for a different identity.*
Bella *throws paper from her bag in the air going round in circles as* **Ronnie** *takes centre stage holding a red shoe. The music plays softly underneath.*

Ronnie   I still love you Bella.

Bella   Really, Ron?

Ronnie   Really, Bella.

Bella   Since when?

Ronnie   The day I saw you walk naked into the river apart from your shoes, Bella. That was a hot day.

Ronnie   It was a lovely day.

Bella   It was a summer's day.

Ronnie   I loved you then, Bella.

Bella   The river stones hurt my feet.

Ronnie   Your breasts were heavy and white.

Bella   I needed a holiday.

Ronnie   Your nipples were hard.

Bella   The river was cold.

Ronnie   You let your hair down over your shoulders.

Bella   I'd forgotten to wash it, it needed a wash.

Ronnie   I watched you swim.

Bella   You should have come in.

Ronnie   I couldn't swim.

Bella   But you can now.

Ronnie   I couldn't then and we are talking about then . . .

Bella   I could have fucked you then.

Ronnie   And now?

Bella   With my shoes on.

Ronnie   Bella?

Bella   In the river.

Ronnie   Bella.

Bella   With my hardened nipples and heavy breasts.

Ronnie   BELLA! You are not listening to me!

Bella   You were afraid.

Ronnie   I wasn't.

Bella   Of me.

Ronnie   Of water.

Bella   You should have come in.

Ronnie   I paddled, you saw me paddle.

Bella   I did but I was already out on the other side.

Ronnie   You could have come back.

Bella   I was breathless.

Ronnie   We were supposed to be together.

Bella   The water parted us.

Ronnie   It was only a river.

Bella   Perhaps a symbol.

Ronnie   The river? Of what?

Bella   Who knows?

Ronnie   Don't talk shit.

Bella   I am not talking shit.

Ronnie   Everything's a symbol according to you.

Bella   Perhaps everything is.

Ronnie   But what if everything isn't?

Bella   Then I would have made a mistake.

Ronnie   So then what would you say?

Bella   I'd say I'd ruined my shoes for a swim in a meaningless river for which you call me a fool and we sit on the bank a few minutes later eating a picnic in silence and drinking.

Ronnie   Champagne.

Bella   What?

Ronnie   I bought champagne that day, I remember going up to the counter with the bottle asking for fags when . . .

Bella   What?

Ronnie   There was a snag.

Bella   A hitch?

Ronnie   A balls-up.

Bella   How typical.

Ronnie   I only left my wallet in the suitcase, Bella.

Bella (*she slowly exits, leaving* **Ronnie** *alone*)   So there was no champagne.

Ronnie   Not quite. I found a tenner in my top left-hand pocket. I must have left it there the day I got pissed on international day; we lost 12:10. Alastair McHarg broke his ribs, a bloke standing next to me fell over and broke his ankle bad, it was a compound fracture, the same kind of fracture Ian Hall had during our midweek defeat by the All Blacks in 1974 when Ian Kirkpatrick picked the ball up at the base of the scrum, ran straight for a try past Phil Bennet under the posts.

Pause.

The crowd went quiet, Bella, I've never heard such a silent crowd. It was AS IF THERE WAS NO ONE THERE.

Ronnie *looks around realizing that* **Bella** *has gone. Fade in the sound of a loud express train passing which drowns out* **Ronnie**'*s cries.*

Ronnie   BELLA, BELLA, BELLA!

Ronnie *exits. Enter* **Trampas** *stripped to the waist, splattered in blood and bandaged around the wrists.* **Bella** *watches him as the train noise fades away.*

Trampas   The iron horse from the city moves relentlessly over the snowy plains of a silent country.

Bella   That's nice, Trampas.

Trampas   Do you like it?

Bella   Yes, you should have been a poet.

Trampas   I was once, but I suffered a terrible bout of existential nausea.

Bella   The curse of the sensitive soul.

Trampas   I wasn't that sensitive, Bella, I once starved a minah bird to death for quoting Albert Camus.

Bella   The novelist.

Trampas   Yes. If only he'd kept his gob shut, he'd still be tweeting today.

Bella   Albert Camus?

Trampas   No, Bella, the minah bird

Bella   Of course, I'm sorry, how stupid of me.

Trampas   Forget it.

Bella   Really?

Trampas   Really.

Bella   Thanks.

Pause.

Trampas   I was in the city then. I thought I could be someone.

Bella   I used to go to the city a lot at one time too.

Trampas   Really?

Bella   Yes.

Trampas   To work?

Bella   No, just to have a look, drive around, go to the airport.

Pause.

Did you ever go to the airport, Trampas?

Trampas   Yeah, but I've never flown.

Bella   I could have flown once but I turned down the offer.

Trampas   That's a shame.

Bella   I suppose it is.

*Fade in aeroplane noise. They both look up at the sky. Lights change. During **Bella***'s
*speech mix in the various sounds that she describes and when the dialogue starts **Ronnie***
*uncovers a battered motorbike from under a sheet and becomes **Mr Bratton** while*
Trampas *plays* **Martin Bratton**.

Bella   It was a Wednesday night. I can remember it like yesterday. I was
seventeen. My father locked me in my room: he caught me smoking. My
mother brought me haddock with butter and pepper and vinegar. I never
touched it. I stared out of the window. I saw Mrs Leandro standing on her
doorstep rolling beads between her fingers, came over here after the war from
Spain, never spoke a word of the language or if she did she never spoke it to
me. They'd just turned the street lamps on, they were red turning orange. I
watched the drizzle fall to the sound of a bluebottle banging its head against
my window. Then suddenly it stopped.

The guitar fades out.

There was silence. Perfect silence. I went to the window, opened it and looked
out and knew straightaway that this was the night Martin Bratton would fly.

Fade in sound of rumble and drums and orchestral music low level.

I put on my shoes, climbed out of the window and jumped down into the street.
The place was deserted. I looked in through the downstairs window and saw my
mother knitting and my father asleep in the chair, the weather forecast filling in
the background with the hiss of the gas fire. I looked towards his house and
started running down the street, across the road, through the gate, up the path
and around to the back where I stopped. The back door was open. I went in.

Pause.

Ronnie *enters, dressed as* **Mr Bratton**, *covered in oil.*

Cabbage boiled on the cooker in the kitchen. In the hall, Mr Bratton was
fixing a motorbike. He was covered in oil. He hardly noticed me. I asked him
where Martin was but he didn't answer. He just said.

Mr Bratton   I got into motorbikes on the day Iris lost her marbles,
happened like that. One minute she was with us, next, well she took to keeping
ferrets. What else could I do?

Pause.

Bella I smiled and slid past him as he kick-started the machine and pulled away leaving a stream of oil and smoke behind him.

Pause.

I heard the sound of music from upstairs, I couldn't make it out It sounded like an old song. It reminded me of the days I went to Sunday school in a red velvet dress and red shoes.

Fade in Beth yw'r Haf i mi *at a low level evoking a remembrance of things past.*

Bella I climbed to the top of the stairs where I saw a photo of a man I never knew, a poster of a film I never saw and a bible lying face down next to a vase of plastic flowers. I knocked at Martin's door but there was no answer, so I turned the handle and walked inside.

Fade up the music louder as the lights change and **Trampas** *wrapped in a sheet covered in blood squats, laughing at* **Bella**.

Bella What's all the blood for?

Trampas I'm losing my innocence, coming of age. I'm either going to fly or fall from the sky with a crash.

Pause.

You can come with me if you want.

Bella I can't.

Trampas Why not?

Bella I'm a virgin and besides my mother's got some haddock waiting for me on the table.

Trampas *laughs.*

Trampas You'd better go home then before it gets cold.

Bella That's a cruel thing to say, Martin.

Trampas I can be as cruel as I want. I'm flying away.

Bella Nobody flies, Martin.

Trampas No?

Bella No.

Trampas Then watch this.

Trampas *throws the sheet into the air, to the sound of drums, when the sheet hits the floor, the music stops and there is the sound of wind.* **Bella** *walks to the window and looks out.*

Bella   I might have loved him. He could have been my friend.

Trampas   It's good to make friends, Bella. I had a friend once. Wymff his name was.

Bella   That's nice.

Trampas   We grew up together. We were like brothers. No one could ever separate Wymff and me. We were like that *(crossing his fingers)*. He taught me to hunt, handle a rifle, lay nightlines, he taught me his secrets too.

Bella   What kind of secrets?

Trampas   He told me that if he ever saw Ger Snake out alone on the Cribarth, he'd shoot him dead, no questions asked.

Bella   Really?

Trampas   Really.

Pause.

Trampas   Do you know Ger Snake?

Bella   No. I don't think so, no.

Trampas   You're lucky, Bella, Ger Snake is a bad egg. Wymff was due to go on holiday with his girlfriend, Sharon, to a caravan in Trecco Bay but a week before they went someone broke in and bust it all up. It was unusable!

Bella   Ger Snake.

Trampas   Exactly.

Bella   That's terrible.

Trampas   Ger Snake left town as soon as he knew Wymff was after him.

Bella   I bet.

Trampas   It's the only thing you can do with someone like Wymff after you. I can tell you, Wymff was as hard as nails. He was a miner. Miners are as hard as nails.

Bella   You can say that again.

Trampas   You know a few miners, do you?

Bella   I used to once. My father was one. I lived in a mining village, it's not there anymore, the mine I mean.

Trampas   No.

Bella   It's a shame it's died out, mining.

Trampas   It is.

Bella   It's a real shame.

Trampas   Miners used to bring down governments.

Bella   They did.

Trampas   There were thousands of them.

Bella   Yes.

Trampas   Pits all over the place.

Bella   And now there's none.

Trampas   None.

Bella   None.

Trampas   Just holes in the ground.

Bella   It's funny.

Trampas   It is.

Bella   Hard to believe.

Trampas   Yes.

Bella   But true.

Trampas   Yes. All true.

Pause.

Wymff had no choice but to go to the city. I went with him. We got a job in Johnny Greco's basement in the city centre. He ran a print shop there and a few other things. He used to call Wymff, the kid.

Bella   The kid.

Trampas   Yeah, the kid, from *The Hustler*, a Paul Newman film.

Bella   It was a good film.

Trampas   Wymff was a good kid.

Bella   I'm sure he was.

Trampas   Then one day, Wymff and Greco decided to call me Trampas.

Bella   Why?

Trampas   Because they said I had no home.

Fade in music, **Ronnie** *enters dressed as* **Wymff**. *Like* **Trampas** *he is covered in blood and stripped to the waist. He is a violent man. During the scene Bella switches on the TV to continue the film* A Silent Village. *The film plays right through to the end.*

Wymff   I've just been back home for the weekend to see Sharon.

Trampas   How is she?

Wymff Not too good.

Trampas Why?

Wymff We finished.

Trampas What for?

Wymff Because she said she didn't give a shit any more and she wanted to get out.

Trampas Come to the city?

Wymff Go somewhere else, anywhere, Spain, Russia, Brazil, even England.

Trampas Jesus.

Wymff She says Cwmgiedd is no longer there for her.

Trampas That's bollocks.

Wymff It isn't, Trampas.

Trampas What do you mean?

Wymff What I say. It's finished, changed, fucked off, no longer continues to be.

Trampas That's impossible. It's a village with over a hundred inhabitants, no pub but one post office, a butcher's shop, a chapel and a bridge over a canal leading into it. They even made a film there, Wymff.

Wymff So?

Trampas In the war. 1942. *Silent Village*, they called it. They used local people in it. My father was in it and my grandfather and yours. It was a fucking good film, Wymff.

Wymff That's good. At least it will have something to remember it by.

Trampas Uh?

Wymff It's gone, you go and have a look for yourself. They've changed the canal into a long straight road.

Trampas What?

Wymff Shinkin's butcher's shop's, an old folks' home, and the school's now a place you can buy DIY and cheap furniture of a Sunday.

Trampas Fuck off.

Wymff Fuck off yourself.

Trampas It can't be true.

Wymff As true as I'm standing here.

Trampas   But I was part of the community, Wymff.

Wymff   No community, anymore, man.

Trampas   And you were too, and everybody else. It was a fucking good place.

Wymff   Don't get sentimental, Trampas.

Trampas   I'm not.

Wymff   Cwmgiedd ain't a village no more. It's become part of Ystrad. You go and have a look for yourself.

Trampas   I fucking hate Ystrad.

Wymff   People don't think of them as Cwmgiedd no more.

Trampas   Then who the fuck do they think they are?

Wymff   I don't know. Do you know who the fuck you are?

Trampas   No.

Wymff   So there we go.

Trampas   But neither do you.

Wymff   I know, but I don't care.

Trampas   I don't believe you.

Wymff   I know. You don't but it's true. You go back there, see for yourself, but I'm warning you, you won't like it.

Fade in music. **Wymff** *starts to sing. During the song,* **Trampas** *uncovers his memories of the village while* **Bella** *enters as a bride.* **Wymff** *continues to sing as* **Bella** *tears off her wedding dress and dresses as* **Donna,** *the pizza delivery girl.*

Talking About You and Me

First Verse

I'm not talking about the Sparkling Darkness
I'm not talking about the Strawberry Fields
I'm not talking about a Clockwork Orange
I'm not talking about a Tangerine Dream
I'm not talking about Jack the Ripper
I'm not talking about a Monkey on a Stick
I'm not talking about the Big Dipper
Though it frightened me and made me sick.

Chorus.

I'm just talking about you and me.

Second Verse

I'm not talking about the Glittering City
I'm not talking about the Sparkling Bridge
I'm not talking about Disfigurement
I'm not talking about the Violins
I'm not talking about the Smell of Rum and Coca Cola
I'm not talking about the Girl in the Pretty Dress
I'm not talking about the Twilight
Though it was a thing of loveliness.

Chorus.

Third Verse

I'm not talking about the Swimming Pool
I'm not talking about the Emotional Crush
I'm not talking about the Bandages
I'm not talking about the Shrine of Love
I'm not talking about the Wedding Dress
I'm not talking about the Moon and the Stars
I'm not talking about the Resurrection
Or the Diamonds or the Lilac stars.

Chorus.

Fourth Verse

I'm not talking about the Cult of Beauty
I'm not talking about the Tower Blocks
I'm not talking about evolution
I'm not talking about the Multi-Storey Car Park
I'm not talking about the Cabaret Show
I'm not talking about Narcotic Love on Dark Settees
I'm not talking about Fairy Lights in Cafe Windows
Ah but it looks so lovely

Chorus.

The song ends. **Trampas** *is angry.*

Trampas   I spread my mother's ashes there, man.

Wymff   For fuck's sake, Trampas, grow up will you.

Donna   Pizza for Jones.

Bella *dressed as* **Donna** *stands smiling with a pizza box in her hand.*

Trampas   Jesus Christ.

Trampas *walks aside disgustedly.*

Donna   Is he okay?

Wymff   Yeah, he's fine, he was just mulling over a few things he found upsetting.

Donna   I see.

Wymff   It was nothing to do with you.

Donna   Are you sure?

Wymff   Positive.

Donna   Because I did wonder.

Wymff   Wonder?

Donna   If he was unhappy about the pizza.

Wymff   No. I'm sure it will be fine.

Donna   You didn't talk him into it, then.

Wymff   Talk him into what?

Donna   The pizza. When he could have had a Chinese, or an Indian, a kebab, even fish and chips.

Wymff   No I assure you, I didn't talk him into anything, besides your pizza delivery service is the best in the area by all accounts.

Donna   Really?

Wymff   Really. It's common knowledge honestly.

Donna   This is really good to hear, Mr Jones.

Wymff   Wymff.

Donna   Wymff?

Wymff   Please call me Wymff.

Donna   Ah . . .

Wymff   Is that a problem?

Donna   No, not at all.

Wymff   Because, if it is I can get you some identification.

Donna   No, no, that's alright. I'll take your word for it.

Wymff   Thanks.

Donna   My name is Donna.

Wymff   Pleased to meet you Donna.

Donna   And you, Wymff.

Trampas   Are you talking about me?

Wymff   Course we're not, Trampas. I'm not having a private conversation with my friend Donna here.

Donna   Is your name really Trampas?

Trampas   Yes.

Donna   You were in *The Virginian*, weren't you.

Trampas   I was, yes.

Donna   Can I have your autograph?

Wymff   Donna . . . I . . .

Donna   In a minute, Wymff. It's not every day you meet a TV star.

Trampas   I'm not really a TV star, pizza delivery girl.

Donna   The name's Donna.

Trampas   I'm not really a TV star, Donna. I'm just a saddle-tramp looking for a home.

Donna   God, you're so wonderful.

Wymff   Donna, please I . . .

Donna   Who the hell is this guy?

Trampas   His name is Wymff, he ordered the pizza.

Donna   That'll be twelve-ninety.

Wymff   Ah.

Donna   Ah what.

Wymff   Mr Greco is the cashier in this place. You'll have to wait for him to come back.

Donna   Come back from where?

Wymff   Making coffee.

Trampas   He's been gone a long time, Wymff, aren't you worried about him?

Wymff   No, he'll be okay. He's probably making percolated coffee, it takes a long time to prepare.

Donna   I'd appreciate it, if you'd chivvy him along, Wymff. After all, time is money.

Wymff   Yes, but I . . .

Donna   We have got a business to run, Wymff.

Wymff   I'll see what I can do.

Donna   Thanks, I appreciate that.

Wymff *disgruntled, . . . exits to find* **Greco**.

Donna   He's a funny guy.

Trampas   He's okay. A little excitable but okay.

Donna   I suppose so.

Trampas   Everybody has their problems, Donna.

Donna   Yes, I know, but still.

Trampas   Still what?

Donna   Still waters run deep, Trampas.

Trampas   Do you think so?

Donna   I do. I once had a brother who fell into a river, he drowned. The water was deep, the river was still. I tried to save him but . . .

Trampas   But?

Donna   This is very difficult for me.

Trampas   I understand.

Donna   He was my own flesh and blood and I couldn't save him.

Trampas   Accidents happen, Donna, the world is cruel.

Donna   I turned the river red with the effort. I should have worn shoes. River stones hurt my feet. I cut my bare feet badly, my blood turned the river red.

Trampas   That's really symbolic.

Donna   Is it?

Trampas   It sure is.

Donna   Of what?

Trampas   A red river rising.

Donna   I suppose it is. I should have clocked it.

Trampas   Not one human alive is ever capable of clocking every symbol that arises, Donna.

Donna   No. I suppose not.

Trampas   So don't give yourself a hard time about it.

Donna   I'll try not to.

Trampas   You're a brave woman.

Donna   Thanks.

Trampas   Now. Do you want my autograph or not?

Donna   Yes, yes, of course I do.

Trampas   Have you got a pen?

Donna   Yes, but no paper.

Trampas   I could write on your arm.

Donna   I'll never wash again.

Trampas   You could always have a skin-graft.

Donna   Yes, yes, I suppose I could.

Trampas   You could preserve it in formaldehyde then frame it in a glass case.

Donna   That's exactly what I've done with my brother Clint's head.

Trampas   Really.

Donna   Yes. I got a taxidermist friend to add the final touches. It made all the difference. Mind you he wasn't cheap.

Trampas   Taxidermy is an expensive business these days.

Donna   I know, and a lot of people frown upon it.

Trampas   A lot of people frown upon a lot of things, Donna, it's the way things are.

Donna   Do you get frowned upon too, Tramp?

Trampas   I'm afraid I do. No one wants a saddle-tramp for a lover, Donna.

Donna   I didn't know you still were Tramp. You don't mind me calling you Tramp, do you?

Trampas   No. Life is short. Why shouldn't a man's name be abbreviated.

Donna   Shortening my name to Don gives me awful identity crises.

Trampas   Don's a different case altogether.

Donna   That's the way I look at it, Tramp.

Trampas   It's good to see eye to eye with you, Donna.

Donna   It is.

Pause.

Can I ask you a question?

Trampas   Sure.

Donna   Why aren't you on the TV any more. I miss you terribly and not only I miss you, a whole generation misses you, Trampas.

Trampas   I don't know. The producers just reckoned we'd gone past our sell-by date, that's all.

Donna   Producers are so short-sighted.

Trampas   I know, but what could I do?

Donna   You could have gone into feature films.

Trampas   I sort of did, I did a couple of Disney films then work sort of dried up.

Donna   So you no longer ride a horse.

Trampas   Nope. I got rid of my horse the other side of Trapp. He was a race-horse trainer who also took old horses for grazing.

Donna   That's really sad, Tramp.

Trampas   The world must go on Donna. I now travel by train.

Donna   The iron horse of the plains.

Trampas   That's the one.

Donna   But how do you earn a living in these parts, Trampas?

Trampas   I double in a few things, casual work moving from contract to contract.

Donna   What do you do mostly?

Trampas   Contract killing.

Donna   Wow!

Trampas   I kill people for a living, Donna.

Donna   Are you on a job at the moment, Tramp?

Trampas   I usually keep that sort of information to myself.

Donna   Yes, yes of course you do.

Trampas   It's confidential.

Donna   Absolutely.

Trampas   But I'll go so far as to say that I'm involved in a private investigation.

Donna   I understand. I won't say any more.

Trampas   But I'm also open to offers.

Donna   I don't think that I could afford the fee.

Trampas   The fee is negotiable, Donna.

Donna   Really?

Trampas   Yes.

Donna   What's your bottom price?

Trampas   Love.

Donna   Love?

Trampas   Love. I could kill for love, Donna.

Pause.

Donna   I think you've over-stepped the mark, Trampas.

Trampas   I'm sorry.

Donna   I don't mean to get heavy but I . . .

Trampas   I was only trying to make conversation, Donna, trying to relax, unwind, confront . . . my own situation.

Donna   I understand, Trampas.

Trampas   I'm a very lonely person, Donna.

Donna   I can see that.

Trampas   Loneliness shines out of every pore of my body. I . . .

Donna   Stop it, please, you're making me feel uneasy.

Trampas   Sorry.

Donna   Can we start the conversation somewhere else?

Trampas   If you like.

Donna   Shall we try over there?

Trampas   That's fine by me.

Donna   Okay. Let's go over there.

Donna *and* **Trampas** *walk over to another spot on the stage.*

Pause.

Donna   I don't know . . .

Trampas   What . . .?

Donna   You meet the funniest people in my job.

Trampas   I can imagine.

Donna   People are funny.

Trampas   Yes.

Donna   Do you know sometimes you can tell the kind of person somebody is by the pizza they buy.

Trampas   Is that right?

Donna   Yes. I've made a study of it. Often the people who want loads and loads of fillings on a deep pan pizza are filling a void in their lives. And those people who want a plain cheese and tomato pizza thin crust are more contented.

Trampas   It's an interesting theory.

Donna   Those who order artichoke like the exotic.

Trampas   Hmm.

Donna   Do you like the exotic, Trampas?

Trampas   I don't know.

Donna   Are you married, Trampas?

Trampas   No. Are you married, Donna?

Donna   No. But I'm living with someone.

Trampas   Are you happy?

Donna   No, his name is Clive. Not that his name is the reason I'm not happy, if you know what I mean.

Trampas   Yes.

Donna   I mean, what's in a name.

Pause.

He's in the Merchant Navy. He has affairs.

Trampas   Have you thought of leaving him?

Donna   I have but I stay for my daughter's sake. Her name is Cheryl. She's seven.

Trampas   That's nice.

Donna   You wouldn't believe the time I've stared at the walls and looked at the ceiling praying for something good to happen.

Trampas   I know the feeling.

Donna   You stare at ceilings too.

Trampas   I do. Sometimes I think it's the ceilings that stop us from seeing the sky.

Donna   That's very deep, Trampas.

Trampas   I can be a deep kind of guy.

Donna   I must admit, I've always like the deep type.

Pause.

Trampas   I could love you, Donna.

Donna   I hope Mr Greco hurries up. The pizza's getting cold.

Trampas   I could get rid of Clive and we could live together.

Donna   He must have run out of coffee.

Trampas   I'd be a good step-father to Cheryl.

Donna   Either that or he needs a new percolator.

Trampas   I'll build a new house.

Donna   I bought a new percolator only the other day. It even made cappuccino. Clive was ever so happy.

Trampas   A house of love.

Donna   He loves his coffee with a lot of froth and a light sprinkling of chocolate chips.

Trampas   Here, East from the gantry you . . .

Donna   I think what you need Trampas is a new coffee maker. You should shop around.

Trampas   I love you, Donna.

Donna   There are bargains to be found still.

Trampas   I can kill for love.

Donna   The shops are open on Sunday now.

Trampas   Please listen to me Donna, please..

Donna   Perhaps Mr Greco can pay next time. I'm sure we can give him credit I . . .

Trampas   Why can't you love me?

He grabs her.

Silence.

Donna   Let me go, Trampas.

Trampas   I . . .

Donna   Please.

He releases her.

I'm sorry.

Donna *starts to back off cautiously.*

You'll be okay, you'll find someone, somewhere, but not me. It can't be me Trampas, not this time.

Trampas   What about the autograph?

Donna   I'll get it off you when I've got a pen and paper.

Trampas   What about the pizza?

Donna   Tell Mr Greco that he can pay next time.

Trampas   I . . .

Donna   I've got to go, Trampas, business calls.

Donna *exits, fade in music as* **Trampas** *looks round the messy, memory-filled set. As the music fades there comes a noise from a wooden box on the corner of the stage.* **Trampas** *looks round.*

Box   Psssst.

Trampas   Who's that?

Box   It's me, Clint.

Trampas   Clint?

Box   In the box.

Trampas   Fucking hell.

Box   Come here.

Trampas   Fucking, fucking hell.

Box   Open the box.

Trampas *nervously approaches the box. He slowly opens it, revealing the head of* **Clint,** *played by* **Ronnie**.

Clint   Did anyone ever tell you, you look like Burt Reynolds.

Trampas   Aaaarrrrgggghhhh!!!

Clint   Not so loud man, do you want the whole world to know?

Trampas   No.

Clint   Good, this is a secret, pal, between me and you, you got me?

Trampas   I got you, yeah.

Clint   Good, now, have you got a fag?

Trampas   I have . . . yes . . . but they're bad for you.

Clint   Bad for you, he says, bad for you, what do you think living in a box full of formaldehyde does to a man?

Trampas   I . . .

Clint   Do you think I like it?

Trampas   No.

Clint   Would you like it?

Trampas   No . . . No . . . I wouldn't . . . I . . .

Clint   My sister Donna means well pal, but fuck, she treats me like an exhibit, man.

Trampas   I can imagine.

Clint   Can you? Can you?

Trampas   No, I suppose I can't.

Clint   Exactly, nobody can imagine it.

Trampas   It must be tough.

Clint   It is tough, yes, now give me a fag.

Trampas   Right.

Clint   Thank Christ for that.

Trampas   *holds his head as he puts a fag in his mouth.*

Clint   Not so rough man, I'm not a football.

Trampas   I'm sorry.

Clint   Now light the fag.

Trampas   *lights it.* **Clint** *pulls contentedly at it.*

Trampas   Happy?

Clint   Oh man . . . yeah . . . Jesus . . . it's heaven man.

Trampas   That's good.

Clint   You're a good man, Burt.

Trampas   My name's not Burt.

Clint   I don't care what your name is, man, you look like Burt Reynolds.

Trampas   You reckon.

Clint   Sure thing, if my brother Ted saw you he'd be really angry.

Trampas Ted?

Clint He used to model himself on Burt Reynolds. Me and him were inseparable.

Trampas Do you like Burt Reynolds, Clint?

Clint Like him? Jesus man. I think he's a God.

Trampas Which is your favourite film?

Clint *Citizen Kane*.

Trampas Burt Reynolds isn't in *Citizen Kane*, Orson Welles is.

Clint I know.

Trampas So what are you saying?

Clint I'm just saying that *Citizen Kane* is my favourite film, is that a problem to you?

Trampas No. That's not a problem at all I . . .

Clint I'm glad to hear it, it's one of the best films ever made.

Trampas But . . .

Clint No buts, I won't hear a but against it.

Trampas Burt Reynolds isn't in the fucking thing.

Clint I know Burt Reynolds isn't in the fucking thing.

Trampas But I wanted you to tell me which of Burt Reynolds' films you liked best.

Clint Oh Jesus.

Trampas You've got me?

Clint I've got you. I've got you.

Trampas Good. Thank Christ for that.

Pause.

So which one?

Clint None. I think all Burt Reynolds films are crap.

Trampas What about *Deliverance*?

Clint What about it?

Trampas It's a good film.

Clint I think it's crap.

Trampas I don't. I like the inbred Southern kid playing the banjo.

Clint   How do you know he's inbred?

Trampas   It's obvious.

Clint   Just because he plays the guitar upside down?

Trampas   That's one reason.

Clint   Jesus, you're thick.

Trampas   Don't you call me thick.

Clint   I'll call you thick if I want to.

Trampas   I am not thick.

Clint   No wonder nobody loves you.

Trampas   That's not true.

Clint   Donna wouldn't come anywhere near you.

Trampas   That's because Donna's loyal. She's got a bloke. Clive his name is.

Clint   She left Clive over eight months ago, Burt.

Trampas   Not true.

Clint   She found you repulsive.

Trampas   Shut it.

Clint   Couldn't stand the sight of you.

Trampas   Fuck up, I said.

Clint   Wouldn't have shagged you if you were the last man on earth.

Trampas   Aaaarrrrgggghhh!!!!

To the sound of crashing drums, **Trampas** *goes wild and starts to throttle the hapless* **Clint,** *suffocating him in some of the set's discarded clothing, wrestling him on the floor. The music fades as* **Trampas** *realises that he's killed* **Clint.** *He looks at him sadly.*

Trampas   I'm sorry, Clint.

Pause.

I didn't mean to do it.

Pause.

I thought I could be somebody, that's all, that I'd make it . . . get re-born, start again.

Pause.

I thought the stars would shine down on me, it would be there, in front of me, within grasp, reachable, to be had, felt, taken in hand and held, squeezed, there, in front of me, a light flickering, a good thing, not far away, mine . . .

Pause.

I wanted it bad . . .

Pause.

I once thought I saw it.

Pause.

I put out my arms, I opened them, I shut my eyes expecting a touch, on my lips, in my mind, I once thought it touched the tips of my fingers and I think I smiled, you know the way you smile when something good is going to happen? Is on the verge of happening so close you can really smell it? A perfume, a strange perfume, a wisp, a tail, a stream of smoke coiling around me, a serpent hissing, strange perfume in the boots of cars, buses, faces, my eyes are shut, my lips right over my teeth and music, strange music, like I imagine tomorrow's song, song of tomorrow, my head is on fire, I feel as if I'm burning, my skin is melting, my fingers reach, are reaching, I could have been, I nearly did, I saw it as clear as day.

Pause.

Then I opened my eyes on the bitter silence of now.

Pause.

Maybe I opened my eyes too soon. Maybe I should have waited, I had time, I mean, I'm not that old, I was so near, I was so fucking near then it was gone . . . do you know what I'm saying?

Pause.

I told Greco I was going home. At first he said nothing, then he laughed and said, 'Home?'. I said 'Yes, home, what's wrong with that?'

Pause.

He stubbed out his fag in the ash-tray and said 'You haven't got a home man,' he said, 'it don't exist, it disappeared, it shrunk, it fucked off, it took a walk, it died, it no longer continued to be.'

Pause.

I finished my drink, walked out of the pub and I haven't seen him since. And I don't think I ever will again.

Trampas lights a match, fade in the sound and light of a fire as smoke engulfs the stage. **Trampas** *fans it and exits.* **Bella** *and* **Ronnie** *enter into cold blue light.* **Bella** *stands at the window. Sounds fade.*

Bella They say it's general.

Ronnie   What is?

Bella   The snow.

Ronnie   Jesus Christ.

Bella   Don't you think it's effective for making the ugliest thing attractive, even beautiful!

Ronnie   No.

Bella   A few days ago, I walked passed the old iron works on Ynyscedwyn Road. I was struck by its fierce, if bleak beauty, the dereliction was overwhelming, the falling snow a balm of forgetfulness, I called into the tavern for a drink. I lit a cigarette and stood by the window.

Ronnie (*disgusted*)   Fucking hell!

Bella   I looked up at the TV set in the corner, the weatherman said there would be drifts. I think his name was Michael Fish.

Ronnie (*suddenly interested*)   Who is Michael Fish?

Bella   The weatherman.

Ronnie   What did he look like?

Bella   He had a moustache and glasses and a sort of greeny-brown check sports jacket.

Ronnie   Is that all?

Bella   I think so yes, why?

Ronnie   I don't believe you, that's why.

Bella   I saw him clearly, Ronnie.

Ronnie   No weatherman worth his salt would forecast a snow drift wearing only a sports jacket, glasses and moustache. What the fuck do you take me for, Bella?

Bella   I didn't mean that's all that he had on, Ronnie.

Ronnie   But that's what you said.

Bella   I was just outlining his most distinctive characteristics that's all, I . . .

Ronnie   Since when has a greeny-brown check sports jacket ever been distinctive.

Bella   Never.

Ronnie   Exactly.

Bella   But it's not what I meant.

Ronnie   I think you fantasize about him.

Bella   What?

Ronnie   Has he got a big penis, is that it?

Bella   Ronnie.

Ronnie   Is he circumcised?

Bella   I'm not going to . . . (answer this.)

Ronnie   Will you take him as a lover? . . . quickly, passionately, on the floor? . . . with the weather signs above your head? . . . will you, Bella, will you?

Bella   You're insane, Ronnie.

Ronnie   I know but you're the one who turns a perfectly innocuous television weather forecast into lurid fantasy, not me.

Bella   There was no lurid fantasy I . . .

Ronnie   There was. You imagined Michael Fish naked, you imagined that he was talking just to you, enticing you with soft words of snowdrifts, he probably knew how much you love the snow, how effective you think snow is for making the ugliest thing attractive, even beautiful, he took advantage of you, Bella, caught you at your weakest, when I wasn't around, he's a bastard Bella, a complete and utter bastard and you're no better because you probably egged him on.

Bella   I did not egg him on, Ron, I was having a quiet drink in a cosy tavern with a few afternoon customers studying *The Sporting Life*, in front of a roaring fire.

Ronnie   How can you talk about a roaring fire in front of me?

Bella   What?

Ronnie   When you burnt down our house!

Bella   That is outrageous. It was an accident.

Ronnie   If only you'd come to bed when I called you.

Bella   I was watching a film.

Ronnie   Smoking a cigarette.

Bella   That is no crime, Ronnie.

Ronnie   It is when it burnt down a house and almost everything in it.

Bella   The cigarette was not the cause.

Ronnie   That's not what the fireman said.

Bella   The fireman could only speculate.

Ronnie   He is a professional man.

Bella   It could have been electrical.

Ronnie   And how come it was I who discovered the fire?

Bella   I went for a walk. I needed some air.

Ronnie   But you said it was a horror film.

Bella   It was.

Ronnie   You said it scared you out of your wits.

Bella   It did.

Ronnie   Then why did you go for a walk when you were scared out of your wits and petrified.

Bella   I have never been afraid of walking the mountains at dark!

Ronnie   Bollocks, Bella, Bollocks!

Bella   How many more times must we go over this, Ronnie?

Ronnie   Until I find out the truth.

Bella   The truth is . . .

Ronnie   That you started the fire deliberately.

Bella   That you are a jealous bastard.

Ronnie   I'm not I . . .

Bella   Then why the fuck else did you shoot that cat?

Pause.

Ronnie   It was an accident.

Bella   You're a jealous and paranoid bastard, Ronnie, and you know it.

Ronnie   It was a mistake, Bella.

Bella   It was no mistake, Ronnie, you never gave it a chance.

Ronnie   I . . .

Bella   Boom, boom, Ronnie John, comes out of his lair like a frightened rabbit in his underpants with his gun in his hands and blows the poor thing to smithereens. There was nothing left of it, Ronnie.

Ronnie   I over-reacted, Bella, that's all.

Bella   That's all.

Ronnie   Besides, I never shot him in my pants. I had my trousers on.

Bella   Oh good God, that makes all the difference, does it?

Ronnie   No, but you never let me explain I . . .

Bella There is nothing to explain, Ronnie, it was cold-blooded murder you . . .

Ronnie I thought it was Martin fucking Bratton.

Silence.

Bella What?

Ronnie You heard.

Bella I don't believe it.

Ronnie It's the truth.

Bella Are you mad?

Ronnie I am but on this occasion it's got nothing to do with what happened.

Bella But you said . . .

Ronnie It was my dream that gave him away.

Bella What dream?

Ronnie It was a clear day . . .

Fade in guitar music low level, lights change to moonlight. Mix in appropriate sound FX.

The house was rebuilt with ranch fencing all around it, two apple trees in flower stand on one side, a hammock is suspended in the middle and I am dozing in it. I am wearing shorts, my legs are sun-burned, a book rests on my chest, a cool drink sits on a small table nearby. I listen to the sound of a bee buzzing from the depths of a purple foxglove which we planted together the year before. I watch you approach in a white dress, you are playing with the stalk of a flower, you are smiling. You are carrying a musical box which you lay on the table next to the hammock. You open the box and some music plays and a dancer goes round and round in a mirror. Perhaps she is admiring herself.

Sound of the musical box.

You put your hand on the inside of my thigh, your fingers are cool, you are stroking me gently, you undo the buttons on my shorts you move your hand inside, slowly, slowly. You are driving me wild with desire, I reach up to your breast. I stroke it, my lips are dry, your nipples erect, you take my heavy cock in your hands, I am on fire, I am . . .

The music stops.

The music stops, my hand stops, your hand stops, the bee leaves the foxglove, the ice melts in my drink and the novel falls from my chest to the floor with a thud. Foolishly I ask you whether you would rather make love or pay a visit to the garden centre to get a new fan belt for the lawn mower.

Bella *laughs.*

Bella   Ronnie.

Ronnie   And you laugh, like you are laughing now and then the music stops.

Silence.

Summer turns to winter and snow begins to fall.

Snow falls.

You take your hand away and walk back towards the house. I follow you to bed but before I turn out the light I look out at the snow-covered landscape. And I see him.

Guitar comes to an end.

Then I woke up, Bella, went to the window and there he was, clear as day.

Bella   Where?

Ronnie   Out in the field in the back, he was leaning against a tree, smoking, watching the house. I ran downstairs to get my gun but by the time I got there he was gone.

Pause.

I thought he'd come back for you Bella, but he isn't going to get you.

Bella   It wasn't Martin Bratton, Ronnie.

Ronnie   It was, he was your first love and you are still in love with him.

Bella   No Ronnie.

Ronnie   You said he'd come back for you, you said you saw him fly east from the gantry.

Bella   I know what I said Ronnie, but he never made it.

Ronnie   What?

Bella   He's dead Ronnie.

Fade in the music of Beth Yw'r Haf i Mi *at a low level.*

Bella   I went home to my house, to eat my haddock. I told my parents what I saw. 'Martin Bratton's flown away' I said. 'No, he hasn't,' said my father. 'He jumped out of his bedroom window and killed himself. It's been on the news, isn't that right, Beth?' 'Your father's right' said my mother. 'We heard the ambulance driver speaking to a reporter. The man reading the news said teenage suicides were rising. I put it down to all this snow.' 'It's not true, Mam,' I said 'I saw him fly east from the gantry.'

Pause.

Bella *picks up the blood-soaked sheet and wraps herself in it.*

My mother and my father looked at each other before calling the doctor to me and giving me a sweet cup of tea. She's in shock, they told the doctor. She saw it happen. He was her boyfriend. The doctor said he thought it was sad and then my mother said that they thought it was sad too.

Pause.

Music fades.

Ronnie   I'm sorry, Bella.

Bella   Forget it.

Ronnie   I didn't mean to . . .

Bella   No.

Bella *moves away from him.*

Ronnie   Then who was it I saw in the snow?

Bella   That was probably Trampas.

Ronnie   Trampas?

Bella   Trampas.

Fade in music as **Trampas** *enters, washed and wearing jeans and a T-shirt. Music fades. All three look at each other for a moment.*

Bella   Ronnie, Trampas. Trampas, Ronnie.

Ronnie   Hello, Trampas.

Trampas   Hello, Ronnie.

Bella   I was thinking, perhaps Trampas would like to stay for dinner with us Ron.

Ronnie   Dinner . . . yes . . . yes.

Trampas   Are you sure?

Bella   Positive, aren't we Ron?

Ronnie   Yes . . . yes.

Bella   Besides we ordered a King Size pizza not long ago. There'll be plenty for three.

Trampas   Well, I don't want to impose.

Bella   You're not imposing at all, is he Ron?

Ronnie   No . . . no . . . do you like pepperoni Trampas?

Trampas   Umm . . . yes.

Bella   We ordered pepperoni instead of anchovy I hope you don't mind.

Trampas   No, no . . . it's one of my favourite fillings.

Bella   So that's settled then.

Trampas   Yes . . . thank you.

Pause.

Have you ever heard of a man called Wymff, Ronnie?

Ronnie   No. I can't say as I have.

Bella   Wymff was Trampas's friend, Ronnie.

Trampas   I say it because, to be perfectly frank, you're his spitting image, Ronnie.

Ronnie   Really?

Trampas   Really.

Ronnie   A lot of people look alike, Trampas.

Trampas   Yeah, I suppose they do.

Pause.

Bella   I think I'll go and put on some coffee.

Ronnie   That would be nice, Bella.

Bella   Coffee, Trampas?

Trampas   Thank you, white, two sugars.

Bella   Fine, I won't be long.

Bella *exits.*

Trampas   She's a remarkable woman.

Ronnie   She is, but she's prone to the strangest behaviour.

Trampas   Really.

Ronnie   Yes, she once brought a pair of man's hands home in her handbag.

Trampas   That's interesting.

Ronnie   I was amazed.

Trampas   Had she done this sort of thing before?

Ronnie   Not really, no.

Trampas   Perhaps you could ask the doctor to prescribe some drugs.

Ronnie   Impossible, he's insane, he keeps sending love-letters. I intercept them at the T-junction at the foot of the mountain.

Trampas   I know that T-junction.

Ronnie   Really?

Trampas   Yes, it used to be a canal and now it's a long straight road.

Ronnie   Things change.

Trampas   I know.

Ronnie   It's a crazy world, with crazy people.

Trampas   Especially on trains.

Ronnie   I'm sorry.

Trampas   I left the city by train. I was looking to find myself. Instead I found a skinhead with 'Born in Newport' on his forehead, wearing only boots and trousers, when I asked him if he knew me, he just said, 'No man, I don't know who the fuck you are.'

Ronnie   That's really tough.

Trampas   It sure is and we rode across the plain like Casey Jones.

Ronnie   The train driver.

Trampas   Yes.

Ronnie   He always struck me as a man you could trust.

Trampas   Oh he was . . . he was.

They smile.

Pause.

Ronnie   I'm going to rebuild this house one day, see Trampas. Make it good and strong and open, so when we have visitors we can entertain them properly.

Trampas   It'll be a long job, Ron.

Ronnie   I know but with a bit of help, I could do it, start again, fresh, east from the gantry.

Pause.

It might be a good place one day, Trampas.

Pause.

That's my dream, man.

Trampas   That's fair enough, Ron.

Pause.

Ronnie   What about you, Trampas?

Trampas   I don't know, I reckon the Cwmgiedd I know has gone forever.

Ronnie   I suppose it has, Trampas.

Trampas   Wymff and Johnny Greco were right.

Ronnie   Were they?

Trampas   They said I had no home.

Ronnie   It's a shame.

Trampas   And I can't go back to the city no more.

Pause.

Ronnie   So what will you do?

Trampas   Make a new start I suppose.

Ronnie   A new Cwmgiedd.

Trampas   Who knows?

Ronnie   Cwmgiedd II.

Trampas   Yeah.

Pause.

First thing I'll do is change my name. I made Trampas up.

Ronnie   What's your real name then?

Trampas   They used to call me Boyo.

Ronnie   Boyo.

Trampas   Boyo. But my real name's Billy.

Ronnie   Call yourself Billy then.

Trampas   I guess I will.

Pause.

Ronnie   Hello, Billy.

Trampas   Hello, Ronnie.

Pause.

Ronnie   Bella isn't Bella's name either.

Trampas   No?

Ronnie   No, her real name's Gwenny, she's got it from a play she saw once.

House Of America or something, they called it.

Trampas I knew a Gwenny a few years ago.

Ronnie A popular name.

Trampas I suppose it is.

Pause.

Ronnie Nothing like a good pizza see.

Trampas No.

Ronnie Or Chinese.

Trampas Mm.

Ronnie Or Indian.

Trampas No.

Ronnie To be honest, I'll eat anything me.

Trampas That's good.

Pause.

Ronnie You couldn't have loved, Bella, see Trampas.

Trampas No?

Ronnie No.

Trampas Why not?

Ronnie She's in love with Michael Fish.

Trampas Who's Michael Fish?

Ronnie Just a weatherman.

Trampas Oh.

Fade in Dean Martin's Memoiries *as* **Bella** *enters and hands an apple each to the men.* **Trampas** *puts it on his head,* **Ronnie** *shoots an imaginary gun at it. They smile.* **Bella** *bites into her apple as the music plays to blackout.*

Why Can't This Crazy Love Be Mine?
An introduction to Edward Thomas and Y Cwmni

Many of Edward Thomas's characters awake and look around them, at four grey walls that surround them, and realize that, yes, they were only dreaming. The point is, whose dreams were they dreaming? And how? And why?

Some say that a man or woman is made up by their memories. But memory is a selective process, drawing on imaginative experience. Memories might revolve around something that can be verified by so-called objective witnesses; but, also and equally, they might not. Thomas's plays show how relationships break down when one person insists on the exclusive truth of their own point of view, and in so doing blocks their partner's capacity to improvise, sustain and develop alternatives – in other words, blocks their capacity to play, in the most full and vital sense, which is a large factor in human dignity. When people limit other people's abilities to dream and transform, they limit their own: they sacrifice strangeness, preferring familiar, reiterative patterns of possibility which mount up in the form of depression.

On the other hand, the creative imagination works, and plays, through transferring qualities from one thing to another – the dynamics of metaphor – in a way which is quite different to what is familiar. As the French philosopher Jean-François Lyotard says in his essay 'Lessons in Paganism': 'How can you possibly grumble when the intimate and infinite power of stories is unleashed, even if you do find those who spread them despicable? If you think their version is worthless, you have only to come up with a different version.' This is why he calls for a politics based on narrative – 'after all, anyone can tell stories'. Unlike theories, narratives are social elements which challenge the very things that political parties and authoritarian regimes depend upon: namely, an exclusive monopoly on identifying what is historical, factual, valuable and possible. Lyotard suggests that one way to respond to the tyranny of ideologies is not to 'tell the truth and save the world', but instead 'to will the power to play out, listen to and tell stories'.

In his book *Cold War Theatre*, John Elsom pertinently asserts: 'The one thing we know about theatre is that it is not real life. It gives us the chance to test assumptions in our imaginations', and 'the advantage of live theatre, as opposed to TV drama, is that myths are tried out within small groups of people'. Elsom describes myths as unprovable revelations, 'aids to perception, embedded in language': they may not be provable factually, 'they may be provably false', but this does not necessarily deny their usefulness or significance: 'If governments defend their myths to the point of excluding all others, societies become brittle. There are no ways of looking at the world than those provided by the state' (hence, 'the question raised by arts subsidy is not how much money should be given to the arts, but how much power should be given to governments').

In 1988, Edward Thomas formed Y Cwmni – in English, simply 'The Company' – a gang of disaffected Welsh artists with an arrogant, unashamed edge to their insistence on expression: not striving for 'making history' on the terms of somebody else's authority, or lamenting some golden age lost forever, but exercising the right to remake history, in the company of wild astonishment and artful challenge, and so create new presents and new futures for a living. As artistic director of Y Cwmni, Thomas has led his squad of voracious anarchists in a series of consciously excessive tours, based around performances of his purposefully impossible plays.

The first play, *House of America* (written 1988) shows a microcosmic Welsh family reduced to playing out other people's stories, suffering from being made subservient to technologically transmitted images which they have not created and cannot control. A taut, relentless and profoundly harrowing tragedy, *House of America* discovers a world on the edge, where the last remaining fugitive excitement seems to be in versions of glamorous doom, driving out towards a frontier of death: the grass of this imposed mythic landscape may look greener, but may also finally demand that you be laid beneath it.

Adar heb Adenydd was written in 1989 and revised and translated as *The Myth of Michael Roderick* for 1990. In the first critical article on Thomas and Y Cwmni to be published, Charmian C Savill described the latter version as 'a precisely constructed labyrinth delving into possibilities of salvation', where characters seek to break through indifference and nostalgia through ritual, 'wrenching and distorting themselves in efforts to create or sustain their own individual myths in a bid for vibrant rebirth' ('Wales is Dead!', in *Planet* 85, Feb–Mar 1991, 86–91). The play also exposes all forms of determinism and integration into the fictitious cult of normality as essentially fears of freedom.

Flowers of the Dead Red Sea (written 1991) was a more gruelling prize-fight of a play. Two slaughtermen attempt to empower themselves through language, in a shrinking island of diminishing possibilities. They plunge into vicious cancellations of their selves and each other, even as they hurtle back and inwards to find something or someone to hold onto, amidst the grim sense of time running out. They suffer from believing others' truths for the sake of 'general good', yet express a need to respond, break the silence and discover a new way of saying 'I am still here' – begging the question, who is willing to listen?

East from the Gantry (written 1992) turns from a bloodied sea to hills masked in snow, from submergence to reflective expansiveness. Some familiar Thomas characters show up in new incarnations, as if rinsed out by time: the mythical birdman Martin Bratton might be a reanimation of the title character from *The Myth of Michael Roderick*; the final divulging of Trampas and Bella's previous names, Boyo and Gwenny, recalls the brother and sister apparently locked into doom at the end of *House of America*; again, Tom Jones provides some of the soundtrack for what threatens to become a dance of death. But *East from the Gantry* unlocks new possibilities as characters play in the knowledge that their lives depend upon it, reinventing themselves through assuming various identities. All pursuing different searches, together they find time and space to reclaim memories, to recover stories, however treacherous, beautiful, erotic or painful, and to develop them anew, with someone listening.

East from the Gantry, and other Thomas plays, deal in self-authorization: the painful cost and the terrible release involved in making yourself up, becoming the reader and writer of your own life, answerable only to other people's equal power to do the same. Thomas's men and women rise or fall to the challenge of showing their potential, the extent to which they, like Bob Dylan's mythical Jokerman, can keep 'Shedding off one more layer of skin/Keeping one step ahead of the persecutor within'. But then, as Richard Lynch, leading actor in Y Cwmni, says: art, like life, is a matter of demonstrating soul, courage and instinct. *East from the Gantry* invites the audience to join in, changing the past in order to change the future, building new stories out of ruined hopes, making a landscape fit to live in. As Ronnie, Bella and Trampas find out, it's a fragile and dangerous business, which flies in the face of rationalism and realism; but when they work together with all their imagination and will, there is in fact *no* reason why that crazy love cannot be theirs.

David Ian Rabey
Senior Lecturer in Drama, The University of Wales, Aberystwyth
February, 1993

Edward Thomas was born in Abercraf, South Wales in 1961. He has worked extensively in radio, film and television as an actor, writer and director and is currently artistic director of *Y Cwmni,* a small independent theatre and television company based in Cardiff.

Since forming the company in 1988, he has written five plays, all of which he has directed: *House of America* (1988), (which won the Time Out/01 for London award in 1989), the Welsh language play *Adar Heb Adenydd* (1989), *The Myth of Michael Roderick* (1990), *Flowers of the Dead, Red Sea* (1991) and most recently, *East from the Gantry* (1992) which premièred at the Tramway, Glasgow before touring in Wales and the Ukraine.